Android®
Tablets

for
dummies®
A Wiley Brand

Android®
Tablets

4th edition

by Dan Gookin

A Wiley Brand

Android® Tablets For Dummies®, 4th Edition

Published by: **John Wiley & Sons, Inc.**, 111 River Street, Hoboken, NJ 07030-5774, www.wiley.com

Copyright © 2017 by John Wiley & Sons, Inc., Hoboken, New Jersey

Published simultaneously in Canada

For general information on our other products and services, please contact our Customer Care Department within the U.S. at 877-762-2974, outside the U.S. at 317-572-3993, or fax 317-572-4002. For technical support, please visit https://hub.wiley.com/community/support/dummies.

Wiley publishes in a variety of print and electronic formats and by print-on-demand. Some material included with standard print versions of this book may not be included in e-books or in print-on-demand. If this book refers to media such as a CD or DVD that is not included in the version you purchased, you may download this material at http://booksupport.wiley.com. For more information about Wiley products, visit www.wiley.com.

Library of Congress Control Number: 2016955198

ISBN: 978-1-119-31073-0; 978-1-119-31074-7 (ebk); 978-1-119-31075-4 (ebk)

Manufactured in the United States of America

10 9 8 7 6 5 4 3 2

Contents at a Glance

Table of Contents

Introduction

Somewhere between a smartphone and a computer lies the premiere device of the 21st century. It's probably something you've never used but will soon be unable to live without. It's the tablet — specifically, an Android tablet.

The Android tablet is a gizmo that could fully replace your computer, as well as several other pieces of electronics you may tote around. It's an all-in-one, light-weight, battery-powered, long-lasting, fully mobile, telecommunications, information, and entertainment gizmo.

Oh, but I do go on.

As an Android tablet owner, or someone who's interested in purchasing such a device, you want to get the most from your technology. Perhaps you've attempted to educate yourself using that flimsy *Getting Started* leaflet that comes with the thing. Now you're turning to this book, a wise choice.

New technology can be intimidating. Frustrating. No matter what, your experience can be made better by leisurely reading this delightful, informative, and occasionally entertaining book.

About This Book

Please don't read this book from cover to cover. This book is a reference. It's designed to be used as you need it. Look up a topic in the table of contents or the index. Find something about your tablet that vexes you or something you're curious about. Look up the answer, and get on with your life.

The overall idea for this book is to show how things are done on an Android tablet and to help you enjoy the device without overwhelming you with information or intimidating you into despair.

Sample sections in this book include:

>> Unlocking the tablet

>> Activating voice input

- » Importing contacts from a computer
- » Adding more email accounts
- » Placing a Hangouts phone call
- » Running Facebook on your tablet
- » Helping others find your location
- » Buying and renting movies
- » Flying with an Android tablet

You have nothing to memorize, no sacred utterances or animal sacrifices, and definitely no PowerPoint presentations. Instead, every section explains a topic as though it's the first thing you've read in this book. Nothing is assumed, and everything is cross-referenced. Technical terms and topics, when they come up, are neatly shoved to the side, where they're easily avoided. The idea here isn't to learn anything. My philosophy while writing this book was to help you look it up, figure it out, and get on with your life.

How to Use This Book

This book follows a few conventions for using an Android tablet. First of all, no matter what name your tablet has, whether it's a manufacturer's name or a pet name you've devised on your own, this book refers to your tablet as an *Android tablet* or, often, just *tablet*.

The way you interact with the Android tablet is by using its touchscreen — the glassy part of the device as it's facing you. The device also has some physical buttons, as well as some holes and connectors. All these items are described in Chapter 1.

The various ways to touch the screen are explained and named in Chapter 3.

Chapter 4 covers text input on an Android tablet, which involves using an onscreen keyboard. When you tire of typing, you can dictate your text. It's all explained in Chapter 4.

This book directs you to do things by following numbered steps. Each step involves a specific activity, such as touching something on the screen; for example:

1. **Tap the Apps icon.**

This step directs you to tap or touch the graphical Apps icon on the screen. When a button is shown as text, the command reads:

1. **Tap the DOWNLOAD button.**

You might also be directed to choose an item, which means to tap it on the screen.

 Various settings can be turned off or on, as indicated by a master control, which looks like the on/off toggle. Tap the master control to enable to disable the feature, or slide its button to the right or left. When the feature is enabled, the master control icon appears in color, as shown in the margin.

Foolish Assumptions

Even though this book is written with the gentle handholding required by anyone who is just starting out, or who is easily intimidated, I've made a few assumptions. For example, I assume that you're a human being and not a colony creature from the planet Zontar.

My biggest assumption: You have or desire to own a tablet that uses Google's Android operating system. Your tablet might be an LTE tablet (one that uses the mobile data network) or a Wi-Fi–only model. This book covers both.

The Android operating system comes in versions, or flavors. This book covers all current Android versions 4.3 through 7.0. These versions are known by the flavors Jelly Bean, Kit Kat, Lollipop, Marshmallow, and Nougat. To confirm which Android version is used on your tablet, follow these steps:

1. **At the Home screen, tap the Apps icon.**

   Refer to Chapter 3 for a description of the Apps icon.

2. **Tap to open the Settings app.**

3. **Choose About Tablet.**

   This item might be named About Device. If you're using a Samsung Galactic tablet, you might have to first tap the General tab atop the screen to locate the About Device item.

4. **Look at the item titled Android Version.**

   The number that's shown indicates the Android operating system version.

Don't fret if these steps confuse you: Review Part I of this book, and then come back here. (I'll wait.)

More assumptions:

You don't need to own a computer to use your Android tablet. If you have a computer, great. The Android tablet works well with both PC and Mac. When directions are specific to a PC or Mac, the book says so.

Programs that run on your Android tablet are *apps*, which is short for applications. A single program is an *app*.

Finally, this book assumes that you have a Google account, but if you don't, Chapter 2 explains how to configure one. Do so. Having a Google account opens up a slew of useful features, information, and programs that make using your tablet more productive.

Icons Used in This Book

TIP

This icon flags useful, helpful tips or shortcuts.

REMEMBER

This icon marks a friendly reminder to do something.

WARNING

This icon marks a friendly reminder not to do something.

TECHNICAL STUFF

This icon alerts you to overly nerdy information and technical discussions of the topic at hand. Reading the information is optional, though it may win you the Daily Double on Jeopardy!

Where to Go from Here

Start reading! Start at Chapter 1, which is probably numbered "one" and not Chapter 12, which is more toward the middle of the book. And, as I admonished earlier, please don't read the book from cover to cover. It's not a novel.

My email address is dgookin@wambooli.com. Yes, that's my real address. I reply to every email I receive, and more quickly when you keep your question short and specific to this book. Although I enjoy saying Hi, I cannot answer technical support questions, resolve billing issues, or help you troubleshoot your tablet. Thanks for understanding.

My website is wambooli.com. This book has its own page on that site, which you can check for updates, new information, and all sorts of fun stuff. Visit often:

wambooli.com/help/android/tablets

The publisher maintains a support page with updates or changes that occur between editions of this book. Go to www.dummies.com, search for *Android Tablets For Dummies*, then open the Extras tab on this book's specific page to view the updates or changes. Or click the Cheat Sheet link to view helpful information pulled from throughout the text.

Enjoy this book and your Android tablet!

1
Getting Started with Android Tablets

Chapter **1**

That Out-of-the-Box Experience

To begin your Android tablet adventure, open the device's box. Sure, you've probably already done that. I don't blame you; I had already opened the box that my Android tablet came in before I read this chapter. No problem. Yet your new adventure is made smoother when you can accompany that out-of-the-box experience with a gentle introduction and handholding.

Initial Procedures

If you've purchased a cellular or LTE tablet, the folks who sold it to you may have already done some configuration before you left the store. That's great because an LTE tablet requires some extra setup before you can use the device. That duty is explained in Chapter 2. For now, all tablet owners — LTE and Wi-Fi — need to perform two basic tablet activities: Get it out of the box, and charge the battery.

ANDROID TABLET PURCHASING TIPS

The major things to look for when purchasing an Android tablet are the screen size and whether you want an LTE or a Wi-Fi–only device.

Larger screens are more visible and easier to read, but a larger tablet requires two hands to operate. A smaller-size tablet might be more convenient. The only way to know which size works best for you is to manhandle an Android tablet at the store before you buy.

LTE tablets use the mobile data network to access the Internet, just like a smartphone. That capability comes with a monthly bill, but if you need Internet access anywhere, it's worth the price. Both LTE and Wi-Fi–only tablets can access Wi-Fi networks.

Some tablets feature removable storage in the form of a microSD card. This feature allows you to expand the device's storage and more easily share files with a computer.

Ensure that the tablet has both front and rear cameras. The camera resolution isn't vital, but if your tablet will be your only digital camera, getting a high-resolution rear camera is a plus. Also confirm that the rear camera has a flash.

Beyond these basic items, most Android tablets are the same, with only subtle software differences. Do ensure, however, that your tablet uses the Android operating system and can access and use Google Play. Some low-price, bargain tablets restrict your purchases to the manufacturer's own app store. I would avoid such devices.

Liberating the tablet from the box

Thanks to an excess of funds, your federal government has conducted numerous studies on how people use electronic devices. Men and women wearing white lab coats and safety goggles have determined that using an Android tablet works best when you first remove it from its box. Thank you, federal grant!

I assume that you're pretty good at the box-opening thing, so I probably don't need to detail that procedure. I can affirm, however, that it's perfectly okay to remove and throw away those protective plastic sheets clinging to the front, back, and sides of the tablet. And don't be embarrassed when, three weeks from now, you find yet another plastic sheet you haven't removed. Feel free to remove and throw away the plastic sheets.

Along with the tablet, you'll find the following items in the box:

>> **USB cable:** You can use it to connect the tablet to a computer or a wall charger.

- » **Power adapter:** Use this thing (and the USB cable) to charge the tablet's battery. The adapter may come in two pieces, both of which must be assembled.

- » **Power charger and cable:** These are included with some tablets that don't use the USB cable to charge the battery.

- » **Useless pamphlets:** If your tablet is like mine, you'll find that the safety and warranty information is far more extensive than the flimsy setup guide. That shows the priority our culture places on lawyers versus technology writers.

- » **The 4G SIM card holder:** For an LTE tablet, you need a 4G SIM card. If you purchased your tablet at a phone store, someone there may have tossed the SIM card holder into the box as well. You can throw it out.

TIP

Keep the box for as long as you own your Android tablet. If you ever need to return the thing, or ship it anywhere, the original box is the ideal container. You can shove all those useless pamphlets and papers back into the box as well.

Charging the battery

The very first thing that I recommend you do with your tablet is give it a full charge. Follow these steps:

1. If necessary, assemble the charging cord.

Attach the charging head (the wall adapter) to the USB cable that came with the tablet.

2. Plug the charging-head part of the USB cable into a wall socket.

3. Plug the other end of the USB cable into the tablet.

4. Wait.

As the tablet charges, you may see the Charging icon appear on the touchscreen. This icon lets you know that the tablet is functioning properly — but don't be alarmed if the battery icon fails to appear.

It's okay if the tablet turns on when you first charge it, but read Chapter 2 to discover how to run initial setup on your Android tablet.

- » Some tablets use their own charging cord, not the USB cable.

- » Even if your Android tablet comes fully charged from the factory, I still recommend giving it an initial charge, to at least familiarize yourself with the process.

>> The battery charges more efficiently if you plug it into a wall, as opposed to charging it from a computer's USB port. Speaking of which:

>> The tablet won't charge when it's connected to the USB port on a computer that isn't turned on.

>> Feel free to use the tablet while the battery is charging. And you don't have to wait for a full charge, either.

>> Some tablets can charge wirelessly, but only when you purchase a special wireless charger.

>> It's been a long time since I've seen an Android tablet come with a removable battery. The only problem with having a nonremovable battery is that if the tablet won't charge, you need to return the entire thing for a refund or replacement.

Tablet Exploration

Everyone loves a good game of hide-and-seek — except when it comes to technology. It's important that you know where certain key items are found on your Android tablet. The problem is that the location of these items isn't consistent, even when two tablets are made by the same manufacturer.

Finding things on the tablet

Take heed of Figure 1-1, which is my attempt at illustrating a generic Android tablet's hardware features. Use this figure as a guide as you follow along on your own tablet to locate some key features.

Important items you'll find on the front of the tablet include the items in this list:

Touchscreen: The biggest part of the tablet is its touchscreen display, which occupies almost all the territory on the front of the device. The touchscreen is a look-touch gizmo: You look at it but also touch it with your fingers to control the tablet.

Front camera: The Android tablet's front-facing camera is found above the touchscreen. On larger tablets, the camera is on top when the tablet is oriented horizontally. (Refer to the left side of Figure 1-1.) On small-format tablets, the camera is on top when the tablet is oriented vertically. (Refer to the right side of Figure 1-1.)

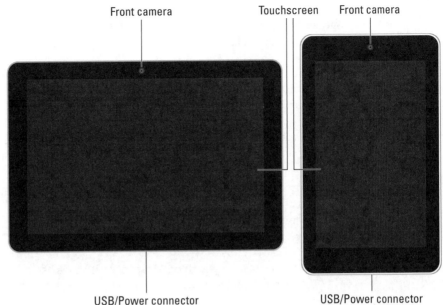

Front camera   Touchscreen   Front camera

FIGURE 1-1:
Things to
find on your
Android tablet.

USB/Power connector   USB/Power connector

Navigation icons: The bottom of the touchscreen shows the Android navigation icons. On some tablets, these icons are physical buttons found below the touchscreen. Refer to Chapter 3 for information on the navigation icons.

Important items found on the tablet's edges include the following:

Power/Lock key: This button, or key, turns the tablet on or off, or locks or unlocks the device. Directions for performing these activities are found in Chapter 2.

Volume key: The tablet's volume control is two buttons in one. Press one side of the key to set the volume higher or the other side to set the volume lower. This key is often found next to the Power/Lock key. It's the larger of the two.

USB/Power connector: This slot is where you connect the USB cable, which is used both to charge the battery and to connect your Android tablet to a computer.

Removable storage slot: Into this slot you insert a microSD card, which expands the tablet's storage. Details are covered in the next section.

SIM card cover: This spot is used to access an LTE tablet's SIM card, which is inserted into a slot beneath the cover.

Headphone jack: This hole is where you can connect standard headphones.

Speaker(s): Stereo speakers are found left and right on the tablet, although smaller-format tablets may have their speakers on the back.

Microphone: A miniscule, circular opening serves as the device's microphone. Some tablets may feature two microphone holes. Don't worry if you can't find them; they're there.

On the back of your Android tablet you'll find one or more logos, plus the tablet's main, or rear, camera. The camera may or may not feature an LED flash.

>> Samsung tablets feature the Home button directly below the touchscreen. This physical button serves the same purpose as the Home navigation icon on other Android tablets.

>> Samsung tablets also feature touch-sensitive Recent and Back buttons.

>> Be careful not to confuse the SIM card slot with the external storage slot. They're not the same thing. You'll rarely, if ever, need to access the SIM card.

TECHNICAL
STUFF

>> SIM stands for Subscriber Identity Module. The SIM card is used by a cellular provider to identify your tablet and keep track of the amount of data transmitted over the mobile data network. Yep, that's so that you can be billed properly. The SIM also gives your LTE tablet a phone number, though it's merely an account number and not something you can dial into or use for sending a text message.

Inserting the microSD card

Some Android tablets offer removable storage in the form of a microSD card. It's used to store photos, videos, music, evil plans, and so on.

The microSD card is teensy. (That's a scientific description.) The card fits into a slot on the edge of your tablet but can also be inserted into an adapter and read by a computer, like any removable media card.

To insert a microSD card into your tablet, heed these directions:

1. **Locate the microSD card hatch on the tablet's edge.**

Figure 1-2 illustrates the hatch's appearance, although it may look subtly different on your tablet. The card may be labeled *microSD*. Do not confuse it with the SIM card cover.

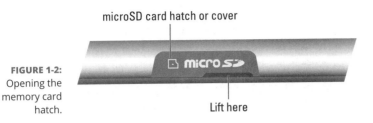
microSD card hatch or cover

Lift here

FIGURE 1-2:
Opening the
memory card
hatch.

2. **Flip open the teensy hatch on the microSD card slot.**

   Insert your thumbnail into the tiny slot on the hatch. Flip the hatch outward. It's attached on one end, so it may not completely pop off.

   Some hatches may pop up when you insert a tiny pin into a hole.

3. **Insert the microSD card into the slot.**

   The card goes in only one way. If you're fortunate, a little outline of the card illustrates the proper orientation. If you're even more fortunate, your eyes will be good enough to see the tiny outline.

   The card makes a faint clicking sound when it's fully inserted. If the card keeps popping out, you're not shoving it in far enough.

4. **Close the hatch covering the microSD card slot.**

If the tablet is on (and has been configured), you may see an onscreen prompt. If so, ignore the prompt and just tap the OK button.

>> It's okay to insert the microSD card when the tablet is on.

>> The tablet works with or without a microSD card installed.

>> The microSD card is a purchase you must make in addition to your Android tablet. Check the tablet's documentation (on the box) to see which capacities are compatible with your tablet.

>> To use a microSD card with a computer, you need an SD card adapter. Insert the microSD card into the adapter, and then plug the SD card adapter into the computer. The adapter is an extra purchase, though some microSD cards come with such an adapter.

>> SD stands for Secure Digital. It is but one of about a zillion media card standards.

>> A microSD card comes in a capacity rated in gigabytes (GB), just like most media storage or memory cards. Common microSD card capacities are 8GB, 16GB, 32GB, and higher. The maximum capacity depends on the tablet.

TECHNICAL STUFF

>> In addition to the microSD card, your Android tablet features internal storage. That storage is used for the programs you install on the tablet, as well as for the tablet's operating system and other control programs.

>> Refer to Chapter 17 for more information on storage.

Removing the microSD card

Most of the time, the microSD card dwells contently inside your Android tablet. When the urge arises to remove it, heed these steps:

WARNING

1. **Turn off your Android tablet.**

   You can damage the media card if you just yank it out of the tablet, which is why I recommend turning off the tablet first. Specific directions for turning off an Android tablet are found in Chapter 2.

2. **Open the itty-bitty hatch covering the microSD card slot.**

3. **Use your fingernail to press the microSD card inward a tad.**

   The microSD card is spring-loaded, so pressing it in eventually pops it outward.

4. **Pinch the microSD card between your fingers and remove it completely.**

The microSD card is too tiny to leave lying around. Put it into a microSD card adapter for use in your PC or another electronic device. Or store it inside a miniature box that you can label with a miniature pen in miniature letters: *microSD Card Inside.* Don't lose it!

TECHNICAL STUFF

It's possible to remove the microSD card without turning off the tablet. To do that, you need to unmount the card while the tablet is running. This technical procedure is explained in Chapter 17.

Optional Accessories

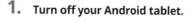

Your credit card company will be thrilled when you discover that an assortment of handy Android tablet accessories are available for purchase. You can find them at the place where you obtained your tablet, online, or in the real world. Here are just a few of the items that you can consider getting to complete your tablet experience:

Earphones: You can use any standard cell phone or portable media player earphones with an Android tablet. Plug the earphones into the headphone jack on the tablet's edge and you're ready to go.

Covers, pouches, and sleeves: Answering the question "Where do I put this thing?" is the handy Android tablet pouch or sleeve accessory. Special pouches that double as covers or tablet stands are also available. Currently popular are covers that feature a wireless keyboard.

Screen protectors: These plastic, clingy things are affixed to the front of the tablet, right over the touchscreen. They help defend the touchscreen glass from finger smudges and sneeze globs while still allowing you to use the touchscreen.

Vehicle charger: Use the vehicle charger to charge the Android tablet in your car. It's an adapter that plugs into your car's 12-volt power supply, in the receptacle that was once known as a cigarette lighter. The vehicle charger is a must-have item if you plan on using the Android tablet's navigation features in your auto or when you need a charge on the road.

Keyboard: You can purchase and use any Bluetooth keyboard with your tablet. Some might be specifically designed for the tablet, which is better than getting any old Bluetooth keyboard. See Chapter 16 for details on Bluetooth.

Other exciting and nifty accessories might be available for your tablet. Check frequently for new garnishes and frills at the location where you bought your tablet.

REMEMBER

TIP

>> None of this extra stuff is essential to using your tablet.

>> You can use Bluetooth earphones or a Bluetooth headset with any Android tablet.

>> If the earphones feature a microphone, you can use that microphone for dictation, recording, and chatting online with friends.

>> If the earphones feature a button, you can use the button to pause and play music. Press the button once to pause, and again to play.

>> Android tablets generally don't recognize more than one Earphones button. For example, if you use earphones that feature a Volume button or Mute button, pressing that extra button does nothing.

>> Another useful accessory to get is a microfiber cloth to help clean the tablet's screen, along with a special cleaning-solution wipe. See Chapter 22 for more information about cleaning an Android tablet's screen.

Where to Keep Your Tablet

Like your car keys, glasses, wallet, and phaser pistol, your Android tablet should be kept in a safe, easy-to-find, always handy place, whether you're at home, at work, on the road, or orbiting the Klingon home world.

Making a home for the tablet

I recommend returning your Android tablet to the same spot whenever you finish using it. If you have a computer, my first suggestion is to make a spot right by the computer. Keep the charging cord handy, or just plug the cord into the computer's USB port so that you can synchronize information with your computer on a regular basis, not to mention keep the tablet charged.

Another handy place to keep the tablet is on your nightstand. That makes sense because, in addition to using the tablet for nighttime reading or video watching, it can serve as an alarm clock. (See Chapter 14.)

Above all, avoid putting the tablet in a place where someone can sit on it, step on it, or otherwise damage it. For example, don't leave the tablet on a table or counter under a stack of newspapers, where it might get accidentally tossed out or put in the recycle bin.

Never leave the tablet on a chair!

REMEMBER

As long as you remember to return the tablet to the same spot when you're done with it, you'll always know where it is.

Taking the Android tablet with you

If you're like me, you probably carry the Android tablet around with you to or from the office, at the airport, or tucked into your pants while you ride in a police car. I hope you're not using the tablet while you're driving. Regardless, it's best to have a portable place to store your tablet while you're on the road.

The ideal place for the tablet is a specially designed pouch or sleeve. The pouch keeps the device from being dinged, scratched, or even unexpectedly turned on while it's in your backpack, purse, or carry-on luggage or wherever you put the tablet when you're not using it.

Also see Chapter 21 for information on using an Android tablet on the road.

Chapter **2**

Android Tablet On and Off

The bestselling *Pencils For Dummies* has no chapter describing how to turn on a pencil. *Pens For Dummies* does have the chapter "Enabling the Pen to Write," but that's not really an on-off thing, and the author of that book describes in great detail how awkward an On-Off switch or power button would be on a pen. Aren't you and I lucky to live in an age when such things are carefully described?

Your Android tablet is far more complex than a pen or a pencil, and, often, it's more useful. As such an advanced piece of technology, your tablet features not an On-Off button but, rather, a Power/Lock key. This key does more than just turn the Android tablet on or off.

Greetings, Android Tablet

It would be so easy to write, "To turn on your Android tablet, press the button and go." As you may fear, such simple directions aren't possible for a sophisticated gizmo.

TIP

>> Initial tablet setup works best when you already have a Google, or Gmail, account. If you lack such an account, you're prompted to create one during the setup process.

>> The tablet will not start unless the battery is charged. See Chapter 1.

Turning on your tablet for the first time

The very, very first time you turn on your Android tablet, you're required to work through the setup process. It's a must, but it needs to be done only once. If your tablet has already been set up, skip to the later section "Turning on the tablet."

The specifics of the setup-and-configuration process differ subtly from tablet to tablet. For example, some tablets may prompt you to sign in to services like Dropbox. Tablets on certain mobile data networks may require you to run specific setup apps, which you'll read about during the configuration process. Generally speaking, however, the process covers basic steps on all Android tablets.

TIP

I recommend reading through these steps first and then turning on the tablet and working through them afterward. The process goes kind of fast, and the screen may dim if you spend too much time waiting between steps:

1. **Press the Power/Lock key to turn on the tablet.**

You may have to press the button longer than you think; when you see the tablet's logo appear on the screen, release the key.

TIP

It's okay to turn on the tablet while it's plugged in and charging.

2. **Answer the questions presented.**

You're asked to select options for some, if not all, of these prompts:

- Select your language

- Activate an LTE tablet on the mobile data network

- Connect to a Wi-Fi network

- Set the time zone

- Accept terms and conditions

- Sign in to your Google account or create a new account

- Add other online accounts

- Set location information

When in doubt, just accept the options as presented to you during the setup process. Tap the SKIP button to make the setting later.

To fill in text fields, use the onscreen keyboard. See Chapter 4 for keyboard information.

Other sections in this chapter, as well as throughout this book, offer information and advice on these settings. You can't screw up anything at this point; any selection you make can be changed later.

3. **After each choice, tap the NEXT button or icon.**

   The button might be labeled with the text *NEXT,* or it may appear as a triangle icon, shown in the margin.

4. **Tap the FINISH button.**

   The FINISH button appears on the last screen of the setup procedure.

From this point on, starting the tablet works as described in the next section.

After the initial setup, you're taken to the Home screen. Chapter 3 offers more Home screen information, which you should probably read right away, before the temptation to play with your new tablet becomes unbearable.

>> You may find yourself asked various questions or prompted to try various tricks when you first start to use the tablet. Some of those prompts are helpful, but it's okay to skip some. To do so, tap the GOT IT or OK button or select the Do Not Show Again check box.

>> Additional information on connecting your tablet to a Wi-Fi network is found in Chapter 16.

>> Location settings relate to how the tablet knows its position on Planet Earth. I recommend keeping all these items activated to get the most from your Android tablet.

>> It's not necessary to use any specific software provided by the tablet's manufacturer or your cellular provider. For example, if you don't want a Samsung account, you don't need to sign up for one; skip that step.

>> Your Google account provides for coordination between your new Android tablet and your Gmail messages, contacts, Google Calendar appointments, and information and data from other Google Internet applications.

» See the later sidebar "Who is this Android person?" for more information about the Android operating system.

Turning on the tablet

To turn on your Android tablet, press and hold the Power/Lock button. After a few seconds, you see the tablet's start-up logo, enjoy some hypnotic animation, and maybe even hear a tune. Release the Power/Lock key; the device is starting.

Eventually, you see the unlock screen. See the later section "Working the Lock screen" for information on what to do next.

» If you've encrypted the tablet's data, you must work a screen lock before the device fully starts. See Chapter 20 for details on data encryption.

» The tablet won't turn on when the battery charge is too low, even if you plug in the tablet. In that situation, wait for the battery to charge.

Unlocking the tablet

Most of the time, you don't turn your Android tablet off and on. Instead, you lock and unlock it. To unlock it, press the Power/Lock key. A quick press is all that's needed. The touchscreen comes to life and you see the Lock screen, illustrated in Figure 2-1.

To begin using the tablet, swipe the screen as illustrated in the figure. If you have screen lock applied, work the lock; see the next section for details.

Eventually, you find yourself at the Home screen, where you can begin to use and interact with your Android tablet.

» On Samsung tablets, press the Home key to unlock the tablet. The key is centered below the touchscreen.

» On the Samsung Galaxy Note tablet, remove the S Pen to unlock the device.

» If your tablet features a cover, opening the cover unlocks the device.

» Android tablets don't snore while sleeping, but they can dream. See Chapter 23.

Lock Screen notifications

FIGURE 2-1:
The Lock
screen.

Swipe the screen to unlock   Lock Screen app

Working the Lock screen

You must swipe the screen to dismiss the tablet's Lock screen and view the Home screen. That quick step doesn't really make the "Lock screen" seem too secure, does it? To add more security, you can apply a screen lock beyond the simple Swipe lock. These screen lock types include:

Pattern: Trace a preset pattern over the nine dots on the screen.

PIN: Type a number to unlock the device.

Password: Type a password, which can include letters, numbers, and symbols.

Each of these screen locks appears after you swipe the screen and before you can access the Home screen. To apply these locks, see Chapter 20.

>> The Swipe lock is considered the standard Android screen lock: Swipe the screen as directed in the preceding section.

>> Some tablets may offer a screen lock labeled None. When this "lock" is applied, the Home screen appears instantly when the tablet is unlocked.

>> The PIN and Password locks are considered the most secure. To use certain tablet features, you must choose either the PIN or password screen lock.

>> Also see Chapter 20 for information on specialized screen locks, including the fingerprint lock, signature lock, and others.

Unlocking and running an app

Your tablet's Lock screen may feature app icons, such as the Camera icon, shown earlier in Figure 2-1. To unlock that tablet and run that app, drag its icon across the touchscreen.

If you've set a secure screen lock, unlocking and running an app runs only that app. When you attempt to access other tablet features or apps, you're prompted to work the screen lock.

TECHNICAL STUFF

WHO IS THIS ANDROID PERSON?

Just like a computer, your Android tablet has an operating system. It's the main program in charge of all the software (apps) inside the tablet. Unlike a computer, however, Android is a mobile device operating system, designed primarily for use in tablets and cell phones.

Android is based on the Linux operating system, which is also a computer operating system, though it's much more stable and bug-free than Windows, so it's not as popular. Google owns, maintains, and develops Android, which is why your online Google information is synced with your tablet.

The Android mascot, shown here, often appears on Android apps or hardware. He has no official name, though most folks call him Andy.

Add Accounts

Your Android tablet can serve as home to your various online incarnations. The list includes your email accounts, online services, subscriptions, and other digital personas. I recommend adding those accounts to your tablet to continue the setup-and-configuration process.

With your tablet on and unlocked, follow these steps:

1. **Tap the Apps icon.**

   The Apps icon is found at the bottom of the Home screen. It looks similar to the icon shown in the margin, although it has many variations. See Chapter 3 for the variety.

   When you tap the Apps icon, you see the Apps drawer, which lists all apps available on your tablet.

2. **Open the Settings app.**

   You may have to swipe the Apps drawer screen a few times, paging through the various icons, to find the Settings app.

   After you tap the Settings icon, the Settings app runs. It shows commands for configuring various tablet options and features.

3. **Choose the Accounts category.**

   Some tablets may title the item Accounts and Sync.

   Upon success, you see all existing accounts on your tablet, similar to the ones shown in Figure 2-2.

4. **Tap Add Account.**

   The Add Account item is illustrated in Figure 2-2.

5. **Choose an account type from the list.**

   For example, to add a Facebook account, choose Facebook.

   Don't worry if you don't see the exact type of account you want to add. You may have to add a specific app before an account appears. Chapter 15 covers adding apps.

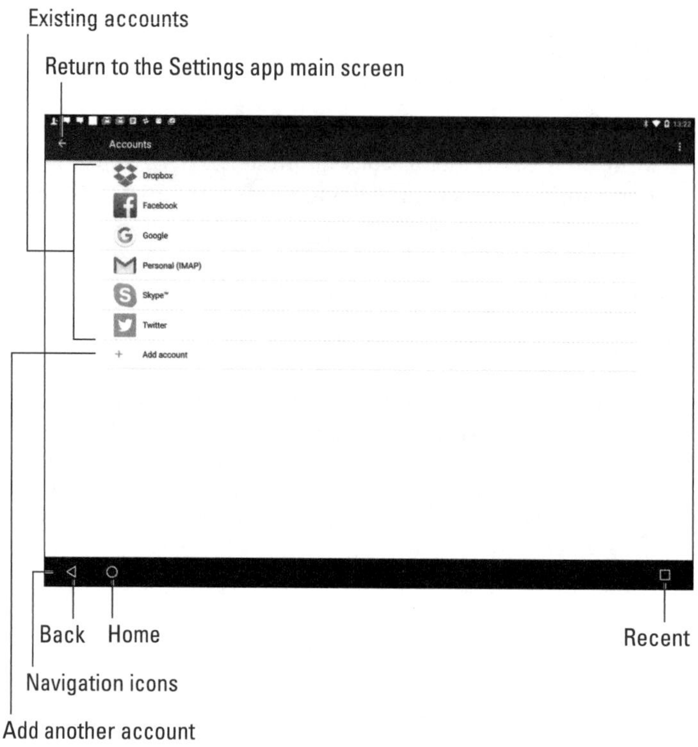

Existing accounts

Return to the Settings app main screen

FIGURE 2-2:
Accounts
listed in the
Settings app.

Back   Home

Recent

Navigation icons

Add another account

6. Follow the directions to sign in to your account.

The steps you take depend on the type of account you're adding. Generally speaking, you sign in using your existing username and password.

Repeat these steps to continue adding accounts. When you're done, tap the Home navigation icon to return to the Home screen.

>> See Chapter 6 for specific information on adding email accounts to your Android tablet.

>> Chapter 9 covers social networking on your tablet. Refer there for specific information on adding Facebook, Twitter, and other social networking accounts.

TRANSFERRING INFORMATION FROM YOUR OLD TABLET

Here's one task you don't need to worry about: All the Google information associated with your old tablet — or your current phone — is instantly transferred to your new Android tablet. This information includes contacts, Gmail, events, and other Googly account data. You can even install apps you've previously obtained (free or purchased).

As you add other accounts to your tablet, the information associated with those accounts is migrated as well. The only category not migrated is media installed on the old device. If you've synchronized the media with an online-sharing service, the information can easily be transferred. Otherwise, refer to Chapter 17 for information on moving over photos, videos, and music to your new Android tablet.

The End of Your Android Tablet Day

I know of three ways to say goodbye to your Android tablet; only one of them involves the application of high explosives. The other methods are documented in this section.

Locking the tablet

Locking the tablet is cinchy: Simply press and release the Power/Lock key. The display goes dark; your tablet is locked.

REMEMBER

>> Your Android tablet still works while locked; it receives email, can play music, and signals alerts. While it's locked, the tablet doesn't use as much power as it would with the display on.

>> The tablet will probably spend most of its time locked.

>> Locking doesn't turn off the tablet.

>> Any timers or alarms you set still trigger when your tablet is locked. See Chapter 14 for information on setting alarms.

>> To unlock your tablet, press and release the Power/Lock key. See the section "Unlocking the tablet," earlier in this chapter.

>> Refer to Chapter 19 for information on setting the automatic timeout value for locking the tablet.

Turning off your Android tablet

To turn off your tablet, heed these steps:

1. **Press and hold the Power/Lock key.**

You see the Device Options card, which may contain only one item: Power Off. Some tablets feature more items on this menu, such as the Samsung version of the Device Options card, shown in Figure 2-3.

Stock Android Device Options card

Power off   **Restart**

FIGURE 2-3:
The Device
Options menu.

Samsung Device Options buttons

If you chicken out and don't want to turn off your tablet, tap the Back icon to dismiss the Device Options card.

2. **Tap the Power Off item.**

If a confirmation message appears, tap the OK button. The Android tablet turns itself off.

The tablet doesn't run when it's off, so it doesn't remind you of appointments and doesn't collect email, nor do you hear any alarms you've set. The tablet isn't angry with you for turning it off, though you may sense some resentment when you turn it on again.

>> Varieties of the Device Options menu on various Android tablets include the Restart command as well as commands to silence the speakers or control vibration. I've also seen a Kid Mode command on some tablets.

>> The tablet can be charged while it's off.

>> Keep your tablet in a safe place while it's turned off. Chapter 1 offers some suggestions.

Chapter **3**

How Android Tablets Work

t used to be that you could judge how advanced something was by how many buttons it had. Starting with the dress shirt and progressing to the first computer, more buttons meant fancier technology. Your Android tablet tosses that rule right out the window. Beyond the Power/Lock key and the volume key, the device is shamefully bereft of buttons.

My point is that in order to use your tablet, you have to understand how a touchscreen works. That touchscreen is the tablet's main input device — the gizmo you use to do all sorts of wondrous and useful things. Knowing how to use a touchscreen is important to getting the most from your Android tablet.

Basic Operations

Your Android tablet's ability to frustrate you is only as powerful as your fear of the touchscreen and how it works. After you clear that hurdle, as well as understand some other basic operations, you'll be on your way toward mobile device contentment.

Touching the touchscreen

Minus any buttons and knobs, the way you control an Android tablet is to manipulate things on the touchscreen with one or two fingers. It doesn't matter which fingers you use, and you should feel free to experiment with other body parts as well, though I find fingers to be handy.

Here are some of the common ways to manipulate the touchscreen:

Tap: The basic touchscreen technique is to touch it. You tap an object, an icon, a control, a menu item, a doodad, and so on. The tap operation is similar to a mouse click on a computer. It may also be referred to as a *touch* or a *press*.

Double-tap: Tap the screen twice in the same location. Double-tapping can be used to zoom in on an image or a map, but it can also zoom out. Because of the double-tap's dual nature, I recommend using the pinch or spread operation to zoom.

Long-press: Tap part of the screen and keep your finger down. Depending on what you're doing, a pop-up menu or card may appear, or the item you're long-pressing may get "picked up" so that you can drag (move) it around. Long-press might also be referred to as *tap and hold*.

Swipe: To swipe, tap your finger on one spot and then move your finger to another spot. Swipes can go up, down, left, or right; the touchscreen content moves in the direction in which you swipe your finger. A swipe can be fast or slow. It's also called a *flick* or *slide*.

Drag: A combination of long-press and then swipe, the drag operation moves items on the screen. Start with the long-press, and then keep your finger on the screen to swipe. Lift your finger to complete the action.

Pinch: A pinch involves two fingers, which start out separated and then are brought together. The effect is used to zoom out, to reduce the size of an image, or to see more of a map. This move may also be called a *pinch close*.

Spread: The opposite of pinch is spread. You start out with your fingers together and then spread them. The spread is used to zoom in, to enlarge an image, or see more detail on a map. It's also known as a *pinch open*.

Rotate: A few apps let you rotate an image on the screen by touching with two fingers and twisting them around a center point. If you have trouble with this operation, pretend that you're turning the dial on a safe.

REMEMBER

You can't manipulate the touchscreen while wearing gloves unless the gloves are specially designed for using electronic touchscreens, such as the gloves that Batman wears.

Using the navigation icons

Below the touchscreen dwell three navigation icons. They can appear as part of the touchscreen itself; or, on some tablets, they may be part of the bezel or may even be physical buttons. These icons serve specific functions throughout the Android operating system.

The traditional three navigation icons are Back, Home, and Recent. Table 3-1 illustrates how the navigation icons look for the most recent releases of the Android operating system.

TABLE 3-1   **Navigation Icon Varieties**

Icon	Lollipop, Marshmallow, Nougat	KitKat and Earlier
Home	◯	⌂
Back	◁	↩
Recent	▢	⧉

Home: No matter what you're doing on the tablet, tap this icon to display the Home screen. When you're already viewing the Home screen, tap this icon to view the main, or center, Home screen page.

Back: The Back icon serves several purposes, all of which fit neatly under the concept of "back." Tap the icon once to return to a previous page, dismiss an onscreen menu, close a card, and so on.

The Back icon changes its orientation, as shown in the margin. Tap this icon to hide the onscreen keyboard, dismiss dictation, or perform other actions similar to the Back navigation icon.

Recent: Tap the Recent icon to display the *Overview,* a list of recently opened or currently running apps. See the later section "Switching between running apps" for more information on the Overview.

The three navigation icons may hide themselves when certain apps run. To access the icons, tap the screen. For some full-screen apps and games, swipe the screen from top to bottom to see the navigation icons.

Setting the volume

The volume key on the tablet's edge controls the noise emitting from the tablet's speaker. Press the top part of the key to make the volume louder. Press the bottom of the key to make the volume softer. When the volume key is on the top edge of the tablet, press the left part to increase volume and the right part to decrease volume.

As you press the volume key, a volume card appears on the touchscreen to illustrate the relative volume level, similar to the one shown in Figure 3-1. You can continue pressing the volume key or use your finger to adjust the onscreen slider and set the volume.

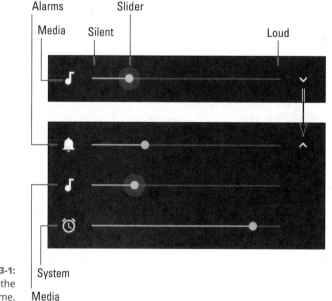

FIGURE 3-1: Setting the volume.

Not every volume card looks like the one shown in Figure 3-1, though they all feature a slider control. Additional controls let you set specific volumes; tap an icon on the card to view details. If the Settings icon appears on the card, tap it to make more specific adjustments.

TIP

>> When the volume is set all the way down, the tablet is muted.

>> The volume key works even when the tablet is locked. That means you don't need to unlock the tablet if you're playing music and you only need to adjust the volume.

>> Some tablets may enter Vibration mode when the volume is muted, though not every tablet features Vibration mode.

>> Refer to Chapter 19 for more details on your tablet's volume controls.

Changing the orientation

Your Android tablet features a gizmo called an *accelerometer.* It determines in which direction the tablet is pointed or whether you've reoriented the device from an upright position to a horizontal one (or vice versa) or even upside down. That way, the information displayed on the tablet's screen always appears upright, no matter how you hold it.

To demonstrate how the tablet orients itself, rotate the tablet to the left or right. Most apps change their orientation to match however you've oriented the tablet, such as the Home screen, shown in Figure 3-2.

FIGURE 3-2:
Android tablet
orientation.

Vertical orientation   Horizontal orientation

The rotation feature may not work for all apps, and it may not even work for the Home screen. In that case, open the web browser app to experiment with rotation.

TIP

» Most games present themselves in one orientation only.

» The onscreen keyboard is more usable when the tablet is in its horizontal orientation. Chapter 4 covers using the onscreen keyboard.

» You can lock the orientation if the rotating screen bothers you. See the section "Making Quick Settings," later in this chapter. Options available include Auto-Rotate, to have the tablet automatically change rotation, or Landscape or Portrait, to lock the tablet in that specific orientation.

» A great app that demonstrates the tablet's accelerometer is the game Labyrinth. You can purchase it at Google Play or download the free version, Labyrinth Lite. See Chapter 15 for more information about Google Play.

Selecting a group of items

Unique to the tablet's touchscreen is the manner in which a group of items is selected. On a computer, you drag the mouse over the items. On a touchscreen, you perform these steps:

1. **Long-press the first item, such as a photo thumbnail in an album.**

   The item is selected, and it appears highlighted on the screen or grows a tiny check mark. Also, the Action Bar appears atop the screen, similar to the one shown in Figure 3-3. It lists icons such as Share and Delete, which manipulate the group of selected items.

FIGURE 3-3: An object-selection Action Bar.

2. **Tap additional items to select them.**

   As long as the Action Bar appears, you tap to keep adding items to the mix. The Action Bar lists the total number of selected items, as illustrated in Figure 3-3.

3. **Do something with the group.**

   Choose an icon from the Action Bar.

To cancel the selection, tap the Cancel (X) icon on the Action Bar, which deselects all items.

There's No Place Like Home Screen

The *Home screen* is where you start your Android day. It's the location from which you start an app. Knowing about the Home screen is an important part of understanding your Android tablet.

 To view the Home screen at any time, tap the Home navigation icon found at the bottom of the touchscreen. Some tablets feature a physical Home button or key, which performs the same duties as the Home navigation icon.

Touring the Home screen

The typical Android tablet Home screen is illustrated in Figure 3-4. Several fun and interesting things appear on the Home screen. Find these items on your own tablet's Home screen:

Status bar: This area at the top of the screen is the status bar. It shows notification icons and status icons, including the current time. The status bar may disappear, in which case a quick swipe of the screen from the top downward redisplays it.

Notification icons: These icons come and go, depending on what happens in your digital life. For example, new icons appear whenever you receive a new email message or have a pending appointment. See the later section "Reviewing notifications."

Status icons: These icons represent the tablet's current condition, such as the type of network connection, signal strength, battery status, as well as other items.

App launchers: These icons represent apps installed on your tablet. Tap a launcher to run the associated app.

Widgets: Widgets work like teensy programs that display information or let you control the tablet, manipulate a feature, access an app, or do something purely amusing.

Folders: Multiple launchers can be stored in a folder. Tap the folder to open it and view the launchers inside. See Chapter 18 for more information on folders.

Wallpaper: The background image you see on the Home screen is the wallpaper.

Folder

Status bar   Notification icons   Status icons

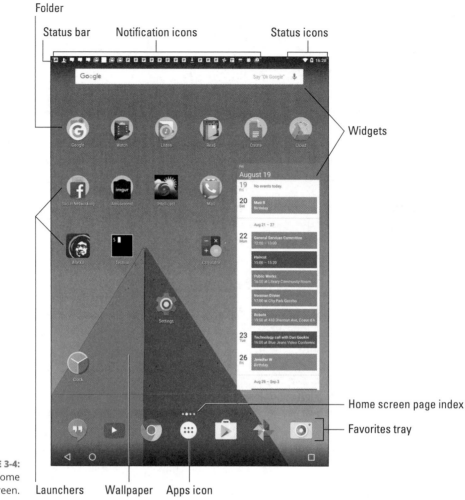

Widgets

Home screen page index

Favorites tray

FIGURE 3-4:
The Home
screen.

Launchers   Wallpaper   Apps icon

Favorites tray: The lineup of icons near the bottom of the screen contains slots for popular launcher icons. The favorites tray shows the same icons at the bottom of every Home screen page.

Apps icon: Tap this icon to view the Apps drawer, a collection of all apps available on your tablet. See the later section "Finding an app in the Apps drawer."

REMEMBER

Ensure that you recognize the names of the various parts of the Home screen. These terms are used throughout this book and in whatever other scant Android tablet documentation exists.

>> The Home screen is entirely customizable. You can add and remove launchers from the Home screen, add widgets and shortcuts, and even change wallpaper (background) images. See Chapter 19 for more information.

>> Touching a part of the Home screen that doesn't feature an icon or a control does nothing. That is, unless you're using the live wallpaper feature. In that case, touching the screen changes the wallpaper in some way, depending on the wallpaper that's selected. You can read more about live wallpaper in Chapter 19.

>> You may see numbers affixed to certain Home screen icons. Those numbers indicate pending actions, such as unread email messages, indicated by the icon shown in the margin.

Accessing multiple Home screen pages

The Home screen is more than what you see. It's actually an entire street of Home screens, with only one Home screen panel displayed at a time.

To switch from one panel to another, swipe the Home screen left or right. There are pages to the left of the main Home screen page, and pages to the right. Use the Home screen page index (refer to Figure 3-4) to determine which Home screen page you're viewing.

>> When you tap the Home navigation icon, you return to the last Home screen page you viewed. To return to the main Home screen panel, tap the Home icon a second time.

>> On some tablets, the main Home screen page is shown by the House icon on the Home screen page index.

>> The number of available Home screen pages depends on the tablet. See Chapter 19 for information on adding or removing Home screen pages.

>> The leftmost Home screen page on some tablets is the Google Now app. See Chapter 14 for information on Google Now.

Reviewing notifications

Notifications appear as icons at the top of the Home screen, as illustrated earlier, in Figure 3-4. To review them, or to pull down the notifications drawer, you drag your finger from the top of the screen downward. The notifications drawer is illustrated in Figure 3-5.

Swipe the list of notifications up or down to review them. To deal with a specific notification, tap it. What happens next depends on the notification or the app that generated it. Typically, the app runs and shows more details.

To dismiss an individual notification, swipe it left or right. To dismiss all notifications, tap the Clear Notifications icon, shown in the margin. Your tablet might instead show the CLEAR button. If the Clear Notifications icon isn't visible, swipe the notifications drawer all the way to the button.

To hide the notifications drawer, tap the Back icon, swipe the screen upward, or tap anywhere else on the Home screen.

>> Notifications can stack up if you don't deal with them!

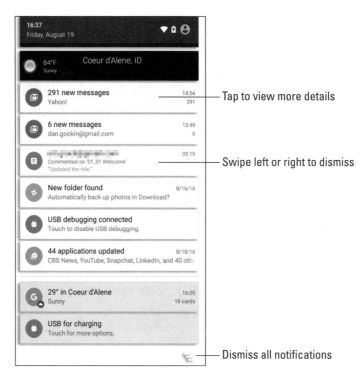

Tap to view more details

Swipe left or right to dismiss

Dismiss all notifications

FIGURE 3-5:
The notifications drawer.

>> When more notifications are present than can be shown, the More Notifications icon appears on the far left end of the status bar, similar to what's shown in the margin.

>> Dismissing some notifications doesn't prevent them from appearing again in the future. For example, notifications to update your apps continue to appear, as do calendar reminders.

>> Ongoing notifications cannot be dismissed. They include items such as USB (refer to Figure 3-5), Bluetooth, and Wi-Fi connections.

» Some apps, such as Facebook and Twitter, don't display notifications unless you're logged in. See Chapter 9.

» Your Android tablet plays a notification ringtone whenever a new notification floats in. You can choose which sound plays; see Chapter 19 for more information.

» Notifications may also appear on the tablet's Lock screen. Controlling which types of notifications appear is covered in Chapter 20.

Making Quick Settings

Many common settings for Android tablet features are found in the Quick Settings drawer, which sits atop the notifications drawer. Use the Quick Settings to access popular tablet features or turn settings on or off, such as Bluetooth, Wi-Fi, Airplane Mode, Auto-Rotate, and more.

To access the Quick Settings, swipe the screen from top to bottom twice. The first time you see the navigation drawer; the second time you see the Quick Settings, similar to what's shown in Figure 3-6.

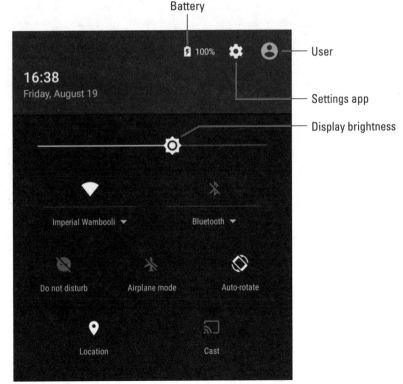

FIGURE 3-6: The Quick Settings drawer.

Samsung tablets always show the Quick Settings atop the navigation drawer. Figure 3-7 illustrates how the icons may look. You can swipe them left or right to view more or tap the downward-pointing chevron to see all available Quick Settings.

To dismiss the Quick Settings drawer, tap either the Back or Home navigation icons.

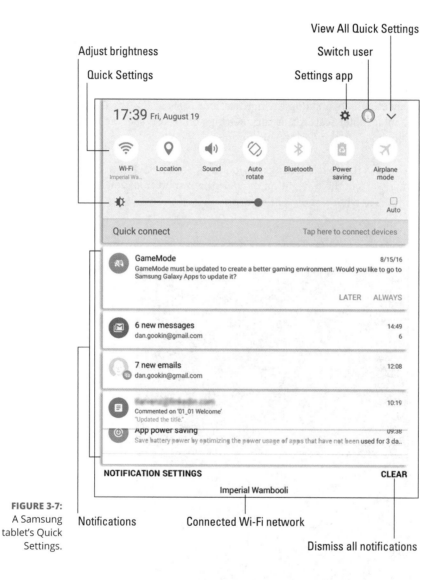

View All Quick Settings

Adjust brightness

Switch user

Quick Settings

Settings app

FIGURE 3-7:
A Samsung
tablet's Quick
Settings.

Notifications

Connected Wi-Fi network

Dismiss all notifications

The World of Apps

You probably didn't purchase a tablet so that you could enjoy the thrill-a-minute punch that's packed by the Android operating system. No, an Android tablet's success lies with the apps you obtain. Knowing how to deal with apps is vital to being a successful, happy Android tablet user.

Starting an app

To start an app, tap its launcher. The app starts.

Apps can be started from the Home screen: Tap a launcher to start the associated app. Apps can be started also from the Apps drawer, as described in the later section "Finding an app in the Apps drawer."

You can also start an app found in a Home screen folder: Tap to open the folder, and then tap a launcher to start that app.

Quitting an app

Unlike on a computer, you don't need to quit apps on your Android tablet. To leave an app, tap the Home icon to return to the Home screen. You can keep tapping the Back icon to back out of an app. Or you can tap the Recent icon to switch to another running app.

TECHNICAL
STUFF

>> Some apps feature a Quit command or an Exit command, but for the most part, you don't quit an app on your tablet — not like you quit an app on a computer.

>> If necessary, the Android operating system shuts down apps you haven't used in a while. You can directly stop apps run amok, which is described in Chapter 18.

Finding an app in the Apps drawer

The launchers you see on the Home screen don't represent all the apps in your tablet. To view all installed apps, you must visit the Apps drawer: Tap the Apps icon on the Home screen. This icon has a different look to it, depending on your tablet. Figure 3-8 illustrates common versions of the Apps icon, though more varieties may exist.

WONDERFUL WIDGETS

Like apps, widgets appear on the Home screen. To use a widget, tap it. What happens after that depends on the widget and what it does.

For example, the YouTube widget lets you peruse videos. The Calendar widget shows a preview of your upcoming schedule. A Twitter widget may display recent tweets. Other widgets do interesting things, display useful information, or give you access to the tablet's settings or features.

New widgets are obtained from Google Play, just like apps. See Chapter 18 for information on working with widgets on the Home screen.

FIGURE 3-8:
Apps icon
varieties.

After you tap the Apps icon, you see the Apps drawer. Swipe through the icons up and down or left and right across the touchscreen.

To run an app, tap its icon. The app starts, taking over the screen and doing whatever magical thing that app does.

TIP

>> As you add new apps to your tablet, they appear in the Apps drawer. See Chapter 15 for information on adding new apps.

>> The Apps drawer may list frequently opened apps at the top of the list. These apps are good candidates for adding to the Home screen. See Chapter 18 for details on adding apps to the Home screen.

>> Some tablets allow you to create folders in the Apps drawer. These folders contain multiple apps, which helps keep things organized. To access apps in the folder, tap the Folder icon.

>> The Apps drawer displays apps alphabetically. On some tablets, you can switch to a non-alphabetical viewing grid. With that feature active, it's possible to rearrange the app icons in any order you like.

Switching between running apps

The apps you run on your tablet don't close when you dismiss them from the screen. For the most part, they stay running. To switch between running apps, or to any app you've recently opened, tap the Recent icon. You see the Overview, similar to what's shown in Figure 3-9.

Swipe the list to view all the apps. Tap the app's card to switch to that app. To exit from the Overview, tap the Back navigation icon.

>> To remove an app from the Overview, swipe it off the list or tap the X (Close) icon, as illustrated in Figure 3-9.

Dismiss an app

Recent apps

Recent icon

FIGURE 3-9: The Overview shows recently used apps.

» Removing an app from the Overview is pretty much the same thing as quitting an app.

» For tablets that lack the Recent icon, long-press the Home icon to see the Overview.

REMEMBER

» The Android operating system may shut down apps that haven't received attention for a while. Don't be surprised if you see an app missing from the Overview. If so, just start it up again as you normally would.

Common Android Icons

In addition to the navigation icons, various other icons appear while you use your Android tablet. These icons serve common functions in apps as well as in the Android operating system. Table 3-2 lists the most common icons and their functions.

TABLE 3-2   ## Common Icons

Icon	Name	Function
◣	Action Bar	Displays a list or menu. This teensy icon appears in the lower right corner of a button or image, indicating that actions (commands) are attached.
⋮	Action Overflow	Displays a list of actions, similar to a menu.
✚	Add	Adds or creates an item. The plus symbol (+) may be used in combination with other symbols, depending on the app.
✕	Close	Dismisses a card or clears text from an input field.
🗑	Delete	Removes one or more items from a list or deletes a message.
🎤	Dictation	Activates voice input.
✓	Done	Dismisses the Action Bar or confirms and saves edits.

Icon	Name	Function
Edit	Edit	Lets you edit an item, add text, or fill in fields.
Favorite	Favorite	Flags a favorite item, such as a contact or a web page.
Refresh	Refresh	Fetches new information or reloads.
Search	Search	Searches the screen, tablet, or Internet for a tidbit of information.
Settings	Settings	Adjusts options for an app.
Share	Share	Shares information via a specific app, such as Gmail or Facebook.
Side Menu	Side Menu	Also called the hamburger, can be tapped to view the navigation drawer available in most Android apps.

Various sections throughout this book give examples of using the icons. Their images appear in the book's margins where relevant.

>> Other common symbols are used on icons in various apps. For example, the standard Play and Pause icons are used as well.

>> The Share icon shown in Table 3-2 has an evil twin, shown in the margin. Both icons represent the Share action.

>> Samsung tablets use the MORE button in place of the Action Overflow icon. In fact, you often see text buttons such as SAVE or CLEAR instead of icons on Samsung tablets.

>> Older Samsung tablets may use the Menu icon to display onscreen menus. This icon serves the same function as the Action Overflow icon, shown in Table 3-2. The icon is featured as a button on the device.

>> Another variation on the Settings icon is shown in the margin. It serves the same purpose as the Gear icon, shown in Table 3-2, although this older Settings icon is being phased out.

Chapter **4**

Creating and Editing Text

Your Android tablet lacks a keyboard — a real one, at least. To sate the tablet's text-input desires, you use something called an onscreen keyboard. It works like a real keyboard, but with the added frustration that it lacks moveable keys. Don't fret! You can add a real keyboard to your tablet, and you can even forgo typing and simply dictate your text.

Behold the Onscreen Keyboard

The onscreen keyboard reveals itself on the bottom half of the tablet's touch-screen whenever text input is required. The stock Android keyboard, known as the *Google Keyboard,* is shown in Figure 4-1.

No matter how the keyboard looks, all onscreen keyboards are based on the traditional QWERTY layout: You see keys from A through Z, albeit not in that order. You also see the Shift key for changing the letter case, and the Delete key, which back-spaces and erases. Your tablet may show more keys — such as Tab and Caps Lock — or it may show fewer keys. Samsung tablets use the Samsung keyboard, illustrated in Figure 4-2. It works similarly to the Google Keyboard, but offers its own special features, such as a Ctrl (control) key and cursor keys, as shown in the figure.

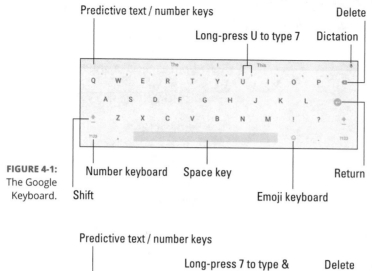

FIGURE 4-1:
The Google
Keyboard.

Predictive text / number keys

Long-press U to type 7   Dictation

Delete

Number keyboard   Space key   Return

Shift   Emoji keyboard

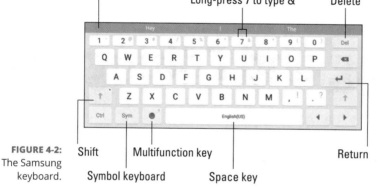

FIGURE 4-2:
The Samsung
keyboard.

Predictive text / number keys

Long-press 7 to type &   Delete

Shift   Multifunction key   Return

Symbol keyboard   Space key

The Return key changes its look, depending on what you're typing. Your keyboard may show these variations graphically or by labeling the key with text, both of which are shown in Figure 4-3.

FIGURE 4-3:
Google
Keyboard
Return-key
variations.

Return   Search   Go   Next   Done

Here's what each key does:

Return: Just like the Return or Enter key on a computer keyboard, this key ends a paragraph of text. It's used mostly when filling in long stretches of text or when multiline input is required.

Search: You see this key appear when you're searching for something. Tap the key to start the search.

Go: This key directs the app to proceed with a search, accept input, or perform another action.

Next: This key appears when you type information into multiple fields. Tap this key to switch from one field to the next, such as when typing a username and password.

Done: This key appears whenever you've finished typing text in the final field and you're ready to submit input.

The large key at the bottom center of the onscreen keyboard is the *Space key.* It's flanked left and right by other keys that may change, depending on the context of what you're typing. For example, the / (slash) key or .com key may appear in order to assist in typing a web page or email address. Though these and other keys may change, the basic alphabetic keys remain the same.

>> To display the onscreen keyboard, tap any text field or spot on the screen where typing is permitted.

>> If you pine for a real keyboard, one that exists in the fourth dimension, you're not stuck. See the nearby sidebar, "A real keyboard?"

>> To dismiss the onscreen keyboard, tap the Back icon. It may appear as the Hide icon, shown in the margin.

>> The Samsung keyboard features a multifunction key. (Refer to Figure 4-2.) Its label varies, showing perhaps the Emoji icon, the Settings icon, or the Dictation icon. Long-press the multifunction key to view its options.

The keyboard changes its width when you reorient the tablet. The keyboard's horizontal presentation is wider and easier for typing.

TIP

A REAL KEYBOARD?

TIP

If typing is your thing and the onscreen keyboard doesn't do it for you, consider getting your Android tablet a real keyboard. A common tablet accessory is a Bluetooth keyboard. They come separate, as part of a docking stand, or integrated into a portfolio cover. The Bluetooth keyboard connects wirelessly, giving you not only a "real" keyboard but also all the divine goodness that wireless brings. You can read more about Bluetooth in Chapter 16.

Everybody Was Touchscreen Typing

In the 21st century, typing has become a basic human activity. Typing on a touchscreen keyboard, however, is still wacky. Don't feel bad if you're the world's fastest typist yet you can only hunt-and-peck on the tablet's screen. That's a limitation everyone has to face. Your Android tablet offers some tricks to make the pain less uncomfortable.

Typing one character at a time

The onscreen keyboard is pretty easy to figure out: Tap a letter to produce the character. As you type, the key you touch is highlighted. The tablet may give a wee bit of feedback in the form of a faint click or vibration.

REMEMBER

>> To type in all caps, tap the Shift key twice. The Shift key may appear highlighted, the shift symbol may change color, or a colored highlight may appear on the key, all of which indicate that Shift Lock is on. Tap the Shift key again to deactivate Shift Lock.

>> Above all, it helps to type slowly until you get used to the onscreen keyboard.

>> A blinking cursor on the touchscreen shows where new text appears, which is similar to how typing text works on a computer.

>> When you make a mistake, tap the Delete key to back up and erase.

>> When you type a password, the character you type appears briefly, but for security reasons, it's then replaced by a black dot.

>> See the later section "Text Editing and Correcting" for more details on editing your text so that you can fix those myriad typos and boo-boos.

Accessing special characters

You're not limited to typing only the characters shown on the alphabetic keyboard. On the Google Keyboard, tap the ?123 key to access two additional keyboard layouts, as shown in Figure 4-4.

To switch from the number keyboard to the symbol keyboard, tap the ~[< key.

Tap the 1234 key to access a numeric input pad.

Tap the ☺ key to view the emoji keyboard.

Tap the ABC key to return to the alphabetic keyboard.

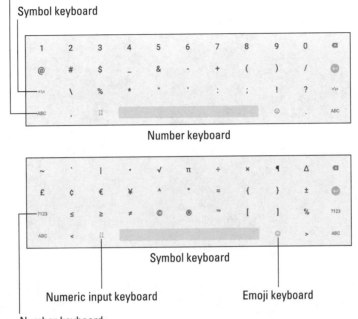

Alpha keyboard

Symbol keyboard

Number keyboard

Symbol keyboard

FIGURE 4-4:
The number
and symbol
keyboards.

Numeric input keyboard

Emoji keyboard

Number keyboard

On the Samsung keyboard, tap the Sym key to access symbols. Use the 1/2 and 2/2 keys to page between the two symbol keyboards.

TIP

Be on the lookout for keys that feature a second character. Refer to Figures 4-1 and 4-2 for examples on the onscreen keyboard's top row. The secret is to long-press those keys to access the second character.

Other keys on the onscreen keyboard also feature special characters, though they're not that obvious. Again, long-press the key to view a pop-up palette of optional characters, similar to those shown for the A key in Figure 4-5.

Choose a character from the pop-up palette. If you choose the wrong character, tap the Delete key on the onscreen keyboard to erase the mistyped symbol.

Using predictive text to type quickly

As you type, you may see a selection of word suggestions just above the keyboard. That's the tablet's predictive-text feature. You can use this feature to greatly accelerate your typing: As you type, tap a word suggestion atop the onscreen keyboard. That word is inserted into the text.

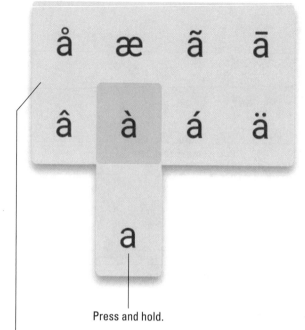

FIGURE 4-5:
Special-symbol
pop-up
palette-thing.

Press and hold.

Drag your finger over a character to select it.

If the desired word doesn't appear, continue typing: The predictive-text feature makes suggestions based on what you've typed so far.

TIP

>> If you see a predictive-text word in boldface, tap the Space key to insert that word. Not every version of the onscreen keyboard supports this feature.

>> If predictive text replaces your correctly typed word with something else, tap the Delete key. The replaced word is restored.

>> With some versions of the onscreen keyboard, you can long-press a word to see similar words.

>> The predictive-text feature is unavailable for typing passwords or when filling in forms.

>> If the predictive-text feature is inactive, see Chapter 19 for information on activating it.

Typing without lifting your finger

If you're really after typing speed, consider using *gesture typing*. It allows you to swipe your finger over the onscreen keyboard to type words. It's like mad scribbling but with a positive result.

To use gesture typing, drag a finger over letters on the onscreen keyboard. Figure 4-6 illustrates how the word *taco* would be typed in this manner.

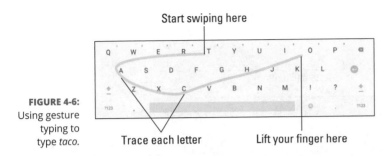

FIGURE 4-6:
Using gesture typing to type *taco*.

Gesture typing is disabled when typing a password or email address, or for other specific typing duties. When it doesn't work, type one letter at a time.

Also see Chapter 19 for information on activating this feature.

Android Tablet Dictation

The Android tablet has the amazing capability to interpret your dictation as text. It works almost as well as computer dictation in science fiction movies, though I can't seem to find the command to locate intelligent life.

>> The dictation is available whenever you see the Microphone icon. This icon appears on the keyboard as well as in other locations, such as search boxes.

>> On Samsung keyboards, the Microphone icon appears on a multifunction key. Long-press that key to choose its dictation function.

>> See Chapter 19 for information on enabling dictation, should you have trouble.

Speaking instead of typing

Talking to your tablet really works, and works quite well, providing that you tap the Dictation key on the keyboard and you don't mumble.

Tap the Dictation key to behold a dictation card at the bottom of the screen, similar to the one shown on top in Figure 4-7. When the text *Speak Now* appears, dictate your text, speaking directly at the tablet. Try not to spit.

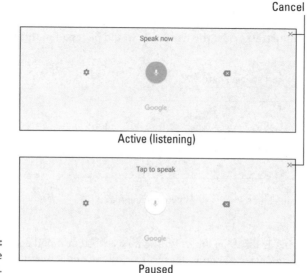

Cancel

Active (listening)

Paused

FIGURE 4-7:
Google Voice
Typing.

As you speak, a Microphone graphic flashes. The flashing doesn't mean that the Android tablet is embarrassed by what you're saying. No, the flashing merely indicates that the tablet is listening, digesting your utterances.

To pause, touch the *Tap to Pause* text, or dictation may pause if you stop talking for a while. To resume, tap the Tap to Speak text.

When you're done dictating, tap the Cancel (X) icon, and the onscreen keyboard returns.

TIP

>> The first time you try voice input, you might see a description displayed. Tap the OK or GOT IT button to continue.

>> Tap misinterpreted words to view a pop-up list of alternatives. Choose an alternative to replace the text.

>> Speak the punctuation in your text. For example, you would say, "I'm sorry comma and it won't happen again" to have the tablet produce the text *I'm sorry, and it won't happen again* or something close to that.

>> Common punctuation you can dictate includes the comma, period, exclamation point, question mark, colon, and new line.

>> You cannot dictate capital letters. If you're a stickler for such things, you have to go back and edit the text.

>> Dictation may not work without an Internet connection.

Uttering s**** words

The Android tablet features a voice censor. It replaces those naughty words you might utter; the first letter appears on the screen, followed by the appropriate number of asterisks.

For example, if *spatula* were a blue word and you uttered "spatula" when dictating text, the Dictation feature would place s****** on the screen rather than the word *spatula*.

Yeah, I know: silly. Or should I say, "s****."

>> The tablet knows a lot of blue terms, including George Carlin's infamous "Seven Words You Can Never Say on Television," but apparently the terms *crap* and *damn* are fine. Don't ask me how much time I spent researching this topic.

>> See Chapter 23 if you'd like to disable the dictation censor.

Text Editing and Correcting

You'll probably do more text editing on your Android tablet than you anticipated. That editing includes the basic stuff, such as spiffing up typos and adding a period here or there as well as complex editing involving cut, copy, and paste. The concepts are the same as you find on a computer, but the process can be daunting without a physical keyboard and a mouse. This section irons out the text-editing wrinkles.

Moving the cursor

The first part of editing text is to move the cursor to the right spot. The cursor is that blinking, vertical line that marks the location where new text appears, edited text changes, or cut/copied text is pasted.

To set the cursor's location, tap the text. To help your accuracy, a cursor tab appears below the text, similar to the one shown in the margin. You can drag that tab to precisely locate the cursor.

After you move the cursor, you can continue to type, tap the Delete key to back up and erase, or paste text copied from elsewhere.

>> You may see the Paste Command button appear above the cursor tab. Use this button to paste in text, as described in the later section "Cutting, copying, and pasting text."

>> Samsung keyboards may feature cursor movement keys. Use those keys to move the cursor as well as the stab-your-finger-on-the-screen method.

Selecting text

Selecting text on an Android tablet works just like selecting text in a word processor: You mark the start and end of a block. That chunk of text appears highlighted on the screen. How you get there, however, can be a mystery — until now!

To select text, long-press a word. Upon success, you see a chunk of selected text, as shown in Figure 4-8.

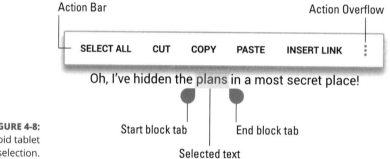

FIGURE 4-8:
Android tablet
text selection.

Drag the start and end markers around the touchscreen to define the block of selected text. Use the Action Bar to choose what to do with the text, as shown in Figure 4-8. Tap the Action Overflow to view additional commands.

To cancel text selection, tap anywhere in the text.

>> See the next section for information on cutting and copying text. To delete selected text, tap the onscreen keyboard's Delete key. To replace the text, type something new. To replace the text with previously cut or copied text, choose the PASTE action.

- » Samsung tablets may display an Action Bar with icons in addition to text. The Action Bar might appear at the top of the screen.

- » The variety of items on the Action Bar depends on the tablet's features and installed apps.

- » Selecting text on a web page works the same as selecting text in any other app. The difference is that text can only be copied from the web page, not cut or deleted.

- » Seeing the onscreen keyboard is a good indication that you can edit and select text.

- » The Action Bar's Select All command marks all text as a single block.

Cutting, copying, and pasting text

Selected text is primed for cutting or copying, which works just like it does in your favorite word processor. After you select the text, choose the proper command from the Action Bar: COPY to copy text or CUT to cut the text.

Just like on a computer, cut or copied text on an Android tablet is stored on a clipboard. To paste any previously cut or copied text, move the cursor to the spot where you want the text pasted.

PASTE

To quickly paste text, tap the cursor tab, and you may see the PASTE button appear, similar to what's shown in the margin. Tap that button to paste the text.

- » Some tablets feature a Clipboard app, which lets you peruse, review, and select previously cut or copied text or images. You might even find the Clipboard button on the Action Bar or onscreen keyboard.

- » You can paste text only into locations where text is allowed. Odds are good that if you see the onscreen keyboard, you can paste text.

Dealing with spelling errrs

Similar to a word processor, your Android tablet may highlight misspelled words. A vicious red underline appears beneath the suspect spelling, drawing attention to the problem and general embarrassment to the typist.

To remedy the situation, tap the red-underlined word. Choose a replacement from the list that's displayed. If the word is correctly spelled but unknown to the Android tablet, choose to add the word to a personal dictionary.

>> Words may be autocorrected as you type them. To undo an autocorrection, tap the word again. Choose a replacement word from the predictive-text list or tap the REPLACE button to see more options.

>> Yes! Your tablet has a personal dictionary. See Chapter 23 for details.

2 Stay in Touch

Chapter **5**

All Your Friends

To best use your tablet as a communications tool, you need to keep track of people. No, it's not spying. It's simply a way to keep your information handy, such as someone's email address, physical address, website, social networking info, and phone numbers because — and this isn't really a secret — it's possible to make phone calls with your tablet. That communication all starts with keeping all your friends' information in a single app.

The Tablet's Address Book

You most likely already have contacts in your Android tablet's address book because your Google account was synchronized with the tablet when you worked through the initial setup process. If you added social networking apps, those contacts might also be stirred into the mix. So you already have a host of friends available. The place where you can access these folks is the tablet's address book.

» The tablet's address book app is named either Contacts or People. The stock Android name is Contacts, though the app has been called People in the past. For the sake of consistency, this chapter refers to the app as Contacts.

» Many apps use contact information from the Contacts app, including Gmail and Hangouts, as well as any app that lets you share information such as photographs or videos.

» Information from your social networking apps is also coordinated with the Contacts app. See Chapter 9 for more information on using the tablet as your social networking hub.

Using the address book

To peruse your Android tablet's address book, open the Contacts app. You may be blessed to find that app's icon on the Home screen, if not directly then in the Google folder. That app is also found in the Apps drawer.

The Contacts app shows all contacts, presented alphabetically by first name. Figure 5-1 illustrates the stock Android Contacts app. In Figure 5-2, you see the Contacts app on a Samsung tablet.

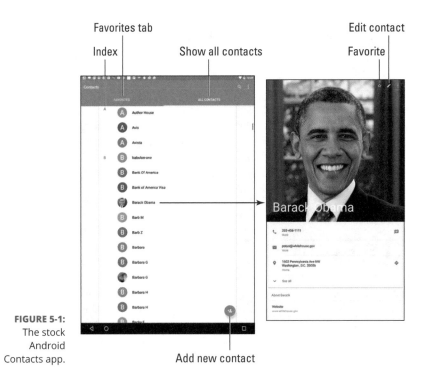

Favorites tab   Edit contact

Index   Show all contacts   Favorite

FIGURE 5-1: The stock Android Contacts app.

Add new contact

Swipe your finger to scroll the list. Use the index (refer to Figures 5-1 and 5-2) to quickly scroll to a specific part of the list.

The number of things you can do with a contact depends on the information shown and the apps installed on your tablet. Here are some common activities:

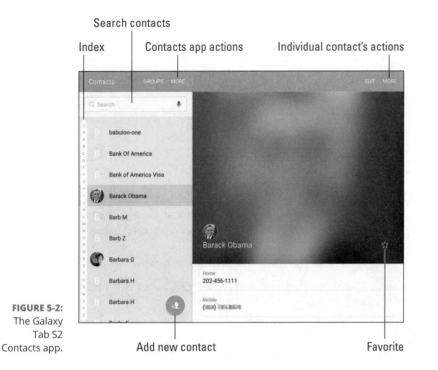

Search contacts

Index   Contacts app actions   Individual contact's actions

Add new contact   Favorite

FIGURE 5-2:
The Galaxy
Tab S2
Contacts app.

Place a phone call. No, an Android tablet isn't a phone, but when you install a phone-dialer app such as the Hangouts Dialer or Skype, tap a contact's phone number to use that app and place a call. See Chapter 8 for details.

Send email. Tap the contact's email address to compose an email message. When the contact has more than one email address, you can choose to which one you want to send the message. Chapter 6 covers email.

View a social networking status. Some address book apps display social networking information on the contact's screen, such as a tweet or Facebook status update. See Chapter 9 for more information on social networking.

View an address on a map. When the contact lists a home or business address, tap that item to view the address in the Maps app. You can then get directions, use Street view to look at the location, or do any of a number of interesting things, as covered in Chapter 10.

Some tidbits of information that show up for a contact don't have an associated action. For example, the tablet doesn't sing "Happy Birthday" whenever you tap a contact's birthday information.

» Some address book apps display contact information side-by-side with the contact index. In Figure 5-1, the contact's information appears on a card. To dismiss the card, tap the Back navigation icon.

» Not every contact has a picture, and the picture can come from a number of sources (Gmail or Facebook, for example). See the later section "Adding a contact's picture" for more information.

» Also see the later section "Joining identical contacts" for information on how to deal with duplicate entries for the same person.

Sorting the address book

The tablet's address book displays contacts in a certain order. Most often, that order is alphabetically by first name. You can change this order if the existing arrangement drives you nuts. Follow these steps when using the Contacts app:

1. **Tap the Action Overflow and choose Settings.**

   In the Samsung Contacts app, tap the MORE button next to GROUPS, and then choose Settings.

2. **Choose Sort By.**

3. **Select First Name or Last Name, depending on how you want the contacts sorted.**

4. **Choose Name Format.**

5. **Choose First Name First or Last Name First.**

   This command specifies how the contacts appear in the list: first name first or last name first.

The Contacts app normally sorts entries by first name and lists them first name first.

REMEMBER

Searching contacts

The Contacts app doesn't provide a running total for all your contacts. Either you have very few friends or a lot of people owe you money. When it's the latter, you can choose to endlessly scroll the list of contacts or employ the powerful Search command to quickly find a contact:

1. **Tap the Search icon.**

    In a Samsung tablet's version of the Contacts app, tap the Search field, illustrated in Figure 5-2.

2. **Start typing a contact name.**

    As you type, a list of matching contacts appears. The list narrows the more you type.

3. **Once you see the matching person, tap that entry.**

To clear a search, tap the X at the right side of the Search text box. To exit the search screen, tap the Back navigation icon.

No, there's no correlation between the number of contacts you have and how popular you are in real life.

REMEMBER

Even More Friends

Having friends is great. Having more friends is better. Keeping all those friends as entries in the Contacts app is best.

Building a contact from scratch

Sometimes it's necessary to create a contact when you actually meet another human being in the real world. Or, maybe you finally got around to transferring information to the tablet from your old date book. In either instance, you have information to input, and it starts like this:

1. **Tap the Add Contact icon in the Contacts app.**

    Refer to Figures 5-1 and 5-2 for what the icon may look like, though different address book apps use subtly different icons.

2. **Choose an account with which to associate the contact.**

    I recommend using your Google account, but if you favor another account, such as Yahoo!, choose it instead.

    I recommend choosing your Google account. That way, the contact is synchronized with the Internet and any other Android gizmos you may own.

TIP

Do not choose the Device account. When you do, the contact information is saved only on your Android tablet. It won't be synchronized with the Internet or any other Android devices.

3. **Fill in the contact's information as best you can.**

   Type text in the various boxes with the information you know. The more information you provide, the better.

   Tap the chevron or Action Bar to the right of a field to set more details, such as whether a phone number is Mobile, Home, Work, or so on.

   To add a second phone number, email, or location, tap the Add New button, which may look like a large Plus icon.

   At the bottom of the Add New Contact screen, you'll find the button More Fields or Add Another Field. Use that button when you can add more details for the contact, such as a birthday or website address.

4. **Tap the Done icon or SAVE button to complete editing and add the new contact.**

If you followed my advice in Step 2, the new contact is automatically synced with your Google account. That's one beauty of the Android operating system: You have no need to duplicate your efforts; contacts you create on the tablet are instantly updated with your Google account on the Internet.

Creating a contact from an email message

Perhaps one of the easiest ways to build up the tablet's address book is to create a contact from an email message. Follow these general steps when you receive a message from someone not already in your Android tablet's address book, or when you receive an email from someone who's in the address book but whose email address you might not have entered:

1. **View the email message.**

   You can't add a contact from the inbox; tap the message to view its contents.

2. **Tap the contact's name or the icon by the contact's name.**

   You see more details about the contact.

3. **Tap the Add Contact icon.**

   If you don't see the Add Contact icon (shown in the margin), tap the CREATE CONTACT or similar button. If so, skip Step 4.

4. **Choose Create New Contact to build a new contact, or choose an existing contact in the list to add that email address to one of your current contacts.**

   If you choose to create a new contact, fill in the contact's information on the card. The email address and perhaps even the name are supplied for you.

These steps may vary, depending on the tablet's incarnation of the Contacts app.

Importing contacts from a computer

Your computer's email program is doubtless a useful repository of contacts you've built up over the years. You can export these contacts from your computer and then import them into your tablet. It's not simple, but it's possible.

The key is to save or export your computer email program's records in the vCard (vcf) file format. These records can then be transferred to the Android tablet and read by the Contacts app. The method for exporting contacts varies, depending on the email program:

In Microsoft Outlook, you don't need to do a thing. Outlook contacts are automatically synchronized when you add your Exchange Server account to the phone. Refer to Chapter 6.

In the Windows Live Mail program, choose Go ➪ Contacts, and then choose File ➪ Export ➪ Business Card (.VCF) to export the contacts.

In Windows Mail, choose File ➪ Export ➪ Windows Contacts, and then choose vCards (Folder of .VCF Files) from the Export Windows Contacts dialog box. Click the Export button.

On the Mac, open the Contacts program and select the contacts you want to export. Choose File ➪ Export ➪ Export vCard to save the vCards as a single file.

After the vCard files are created on your computer, connect the Android tablet to the computer and transfer them. Transferring files from your computer to the tablet is covered in Chapter 17.

With the vCard files stored on your tablet, follow these steps in the Contacts app to complete the process:

1. **Tap the Action Overflow and choose Import/Export.**

   If you can't find this action, choose the Settings action, and then choose Import/Export.

2. **Choose Import from vcf File.**

   The action might be titled Import from SD Card.

3. **Choose the vCard file from the list of Recent items or Downloads.**

   The contacts are imported.

If you're prompted to choose an account for importing, choose your Google account. That way, the new contact is shared with all your Android devices.

See the later section "Joining identical contacts," if the importing process creates duplicates.

Manage Your Friends

Don't let your friends just sit there, occupying valuable storage space inside your tablet! Put them to work. Actually, the tablet does the work; you just give the orders. This section lists some routine and common address book chores and activities.

Editing contact information

 To make minor touch-ups on any contact, locate and display the contact's information. Tap the Edit icon, similar to the Pencil icon, shown in the margin. When the Edit icon isn't visible, tap the Action Overflow and choose Edit.

To change or add information, tap a field and then edit or add new text.

Some contact information cannot be edited. For example, fields pulled in from social networking sites can be edited only by that account holder on the social networking site.

 When you're finished editing, tap the Done icon or the SAVE button.

Adding a contact's picture

Nothing can be more delicious than snapping an inappropriate picture of someone you know and using the picture as his contact picture on your tablet. Then, every time he contacts you, that embarrassing, potentially career-ending photo appears.

I suppose you could use nice pictures as well, but what's the fun in that?

To use the tablet's camera to snap a contact's picture, heed these directions:

1. **Locate and display the contact's information.**

2. **Tap the Edit icon or EDIT button.**

3. **Tap the contact's picture or the picture placeholder.**

4. **Choose Take Photo.**

5. **Use the tablet's camera to snap a picture.**

    Chapter 11 covers using the Camera app. Both the front and rear cameras can be used (but not both at the same time). Tap the Shutter icon to take the picture.

6. **Review the picture.**

    Nothing is set yet. If you want to try again, tap the Retry icon, similar to what's shown in the margin. Repeat Step 5.

7. **Tap the Done icon to confirm the new image and prepare for cropping.**

8. **Crop the image.**

    Adjust the cropping box so that it surrounds only the portion of the image you want to keep. Refer to Chapter 12, which specifically covers how to use the cropping tool.

9. **Tap the DONE button to crop the image.**

10. **Tap the SAVE button to save the image.**

The image you took (refer to Step 4) now appears whenever the contact is referenced on your tablet.

You can also use any image stored on the tablet as a contact's picture. In Step 4, choose the Select New Photo action to view images stored or available on your tablet. Browse for and select an image, and then crop.

Making a favorite

A *favorite* contact is someone you stay in touch with most often. The person doesn't have to be someone you like — just someone that you (perhaps unfortunately) contact often, such as your bookie.

To make a contact a favorite, display the contact's information and tap the Favorite (Star) icon by the contact's image, as shown in Figure 5-1. When the star is filled, the contact is one of your favorites and is stored in the Favorites group.

To remove a favorite, tap the contact's star again and it loses its highlight.

The favorite contacts are all located on the Favorites tab in the Contacts app. Tap that tab to view the lot. (Refer to Figure 5-1.)

>> Removing a favorite doesn't delete the contact, but instead removes it from the Favorites group.

>> By the way, contacts have no idea whether they're among your favorites, so don't believe that you're hurting their feelings by not making them favorites.

Joining identical contacts

Your tablet pulls contacts from multiple sources, such as Gmail, Facebook, and Skype. Because of that, you may discover duplicate contact entries in the tablet's address book. Rather than fuss over which entry to use, you can join the contacts. Here's how:

1. Wildly scroll the address book until you locate a duplicate.

Well, maybe not *wildly* scroll, but locate a duplicated entry. Because the address book is sorted, the duplicates usually appear close together.

2. Edit one of the duplicate contacts.

Display the contact's details, and then tap the Edit icon.

On the Samsung tablet's Contacts app, tap the MORE icon for the contact and choose Link Contacts. Skip to Step 4.

3. Tap the Action Overflow and choose Merge.

The action may be called Join or Link on some tablets.

After choosing the action, you see a list of contacts that the tablet guesses might be identical. You also see the entire list of contacts, in case the guess is incorrect. Your job is to find the duplicate contact.

4. Select a matching contact in the list to join the two contacts.

If necessary, tap the LINK button to complete the action.

The contacts are merged, appearing as a single entry in the address book.

5. **Repeat Steps 3 through 4 if additional, duplicate contacts are found.**

6. **Tap the Done icon to save the joined contacts.**

TIP

Joined contacts aren't flagged as such in the address book, but you can easily identify them: When looking at the contact's information, a joined contact appears as a single, long entry, often listing multiple sources or accounts from which the contact's information is pulled.

Separating contacts

The topic of separating contacts has little to do with parenting, although separating bickering children is the first step in avoiding a fight. Contacts in the address book might not be bickering, but occasionally the tablet may automatically join two contacts that aren't really the same person. When that happens, you can split them. Follow these steps:

1. **Edit the improperly joined contact.**

   As an example, I'm a Facebook friend with other humans named *Dan Gookin*. My tablet accidentally joined my address book entry with another Dan Gookin.

2. **Tap the Action Overflow and choose Separate.**

   The action might also be called Separate Contacts.

3. **Tap the OK button to confirm that you're splitting the contacts.**

You don't need to actively look for improperly joined contacts as much as you'll just stumble across them. When you do, feel free to separate them, especially if you detect any bickering.

Removing a contact

Every so often, consider reviewing your tablet's address book. Purge the folks whom you no longer recognize or you've forgotten. It's simple:

1. **Edit the forlorn contact.**

2. **Tap the Action Overflow and choose Delete.**

   If you don't see the Delete item, the contact is brought in from another source, such as Facebook. You need to use that app to disassociate the contact.

3. **Tap the OK or DELETE button to confirm.**

Poof! They're gone.

 On some tablets, you may find the Delete icon (shown in the margin) directly on the contact's details card. Tap that icon to remove it, and then tap the OK button to remove the contact.

WARNING

>> Because the Contacts list is synchronized with your Google account, the contact is also removed there — and on other Android devices.

>> Removing a contact doesn't kill the person in real life.

Chapter **6**

You've Got Email

The first email message was sent back in the early 1970s. Programmer Ray Tomlinson doesn't remember the exact text but guesses that it was probably something like "QWERTYUIOP." Although that's not as memorable as the first telegraph that was sent ("What hath God wrought?") or the first telephone message ("Mr. Watson, come here. I want you."), it's one for the history books.

Today, email has become far more functional and necessary, well beyond Mr. Tomlinson's early tests. Although you could impress your email buddies by sending them "QWERTYUIOP," you're likely to send and reply to more meaningful communications. Your Android tablet is happily up to the task.

Android Tablet Email

Historically, Android tablets used two apps for electronic mail: Gmail and Email. Recently, Gmail has been updated to handle all email, including Gmail itself as well as everything from traditional ISP email to web email to corporate email. If your tablet doesn't have this update, you'll find the traditional Email app, which you use for all your non–Gmail email.

Confused? Don't worry. The good news is that no matter which apps come with your tablet, both the Gmail and Email apps work the same.

>> Both the Gmail and Email apps are located in the Apps drawer. You may also find launchers on the Home screen. Look for Gmail in the Google folder if you don't find it elsewhere.

>> The Gmail app is updated frequently. To review any changes since this book went to press, visit my website at

```
wambooli.com/help/android
```

>> Though you can use your tablet's web browser to visit the Gmail website, you should use the Gmail app to pick up your Gmail. Likewise, you can use a web page to read most other email, but using the Email (or newer Gmail) app is preferred.

>> If you forget your Gmail password, visit this web address:

```
google.com/accounts/ForgotPasswd
```

Setting up the first Email account

The first email account on your phone is your Gmail account, which is required in order to use an Android mobile gizmo. After that, you add email accounts as described in the later section "Adding email accounts."

If your tablet features an Email app, setting up the first email account works differently than when adding additional accounts. You must know the email account's sign-in (your email address) and password. When you have that information, follow these steps in the Email app to configure that first account:

1. Start the Email app.

Look for it in the Apps drawer. If it's not there, use the Gmail app instead, as described in the next section.

The first screen you see is Set Up Account or Set Up Email. If you've already run the Email app, you're taken to the Email inbox and you can skip these steps. See the next section for information on adding additional accounts.

2. Type the email address you use for the account.

For example, if you have a Comcast email account, use the onscreen keyboard to type your *me@comcast.net* email address in the Email Address box.

Look for a .com (dot-com) key on the onscreen keyboard, which you can use to more efficiently type your email address.

3. **Type the account's password.**

4. **If available, set the default account option.**

   The default account is the one from which email is sent. See the later section "Setting the primary email account."

5. **Tap the SIGN IN button.**

   If you're lucky, everything is connected and you're done. Otherwise, you have to specify the details as provided by your ISP. See the later section "Adding an account manually."

After you configure the account, messages are immediately synchronized with the tablet. You find those messages in the inbox. See the later section "Message for You!" for what to do next.

>> To further configure your email account, see the later section "Setting email account options."

>> If you use Yahoo! Mail, get the Yahoo! Mail app, which handles your Yahoo! mail far better than the Email app (or the Gmail app). The Yahoo! Mail app gives you access to other Yahoo! features you may use and enjoy.

Adding email accounts

The Email app, as well as the newest version of Gmail, can be configured to pick up email from multiple sources. This feature allows you to collect all your email on the tablet without needing multiple apps. So all your Windows Live, Cox Cable, and Yahoo! messages can arrive in one spot.

Both the Email and Gmail apps offer different ways to add a new email account. A more generic approach is to use the Settings app. Obey these directions:

1. **Open the Settings app.**

   It's found in the Apps drawer; tap the Apps icon on the Home screen to view the Apps drawer.

2. **Choose Accounts.**

3. **Tap Add Account.**

   The three options for adding email accounts are

   Personal (IMAP): For web-based email accounts, such as Microsoft Live

Personal (POP3): For traditional, ISP-email accounts, such as Comcast

Exchange or Microsoft Exchange ActiveSync: For a corporate email account hosted by an Exchange Server (Outlook mail)

See the later section "Adding a corporate email account" for information on the Exchange option. The other two options work pretty much the same. In fact, on some tablets, a single option (Email) may replace both.

4. **Choose the proper Personal email account type.**

5. **Type your email address and tap the Next button.**

6. **Continue working through the email setup, providing your password and other account information, as prompted.**

   Most of the preset settings are okay. When asked to give the account a name, you can choose something other than your account name, such as *Main* for your primary, ISP email account.

The new email account is synchronized immediately after it's added, and you see the inbox. See the later section "Checking the inbox."

See the next section if adding the email account doesn't work as you'd expect.

Some Android tablets may add the new email account to the Email app, but others may add the account to Gmail. The only way to tell is to open both apps and look inside for the account's email.

Adding an account manually

TECHNICAL
STUFF

If your email account isn't recognized, or some other boo-boo happens, you have to manually add the account. The steps in the preceding sections remain the same, but you need to provide more specific and technical details. This information includes tidbits such as the server name, port address, domain name, and other incommodious details.

My advice is to contact your ISP or email provider: Look on their website for specific directions on connecting an Android tablet to their email account. Contact them directly if you cannot locate specific information.

The good news is that manual setup is very rare these days. Most ISPs and web-mail accounts are added painlessly, as described elsewhere in this chapter.

Adding a corporate email account

The easiest way to set up your evil corporation's email on your tablet is to have the IT people do it for you. Or you may be fortunate and you'll find directions on the organization's intranet. I present this tip because configuring corporate email, also known as Exchange Service email, can be a difficult and terrifying ordeal.

It's possible to add the account on your own, but you still need detailed information. Specifically, you need to know the domain name, which may not be the same as the outfit's website domain. Other details may be required as well.

Above all, you need to apply a secure screen lock to your tablet to access Outlook email. This means you need to add a PIN or password to the device, which is covered in Chapter 20. You cannot access the Exchange Server without that added level of security.

And there's more!

You also need to grant Remote Security Administration privileges. This means your organization's IT gurus will have the power to remotely wipe all information from your Android tablet. You must activate that feature, which is part of the setup process.

The bonus is that when you're done, you'll have full access to the Exchange Server info. That includes your email messages, as well as the corporate address book and calendar. Refer to Chapter 5 for information on the tablet's address book app; the Calendar app is covered in Chapter 14.

Message for You!

New email arrives into your tablet automatically, picked up according to the Gmail and Email apps' synchronization schedules. On newer tablets, use the Gmail app to read all your email. Otherwise, use the Email app to read non-Gmail email.

Getting a new message

The arrival of a new email epistle is heralded by a notification icon. Each email app generates its own version.

For a new Gmail message, the New Gmail notification, similar to the one shown in the margin, appears at the top of the touchscreen.

For a new email message, you see the New Email notification.

 For email you receive from an Exchange Server, or corporate email, you might even see the New Exchange Mail notification.

Conjure the notifications drawer to review the email notifications. Tap a notification to be whisked to an inbox for instant reading.

Checking the inbox

To peruse your Gmail, start the Gmail app. The Gmail inbox is shown in Figure 6-1.

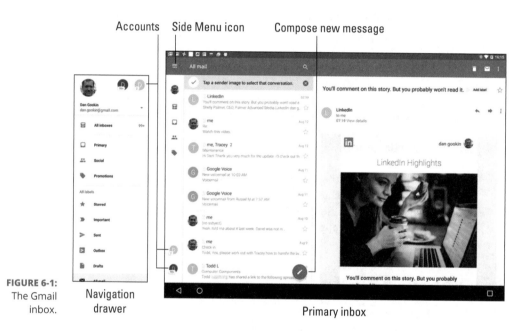

Accounts   Side Menu icon   Compose new message

FIGURE 6-1:
The Gmail
inbox.

Navigation
drawer

Primary inbox

To choose a non-Gmail account, tap the account icon from the navigation drawer. (Refer to Figure 6-1.) You can view only one account's inbox at a time.

If your tablet still uses the Email app, open it to view its inbox. You see a single account's inbox, or you can choose to view the universal inbox, shown as Combined view in Figure 6-2.

REMEMBER

>> Gmail messages don't show up in the Email app. Use the Gmail app to read your Google mail.

>> The Gmail app lacks a combined inbox. To view specific inboxes, tap an account bubble on the navigation drawer, as illustrated in Figure 6-1.

Action Bar

FIGURE 6-2:
Messages in
the Email app.

Compose new message

>> Multiple email accounts that are gathered in the Email app are color-coded.
   When you view the combined inbox, you see the color codes to the left of
   each message — as long as messages from multiple accounts are available.

>> To view an individual account's inbox in the Email app, choose the account
   from the Action Bar, as illustrated in Figure 6-2.

Reading email

To view a specific email message, tap its entry in the inbox, as shown earlier in
Figures 6-1 and 6-2. Or you can choose a new email notification. Reading and
working with the message operate much the same whether you're using the Gmail
or Email app:

>> To read a message, use your finger to swipe the it up or down.

>> Swipe a message left or right to browse between messages.

>> If you don't see the inbox, tap the left-pointing arrow or chevron in the upper
   left corner of the screen.

To work with the message, use the icons that appear above or below the message. These icons, which may not look exactly like those shown in the margin, cover common email actions:

 Reply: Tap this icon to reply to a message. A new message window appears, with the To and Subject fields reflecting the original sender(s) and subject.

 Reply All: Tap this icon to respond to everyone who received the original message, including folks on the Cc line. Use this option only when everyone else must get a copy of your reply.

 Forward: Tap this icon to send a copy of the message to someone else.

 Delete: Tap this icon to delete a message.

If you don't see all these icons, look for them on the message's Action Overflow. You can also try turning the tablet to a horizontal orientation.

Write a New Email Message

I frequently use my Android tablet to check email, but I don't often use it to compose messages. That's because most email messages don't demand an immediate reply. When they do, you'll find that both the Gmail and Email apps are up to the task.

Starting a message from scratch

Creating a new email epistle works similarly in both the Gmail and Email apps. The key is to locate the Compose icon. This icon is illustrated in both Figures 6-1 and 6-2.

After you tap the Compose icon, you're presented with a new message card. Your job is to fill in the blanks, adding a recipient, subject, and message text. Figure 6-3 illustrates how a new message card might look. Its features should be familiar to you if you've ever written email on a computer.

 To send the message, tap the Send icon, shown in the margin, or tap the SEND button.

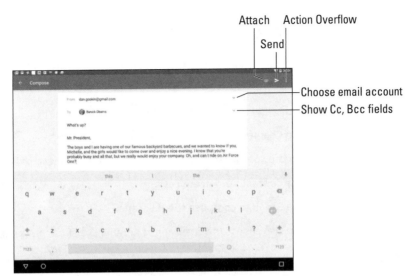

Attach   Action Overflow

Send

Choose email account

Show Cc, Bcc fields

FIGURE 6-3:
Composing
a new email
epistle.

>> To choose an email account for sending, tap the chevron or down arrow next to your name atop the new message card, shown in Figure 6-3. Otherwise, the primary or default email account is used. See the later section "Setting the primary email account."

>> You need only type a few letters of the recipient's name. Matching contacts are instantly fetched from the tablet's address book, and they appear in a list. Tap a contact to automatically fill in the To field.

>> If you can't see the Cc and Bcc fields, tap the chevron, shown in Figure 6-3, to display those fields. Or you can tap the Action Overflow or MORE button to choose the Add Cc/Bcc command.

>> To cancel a message, tap the Action Overflow or MORE button to choose Discard. This action might also be found on the Compose screen. Tap the OK button or DISCARD button to confirm.

>> Save a message by choosing the Save Draft action from the Action Overflow. Drafts are saved in the Drafts folder. You can open them there for further editing or sending.

>> Some versions of the Email app feature a formatting toolbar. Use the toolbar to change the way the text looks in your message.

Sending email to a contact

A quick and easy way to compose a new message is to find a contact and then create a message using that contact's information. Heed these steps:

1. **Open the tablet's address book app.**

   Refer to Chapter 5 for details on the address book app.

2. **Locate the contact to whom you want to send an electronic message.**

3. **Tap the contact's email address.**

4. **Choose Gmail to compose the message.**

   You can also choose the Email app or another specific app, such as Yahoo! Mail or a custom email app you've obtained from Google Play.

At this point, creating the message works as described in the preceding section.

Message Attachments

 The key to understanding email attachments on your Android tablet is to look for the Paperclip icon. When you find that icon, you can either deal with an attachment for incoming email or add an attachment to outgoing email.

Receiving an attachment

Attachments are presented differently between the Gmail and Email apps, yet your goal is the same: to view or save the attachment. Sometimes you can do both!

Figure 6-4 shows both the Gmail app and Email app methods of presenting an email attachment. To deal with the attachment, tap it. In most cases, the attachment opens an appropriate app on your tablet. For example, a PDF attachment might be opened by the QuickOffice app.

Potential actions you can perform with an attachment include

Preview: Open the attachment for viewing.

 Save to Google Drive: Send a copy of the attachment to your Google Drive (cloud) storage.

Save: Save the attachment to the tablet's storage.

Download Again: Fetch the attachment from the mail server.

07 SEP 2016 ▶ 17 SEP 2016 TRIP TO SANTA BARBARA, CA

PREPARED FOR   Santa Barbara Travel Bureau, Inc.
GOOKIN/D   TRAVEL CONSULTANT TR

RESERVATION CODE
AIRLINE RESERVATION CODE   (AS)

Travel Arranger Priority Comments
FOR AFTER-HOURS EMERGENCY CONTACT
ADDITIONAL FEES APPLY FOR THIS SERVICE   ————————— Attachment preview

✈ DEPARTURE: WEDNESDAY 07 SEP Please verify flight times prior to departure

ALASKA AIRLINES   GEG   , SFA   Aircraft: ————————— Download

📄PDF Travel Reser...GOOKIN.pdf   ⬇   🔻   ————————— Save to Google Drive

Gmail attachment

FIGURE 6-4:
Attachment
methods and
madness.

📄	Survery.docx		SAVE
	15 KB (100%)		

Email attachment

As with email attachments received on a computer, the only problem you may have is that the tablet lacks the app required to deal with the attachment. When an app can't be found, you have to either suffer through not viewing the attachment or reply to the message and direct the person to resend the attachment in a common file format.

>> Sometimes, pictures included in an email message aren't displayed. Tap the SHOW PICTURES button to see the images.

>> Common image file formats include PNG and JPEG. Documents are shared by using the HTML (web page), DOCX (Microsoft Word), and PDF (Adobe Acrobat) file formats.

>> You may see a prompt displayed when several apps can deal with the attachment. Choose one and tap the JUST THIS ONCE button to view the attachment. Also see Chapter 18 for information on the default app prompt.

**TECHNICAL
STUFF**

>> Attachments are saved in the Downloads or Download folder on either the tablet's internal storage or its removable storage (the microSD card). See Chapter 17 for details on Android tablet storage, including how to view downloaded files.

Sharing an attachment

When sending an email attachment on an Android tablet, don't think about the method. Instead, think about the attachment: Which app on the tablet created that attachment? When you know that, you're ready to follow these steps to send an email attachment:

1. **Open the app that created the item you want to attach.**

   Popular apps for sharing include Photos, Gallery, the web browser app, Maps, Play Store, Drive or any other cloud storage app, and so on.

2. **View the item you want to share.**

3. **Tap the Share icon.**

   You see a list of apps.

4. **Choose the Gmail or Email app.**

5. **Complete the message as described earlier in this chapter.**

   The item you're sharing is automatically attached to the message or included as a link.

Sharing an item is the Android tablet method of attaching something to an email message. You're probably more familiar with the computer method, which is to compose the message first and then attach. You can still do that: On a new message card, tap the Attachment (Paperclip) icon, similar to the one shown in the margin, or an ATTACH button. Choose an app or category, and then select the item to share.

>> The variety of items you can attach depends on which apps are installed on the tablet.

>> The Gmail and Email apps sometimes accept different types of attachments. If you cannot attach something by using the Gmail app, try using the Email app instead.

Email Configuration

You can have oodles of fun and waste oceans of time confirming and customizing the email experience on your Android tablet. The most interesting things you can do are to customize the account, modify or create an email signature, and assign a default email account.

Setting email account options

To set email account options, follow these potentially confusing steps:

1. **Open the Settings app.**

The app is found on the Apps drawer.

2. **Choose Accounts.**

3. **Tap the email account item.**

It may be titled Personal (IMAP), or Email — it doesn't matter. (That's the confusing part.)

4. **Choose Account Settings.**

Now you see a list of your tablet's email accounts, along with an item titled General Settings. This is the screen where you can modify general email behavior or change aspects of specific accounts.

For example, to modify settings for a specific email account, choose the account (after working through these steps). You can set the account name to something other than your email address, set your name, choose a signature (covered in the next section), select the sync frequency, and so on.

Tap the Back navigation icon when you're done changing email account options.

Creating a signature

Don't be one of the uninformed tablet users whose email signature is the same as everyone else's. Yeah, I know: That message was sent from your Samsung tablet. Boring!

Why not set your own, unique signature? Here's mine:

```
DAN
This was sent from my Android tablet.
Typos, no matter how hilarious, are unintentional.
```

To create a custom signature for your email accounts, follow Steps 1 through 4 in the preceding section and then continue with these steps:

5. **Choose a specific email account from the left side of the screen.**

6. **Choose Signature.**

Any existing signature appears on the card, ready for you to edit or replace it.

7. **Type or dictate your signature.**

8. **Tap OK when you're done.**

You can repeat these steps (5 through 8) for each of your email accounts, applying to each one a unique signature. Or you can select the signature you create in Step 7 and copy-and-paste that text into the other accounts' signature cards.

The signature you set is appended automatically to all outgoing email you send.

Setting the primary email account

When you have more than one email account, the main account — the *default* — is the one used by the Email app to send messages. To change that primary mail account, follow these steps:

1. **Start the Email app.**

2. **From the Action Bar, choose Combined Inbox or Combined View.**

3. **Tap the MORE button and choose Settings.**

4. **On the Email Settings screen, tap the MORE button again and choose Set Default Account.**

5. **Choose an email account from the list and tap the DONE button.**

The messages you compose and send in the Email app are sent from the account you specified in Step 5.

REMEMBER

In the Gmail app, choose the sending account by tapping the chevron next to the From field, as illustrated in Figure 6-3.

Chapter **7**

Tablet Web Browsing

'm certain that the World Wide Web was designed to be viewed on a computer. The monitor is big and roomy. Web pages are displayed amply, like Uncle Blake on the sofa watching a ballgame. The smaller the screen, however, the more difficult it is to view web pages designed for those roomy monitors. The web on a cell phone? Tragic. But on an Android tablet?

Your tablet doesn't have the diminutive screen of a cell phone, nor does it have a widescreen computer monitor. Instead, the tablet's screen is a good size in between, like a younger, thinner version of Uncle Blake. That size is enjoyable for viewing the web, especially when you've read the tips and suggestions in this chapter.

TIP

» If you have an LTE tablet, activate the Wi-Fi connection before you venture out on the web. The mobile data (cellular) connection works, but a Wi-Fi connection incurs no data usage charges.

» Many places you visit on the web can instead be accessed directly and more effectively by using specific apps. Facebook, Gmail, Twitter, YouTube, and other popular web destinations have apps that you may find already installed on your tablet or are otherwise available for free from Google Play.

The Web Browser App

All Android tablets feature a web browsing app. The stock Android app is Google's own Chrome web browser. Your tablet may have another web browser app, which may be named Web, Browser, or Internet.

The good news is that all web apps work in a similar way and offer comparable features. The secret news is that most of those other tablet web browser apps are simply gussied-up versions of the Chrome web browser. And the sobering news is that I'm writing about only one web browser app in this chapter, which is the Chrome app.

>> If your tablet doesn't have the Chrome app, you can obtain it for free at Google Play. See Chapter 15.

>> An advantage of using Chrome is that your bookmarks, web history, and other features are shared between all devices you use on which Chrome is installed. So if you use Chrome as your computer's web browser, it's logical to use Chrome on your Android tablet as well.

>> The first time you fire up the web browser app on certain Samsung tablets, you may see a registration page. Register your device to receive sundry Samsung bonus stuff — or not. Registration is optional.

The Web on a Tablet

It's difficult these days to find someone who has no experience with the World Wide Web. More common is someone who has used the web on a computer but has yet to sample the Internet waters on a mobile device. If that's you, consider this section your quick mobile web orientation.

Viewing the web

When you first open the Chrome app, you see the last web page you viewed. In Figure 7-1, I was just on Wikipedia, so when I fired up Chrome, it returned to that page.

Here are some handy Android tablet web browsing and viewing tips:

» Drag your finger across the touchscreen to pan and scroll the web page. You can pan up, down, left, or right when the page is larger than the tablet's screen.

Back/Forward   Close tab   Incognito tab

Refresh   Tabs   New tab   Address box   Favorite

FIGURE 7-1:
The Chrome app beholds Wikipedia's home page.

Web page content

» Pinch the screen to zoom out or spread two fingers to zoom in.

» The page you see may be the mobile page, or a customized version of the web page designed for small-screen devices. To see the nonmobile version, tap the Action Overflow and choose Desktop View.

» You can orient the tablet vertically to read a web page in Portrait mode. Doing so may reformat some web pages, which can make long lines of text shorter and easier to read.

REMEMBER

Visiting a web page

To visit a web page, type its address in the Address box. (Refer to Figure 7-1.) You can also type a search word or phrase if you don't know the exact address of a web page. Tap the Go button on the onscreen keyboard to search the web or visit a specific web page.

To "click" links on a page, tap them with your finger. If you have trouble stabbing the right link, zoom in on the page and try again. You can also long-press the screen to see a magnification window to make tapping links easier.

>> Look for special keys when typing a web page address. Some tablets display a .com (dot-com) or .www key. Those keys assist you in rapidly typing web page addresses.

>> Long-press the .com key to see other top-level domains, such as .org, .net, and so on.

>> If you don't see the Address box, swipe the web page from the center of the touchscreen downward. If that doesn't work, tap the web page's tab atop the screen.

>> To reload a web page, tap the Refresh icon. (Refer to Figure 7-1.) If you don't see that icon on the screen, tap the Action Overflow icon to find the Refresh or Reload action. Refreshing updates a website that changes often. Using the command can also reload a web page that may not have completely loaded the first time.

>> To stop a web page from loading, tap the Cancel (X) icon that appears by the Address box.

Browsing back and forth

To return to a previously visited web page, tap the Back icon at the top of the screen. (Refer to Figure 7-1.) If that icon isn't visible, tap the Back navigation icon, shown in the margin.

Tap the Forward icon (refer to Figure 7-1) to go forward or to return to a page you were visiting before you tapped the Back icon.

To review web pages you've visited in the long term, visit the web browser's history page. In Chrome, tap the Action Overflow and choose History.

>> See the later section "Clearing your web history" for information on purging items from the History list.

>> If you find yourself frequently clearing the web page history, consider using an incognito tab. See the later section "Going incognito."

Saving a favorite web page (bookmarks)

You might call them bookmarks, but in the mobile world, your Android calls your favorite web pages just that: *favorites.* To mark a web page as a favorite, tap the Favorite (Star) icon that appears in the Address box. Refer to Figure 7-1 for this icon's location.

When you mark a web page as a favorite, or when you load a favorite web page, the Star icon is filled in. To add more details, tap the icon again. You see the Edit Bookmark card, which makes you wonder why it's not called Edit Favorite. See? Consistency is a thing that's lacking in the Android universe. Figure 7-2 shows the Edit Bookmark card, along with the bookmark or Favorites (or whatever) folder tree.

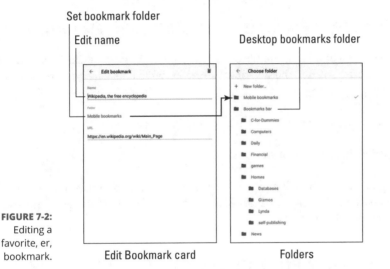

FIGURE 7-2:
Editing a favorite, er, bookmark.

Use the Edit Bookmark card to change the bookmark/favorite's name. The name given is generally longer than is necessary, so tap that item and use the onscreen keyboard to type something brief. For example, edit *Wikipedia, the free encyclopedia* to just *Wikipedia.* Simple.

You can also use the Edit Bookmark card to place the bookmark into a specific folder. Normally, Chrome prefers to shove it into the Mobile Bookmarks folder, as illustrated in Figure 7-2. You can instead choose the Bookmarks bar, in which case the bookmark would also be available to Chrome on any computers you use.

Tap the Back navigation icon when you're done editing the bookmark.

>> To remove the bookmark, tap the Delete (Trash) icon, as illustrated in Figure 7-2.

>> I confess that bookmarks are easier to manage when using a computer.

>> Making a favorite web page isn't the same as saving the page. See the later section "Sharing a web page."

>> A great way to find which sites to bookmark is to view the web page history: Tap the Action Overflow and choose History.

>> The Bookmarks Bar folder was called Desktop bookmarks in older versions of the Chrome app.

Visiting a favorite (bookmarked) web page

To view bookmarks in the Chrome app, tap the Action Overflow icon and choose Bookmarks. You see the Bookmarks screen, which appears in Chrome just like a web page.

Tap a folder to browse bookmarks stored in that folder.

Tap a bookmark to visit that page.

To quickly visit a bookmarked website, just start typing the site's name in the Address box. Tap the bookmarked site from the matching list of results displayed below the Address box.

Managing web pages on multiple tabs

The Chrome app, as well as other tablet web browsers, uses a tabbed interface to help you access more than one web page at a time. Refer to Figure 7-1 to see a couple of tabs marching across the Chrome app's screen, just above the Address box.

You can do various interesting things with tabs:

Open a Blank Tab: To open a blank tab, tap the blank tab stub to the right of the last open tab, shown in Figure 7-1. You can also tap the Action Overflow icon and choose New Tab.

Open a Link in a New Tab: To open a link in another tab, long-press the link and choose Open in New Tab.

Open a Bookmark in a New Tab: To open a bookmark in a new tab, long-press the bookmark and choose Open in New Tab.

To switch between tabs, tap one. The tab shows the web page title. (Refer to Figure 7-1.)

To close a tab, tap its Close (X) icon.

>> The tabs keep marching across the screen, left to right. Swipe excess tabs left or right to view the ones that don't appear on the screen.

>> If you close all the tabs, you see a blank screen in the Chrome app. Tap the Add (Plus) icon to summon a new tab.

Going incognito

TIP

Shhh! For secure browsing, use an incognito tab: Tap the Action Overflow and choose New Incognito Tab. The incognito tab takes over the screen, changing the look of the Chrome app and offering a description page.

When you go incognito, the web browser doesn't track your history, leave cookies, or provide other evidence of which web pages you've visited.

To switch between incognito tabs and regular tabs, tap the Incognito icon in the upper right corner of the Chrome app's screen, as shown in the margin.

To close all incognito tabs, pull down the notification drawer and choose the Chrome notification, Close All Incognito Tabs.

Searching the web

The handiest way to find things on the web is to use the Google Now app, covered in Chapter 14. You can also use the Google Search widget on the Home screen. If it's not there, refer to Chapter 18 for information on adding widgets to the Home screen.

While you're using the web browser app, type search text into the Address bar. Or you can visit any number of search engines. Google would most enjoy it if you used google.com.

Finding text on a web page

To locate text on a web page, tap the Action Overflow and choose Find in Page. Use the onscreen keyboard to type search text. Matching text on the page is highlighted. Use the up and down chevrons to page through found matches.

Tap the Back navigation icon when you've finished searching.

Sharing a web page

There it is! That web page you just have to talk about to everyone you know. The gauche way to share the page is to copy and paste it. Because you're reading this book, though, you know the better way to share a web page. Heed these steps:

1. **Go to the web page you desire to share.**

   Actually, you're sharing a link to the page, but don't let my obsession with specificity deter you.

2. **Tap the Action Overflow icon and choose Share.**

   The command might be called Share Via or Share Page. Either way, you see an array of apps displayed. The variety and number of apps depends on what's installed on the tablet.

3. **Choose an app.**

   For example, choose Gmail to send the web page's link by email, or Facebook to share the link with your friends.

4. **Do whatever happens next.**

   Whatever happens next depends on how you're sharing the link: Compose the email, write a comment in Facebook, or whatever. Refer to various chapters in this book for specific directions.

You cannot share a page you're viewing on an incognito tab.

Another way to share a page is to print it. See Chapter 17 for details.

The Art of Downloading

The most important thing you need to know about downloading is that it's a transfer of information from another source to your gizmo. For your Android tablet, the other source is the Internet. The information that's transferred is accessed on a web page. It can be a picture, a file, or something else that I can't think of right now.

>> The Downloading Complete notification appears after your tablet has downloaded something. You can choose that notification to view the downloaded item.

>> Most people use the term *download* when they really mean transfer or copy. Those people must be shunned.

>> You use the Play Store app to install new apps on your tablet. This topic is covered in Chapter 15. Installing a new app is a type of downloading, but it's not the same as the downloading described in this section.

>> The opposite of downloading is *uploading*. That's the process of sending information from your gizmo to another source, such as the Internet.

TECHNICAL
STUFF

Grabbing an image from a web page

The simplest thing to download is an image from a web page: Long-press the image. You see an action card appear, from which you choose Save Image.

Use the Photos app to view images you download from the web. These images are saved in the Download folder. Follow these steps in the Photos app to view that folder:

1. **Tap the Side Menu icon.**

2. **Choose Device Folders**

Locate the Download folder to peruse images downloaded to your tablet.

Refer to Chapter 12 for information on using the Photos app.

Downloading a file

The web is full of links that don't open in a web browser window. For example, some links automatically download, such as links to Microsoft Word documents or other types of files that a web browser is too frightened to display.

To save other types of links that aren't automatically downloaded, long-press the link and choose the Save Link action. If this action doesn't appear, your tablet is unable to save the link, because either the file is of an unrecognized type or there's a security issue.

Reviewing your downloads

To browse or view items you've downloaded, open the Downloads app. It's found in the Apps drawer.

The Downloads app lists downloaded items alphabetically or by date. To set which way the items appear, look for a sorting icon or tap the Action Overflow to find a Sort or similar action.

To view a download, choose it from the list. The Android tablet uses the appropriate app to view the download. If an app isn't available, an appropriately rude message tells you so.

You can choose the Download notification to quickly review any single downloaded item.

Web Browser Controls and Settings

More options and settings and controls exist for web browser apps than for just about any other Android app I've used. Rather than bore you with every dangdoodle detail, I thought I'd present just a few of the options worthy of your attention.

Clearing your web history

When you don't want the entire Internet to know what you're looking at on the web, open an incognito tab, as described in the earlier section "Going incognito." When you forget to do that, follow these steps to clear one or more web pages from the browser history:

1. **Tap the Action Overflow icon and choose History.**

2. **Tap the X icon next to the web page entry you want to remove.**

    It's gone.

If you want to remove *all* of your web browsing history, after Step 1 tap the button at the bottom of the screen, CLEAR BROWSING DATA. You see the Clear Browsing Data screen. The pre-checked items are what you need, so tap the CLEAR DATA button to purge your tablet's web browsing history.

You don't need to clean up your web browsing history when you use an incognito tab.

Changing the way the web looks

As I rant at the start of this chapter, the web on a tablet will never look as good as the web on a computer. You do have a few options for making it look better.

First and foremost, remember that you can orient the device horizontally and vertically, which rearranges the way a web page is displayed.

You can spread your fingers to zoom in on any web page, but when you find yourself doing that too often, consider resetting the screen text size:

1. **Tap the Action Overflow icon and choose Settings.**
2. **Choose Accessibility.**

   This item might be titled Screen and Text in some web browser apps.

3. **Use the Text Scaling slider to adjust the text size.**

   The preview text below the slider helps you gauge which size works best.

Setting privacy and security options

Pretty much every web browser app available to Android tablets presets optimum security settings. The only issue you should consider is how information is retained and automatically recalled. You may want to disable some of those features. Obey these steps:

1. **Tap the Action Overflow icon and choose Settings.**
2. **Choose Privacy.**
3. **Tap the Clear Browsing Data button.**
4. **Place check marks by those items you want removed from the tablet's storage.**
5. **Tap the CLEAR DATA button.**

Some web browser apps might present options for remembering form data or passwords. If so, remove the check marks by those items. Also, delete any personal data, if that's an option.

TIP

With regard to general online security, my advice is always to be smart and think before doing anything questionable on the web. Use common sense. One of the most effective ways that the Bad Guys win is by using human engineering to try to trick you into doing something you normally wouldn't do, such as click a link to see a cute animation or a racy picture of a celebrity or politician. As long as you use your noggin, you should be safe.

Also see Chapter 20 for information on applying a secure screen lock, which I highly recommend.

Chapter **8**

Text, Voice, and Video

The holy grail of communications has always been video chat. Back in the 1960s, the video phone was touted as the harbinger of the future. The film *2001: A Space Odyssey* features a key character making a video phone call to his daughter on the "Bell network." (Cost: $1.70.) Obviously, seeing and speaking on a phone was considered a big deal.

Years after that film was to have taken place, a video phone call is more commonly known as a *video chat.* It's a feature that your Android tablet is more than capable of offering, along with text messaging, voice chat, and even real phone calls. The future is here — and rather than cost $1.70 for a 2-minute video call, it's free.

Can We Hangout?

The great Googly way to text-message, voice-chat, and video-chat with your online pals is to use the Hangouts app. It's a communications app, designed by Google to let you connect with one or more of your friends to, well, hang out. It's also a great communications tool.

Using Hangouts

You may find the Hangouts app launcher lurking on the tablet's Home screen. Check inside the Google folder. Or locate the app in the Apps drawer.

When you first start the Hangouts app, it may ask whether you want to make phone calls. Of course you do! Install the Hangouts Dialer — Call Phones app. If you're not prompted, get the app from Google Play.

Hangouts hooks into your Google account. You can connect with any one of your contacts who also shares a Google or Gmail account. Obey these steps:

1. **Tap the Side Menu icon.**

2. **Choose Contacts from the navigation drawer.**

3. **Tap a contact.**

4. **Choose whether to text-chat (Hangouts Message), voice-call, or video-chat.**

5. **Connect with the other person.**

If you choose Hangouts Message, you see a screen similar to the text messaging app on your phone. Type a message to the other person. They type back (or not), and so it goes.

In Figure 8-1, you see the main Hangouts app screen. It shows previous conversations and indicates the type of chat: text (no icon), video, or voice.

You can do anything else on the tablet while the Hangouts app stays active. You're alerted via notification of an impending Hangouts request. The notification icon is shown in the margin.

>> Conversations are archived in the Hangouts app. To peruse a previous text chat, tap the Conversation tab and choose a conversation from the list. Video calls aren't archived, but you can review when the call took place and with whom.

>> To remove a previous conversation, long-press it. Tap the Delete icon that appears atop the screen.

REMEMBER

>> Your friend can be on a computer or a mobile device to use Hangouts; it doesn't matter which, but the other person's device must have a camera available to enable video chat.

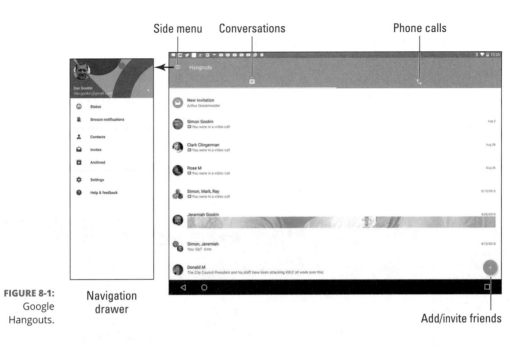

Side menu   Conversations   Phone calls

FIGURE 8-1:
Google
Hangouts.

Navigation
drawer

Add/invite friends

Typing at your friends

Text chatting is one of the oldest forms of communication on the Internet. It's where people type text back and forth at each other, which can be tedious, but it remains popular. To text-chat in the Hangouts app, obey these steps:

1. **Tap the Contacts tab, or to continue a previous conversation, tap the Previous Conversations tab.**

2. **Choose a contact or previous conversation.**

3. **Use the onscreen keyboard to type a message into the Write a Message box, shown in Figure 8-2.**

4. **Tap the Send icon to send your comment.**

   The Send icon changes color when you start to type.

You type, your friend types, and so on until you grow tired or the tablet's battery dies.

>> To add more people to the hangout, tap the Action Overflow and choose New Group Conversation. Select a friend from those listed to invite them into the hangout. Repeat this process to add more friends.

>> Tap an icon below the Write a Message box to add an attachment to the message. (Refer to Figure 8-2.) You can attach a photo or video, take a still shot, record a video, insert an emoji, or insert your current location.

>> When you're chatting, or I should say "hanging out," with a group, everyone in the group receives the message.

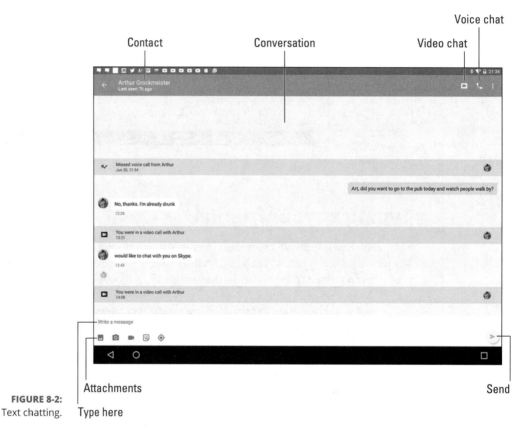

FIGURE 8-2: Text chatting.

Talking and video chat

To take the hangout up a notch, tap the Video Chat icon. (Refer to Figure 8-2.) When you do, your friend receives a pop-up invite, similar to the one shown in Figure 8-3. Tap the Answer button to begin talking.

Figure 8-4 shows what an ongoing video chat might look like. The person you're talking with appears in the big window; you're in the smaller window. If multiple contacts are chatting, their windows appear at the bottom of the screen. Tap one of those windows to view the contact full-screen.

FIGURE 8-3:
Someone
wants to
video-chat!

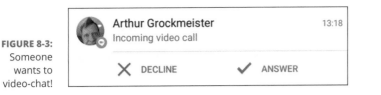

Arthur Grockmeister   13:18
Incoming video call

X   DECLINE   ✓   ANSWER

Person you're calling   Switch cameras   Add contacts

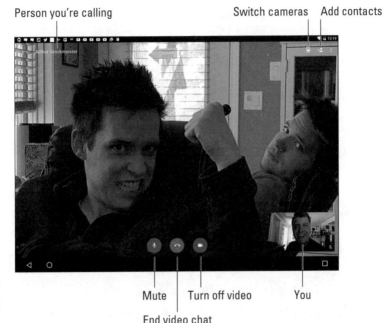

FIGURE 8-4:
Video chat
in the Hang-
outs app.

Mute   Turn off video   You

End video chat

The onscreen controls (shown in Figure 8-4) may vanish after a second; tap the screen to see the controls again.

To end the conversation, tap the End Video Chat button. Well, say goodbye first, and then tap the button.

TIP

>> When you're nude, or just ugly, decline the video-chat invite. After that, you can open the Hangouts app and reply to the caller with a text message or voice chat instead. Explain your embarrassment.

>> If you want to make eye contact, look directly into the tablet's front-facing camera. It's right above the touchscreen, either centrally located or to the left or right.

Placing a Hangouts phone call

If you've obtained the Hangouts Dialer app, you can use Hangouts to place a real, live phone call. It's amazingly simple, and it works like this:

1. **Tap the Phone Calls tab in the Hangouts app.**

    Refer to Figure 8-1 for its location. If you don't see the Phone Calls tab, you haven't yet installed the Hangouts Dialer app.

2. **Type a contact name or a phone number.**

3. **Tap the matching contact, or tap the phone number (when it doesn't belong to a contact) to dial.**

    The call is placed.

 If you'd rather dial a number directly, tap the Dialpad icon, similar to what's shown in the margin. Type the phone number, and then tap the green Dial icon to place the call.

Tap the red End Call icon to end the call.

>> To the person you're calling, an incoming Hangouts call looks just like any other call, although the number may be displayed as *Unavailable.*

>> The good news: Hangouts calls are free!

>> The bad news: You can't use Hangouts to dial every phone number.

Connect to the World with Skype

Skype is one of the most popular Internet communications programs, allowing you to text-, voice-, or video-chat with other Skype users. But the big enchilada is Skype's capability to place honest-to-goodness phone calls, including international calls.

Obtaining Skype for your tablet

The typical Android tablet doesn't come with the Skype app preinstalled. To get Skype, visit Google Play and obtain the Skype app. In case you find multiple apps, get the one that's from the Skype company itself.

To use Skype, you need a Skype account. You can sign up when you first open the app. You will need to confirm your new account, and that confirmation must take place before you can start using the app.

REMEMBER

>> Direct Skype to scour the tablet's address book for contacts. This process may take a while.

>> Skype is free to use. Text chat is free. Voice and video chat with one other Skype user is also free. When you want to call a real phone, or video-chat with a group, you need to boost your account with Skype Credit.

>> It's doesn't cost extra to do a gang video chat in the Hangouts app.

>> Don't worry about getting a Skype number, unless you plan to receive Skype phone calls on your tablet. Those phone calls include calls from any phone, not just a mobile device using the Skype app.

Running Skype

After you initially sign into Skype, the app continues to run on your tablet. Only when you turn off the tablet or deliberately sign out of Skype does the app stop.

You're free to do other things on your tablet while Skype runs. If any text message arrives, a Skype notification appears, similar to what's shown in the margin. Voice and video chats feature full-screen invitations.

To sign out of Skype, tap the Side Menu icon, and in the navigation drawer, choose the Sign Out action. Tap the Sign Out button to confirm.

Chatting with another Skype user

Text chat with Skype works similarly to texting on a cell phone. The difference is, similar to the Hangouts app's text chat, you can only type at other Skype users. If one of them shows up as available in the Skype contacts list, follow these steps to initiate a Skype chat:

1. **At the main Skype screen, tap the People tab to choose a contact.**

The People tab icon is shown in the margin. The Skype user's status appears below the name. A user who is "Available" is theoretically online and willing to chat with you.

2. **Type your text in the Type a Message Here text box.**

The box is found at the bottom of the screen.

Below the box you'll find a row of icons that represent various items you can insert or attach to your text message. These items include emojis, documents, media, your location, and so on.

3. **Tap the Send icon to send the message.**

As long as your Skype friend is online and eager, you'll be chatting in no time.

At the right end of the text box, you find the Smiley icon. Use this icon to insert a cute graphic into your text.

Talking and seeing on Skype

The text chat, covered in the preceding section, is how you initiate communications with other Skype users. To take the call up a notch, you can switch to voice or video chat.

To initiate voice chat, which isn't the same thing as a phone call, start a text chat with someone. You don't even need to type anything; just tap the Voice Chat icon, similar to what's shown in the margin. The other user receives an invite, and soon you're yacking away on Skype.

Rather than voice chat, most people crank up conversation to 11 and go for a face-to-face video chat. To initiate that level of communications, tap the Video Call icon, shown in the margin. The call rings through to the contact, and if that person wants to video-chat, they pick up in no time and you're talking and gawking at each other.

Placing a Skype phone call

Skype can be used to turn your Android tablet into a cell phone. It's an amazing feat. And it works quite well – providing that you have Skype Credit.

To ensure that you have Skype Credit, tap that Side Menu icon in the Skype app and check your Skype Credit quantity on the navigation drawer. If you see $0.00, tap that item to either make a one-time Skype Credit purchase or get a subscription. You don't need a lot of Skype Credit to make calls — the rates are quite cheap.

After you've confirmed your Skype Credit, you can use the tablet to make a "real" phone call, which is a call to any phone number on the planet (Planet Earth). Heed these steps:

1. **Tap the Phone tab.**

   The Phone tab shows any previous calls you've made. Calls can be placed to Skype users or to any phone number, including international numbers.

2. **Tap the Dialpad icon at the bottom of the screen.**

3. **Type the number to dial.**

   Or you can tap the address book icon (near the upper right corner of the screen) to choose a Skype contact. When you do, you're calling their phone, not initiating a new voice chat.

   The preset +1 (prefix) is required for dialing to the United States, even when the number is local. Don't erase it!

4. **Tap the blue phone (Dial) button at the bottom of the screen to place the call.**

5. **Talk.**

   As you talk, the cost of the call is displayed on the screen. That way, you can keep tabs on the toll.

6. **To end the call, tap the End Call button.**

Lamentably, you can't use Skype to receive a phone call on your Android tablet. The only way to make that happen is to pay for a Skype online number. In that case, you can use Skype to both send and receive regular phone calls.

TIP

>> I recommend getting a good headset if you plan on using Skype often to place phone calls.

>> In addition to the per-minute cost, you may be charged a connection fee for making the call.

>> You can check the Skype website at skype.com for a current list of call rates, for both domestic and international calls.

REMEMBER

>> You can use the Hangouts app to place free phone calls, though it doesn't support the broad range of phone numbers as Skype. Hangouts is incapable of placing international calls (as this book goes to press). Refer to the earlier section "Placing a Hangouts phone call."

TECHNICAL STUFF

>> Unless you've paid Skype to let you use a specific phone number, the phone number shown on the recipient's Caller ID screen is something unexpected — often the text *Unknown*. Because of that, you might want to email the person you're calling and let him know that you're placing a Skype call. That way, the call won't be skipped because the Caller ID isn't recognized.

Chapter **9**

Digital Social Life

Long ago, social networking eclipsed email as the number-one reason for using the Internet. It has nearly replaced email, has definitely replaced having a personalized website, and has become an obsession for millions across the globe. Your Android tablet is ready to meet your social networking desires.

Your Life on Facebook

Of all the social networking sites, Facebook is the king. It's the online place to go to catch up with friends, send messages, express your thoughts, share pictures and videos, play games, and waste more time than you ever thought you had.

» The best way to access Facebook is to use the Facebook app. This app is preinstalled on some tablets. If not, you can obtain the Facebook app for free at Google Play. See Chapter 15.

» You can use the Facebook app to sign up for a Facebook account, or you can use your existing account.

» After signing in to Facebook the first time, you have to perform configuration. I recommend choosing the option to synchronize Facebook with your phone's contacts.

TIP

» The Facebook app is updated frequently. Visit my website to review any new information:

```
wambooli.com/help/android
```

Running Facebook on your tablet

The main Facebook screen has several tabs, as shown in Figure 9-1. The tab you'll probably use the most is News Feed. Other options for interacting with Facebook appear on the screen, as illustrated in the figure.

Friend requests   Notifications   Facebook Contacts

News Feed   Menu   Set your status   Upload a photo   Messages

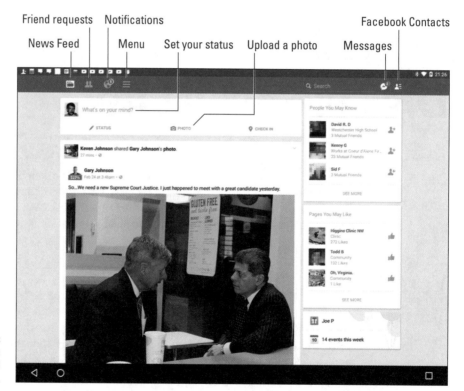

FIGURE 9-1: Facebook on an Android tablet.

To set Facebook aside, tap the Home icon to return to the Home screen. The Facebook app continues to run until you either sign out of the app or turn off your Android tablet.

To sign out of the Facebook app, tap the Menu icon (refer to Figure 9-1) and choose the Log Out action (from the bottom of the list). Tap the LOG OUT button to confirm.

» Refer to Chapter 18 for information on placing a Facebook app launcher or the Facebook widget on the Home screen.

» To update the News Feed, swipe downward on the screen from just below the status bar.

» Use the Like, Comment, or Share icons below a News Feed item to like, comment, or share something, respectively. Existing comments appear only when you choose the Comment item.

» The Facebook app generates notifications for news items, mentions, chat, and so on. Look for them on the status bar along with the tablet's other notifications.

Setting your status

The primary thing you live for on Facebook, besides having more friends than anyone else, is to update your status. It's the best way to share your thoughts with the universe, especially intimate moments like when you're waiting in the doctor's office to have your tonsilloliths removed.

To set your status, follow these steps in the Facebook app:

1. **Switch to the News Feed.**

   Tap the News Feed icon. (Refer to Figure 9-1.)

2. **Tap the Status button at the top of the screen.**

   Look for the text *What's On Your Mind*. Tap that text to view the Post to Facebook screen, where you can type your musings, similar to what's shown in Figure 9-2.

3. **Choose a sharing audience from the button just below your account name.**

   Chose Public so that everyone can see the message, or Friends so that only people you're friends with can see it. Other options are visible when you tap the More action.

4. **Type the post.**

   If necessary, tap the Back navigation icon so that you can see the *What's On Your Mind* text. Anything you type replaces that text.

5. **Tap the POST button to share your thoughts.**

To cancel the post, tap the Back navigation icon. Tap the DISCARD POST button to confirm.

TIP

If you've added the Facebook widget to the Home screen, you can use that widget to share a quick post.

Status update text

Choose sharing audience

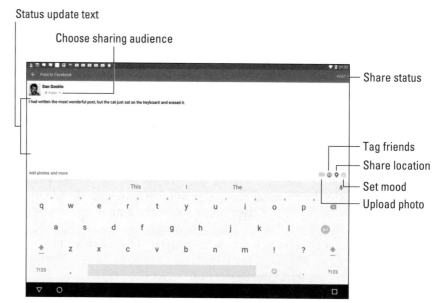

Share status

Tag friends

Share location

Set mood

Upload photo

FIGURE 9-2:
Updating your
Facebook
status.

Uploading a picture or video to Facebook

Your Android tablet features a camera. Mix in the Facebook app and you have an all-in-one gizmo designed for sharing the various intimate and private moments of your life with the ogling throngs of the Internet.

To share a picture or video in the Facebook app, tap the Photo icon. Refer to Figures 9-1 and 9-2 for popular Photo icon locations on the main screen and the Write Post screen. After you tap the Photo icon, you have three choices:

>> First, you can select an image from pictures shown on the screen. These are images stored on your tablet. Tap an image, or tap several images to select a bunch, and then tap the DONE button.

>> Second, you can take a picture and send it to Facebook. Tap the Add Photo icon, shown in the margin, to initiate the process.

>> Third, tap the Add Video icon to use the tablet's camera to record a video.

If you elect to use the camera to take a picture or record a video, the Camera app appears. Snap the photo or record the video. You see a preview screen, similar to the one shown in Figure 9-3. Tap the Retry button to take another image or record another video, or tap the Done icon to get ready to post the media to Facebook. Tap Cancel to abandon your efforts.

Cancel

Done/OK

Retry

FIGURE 9-3: Adding an image to Facebook.

After you select the image or video, it appears on a new post screen. Continue to create the post as described earlier in this chapter. Tap the POST button to present your efforts to the Facebook community. The image can be found as part of your status update or News Feed, and it's also saved to your Mobile Uploads album on Facebook.

>> See Chapter 11 for more information on using the tablet's camera.

>> I find it easier to use the Camera app to take a bunch of images or record video and then choose that item later to upload it to Facebook.

>> The Facebook app appears on the various Share menus available in other apps on the tablet. Tap the Share icon to send to Facebook a YouTube video, an image, a web page, some music, and so on.

Changing the Facebook ringtone

To change or eliminate the noise the Facebook app generates for notifications, follow these steps:

1. **Tap the Menu icon.**

Refer to Figure 9-1 for its location.

2. **Choose App Settings.**

You may have to swipe down the screen to locate this action.

3. **Choose Notifications and then Ringtone.**

4. **If prompted by the Complete Action Using card, select Media Storage and tap the JUST ONCE button.**

See Chapter 18 for information on dealing with the Complete Action Using card, which falls under the topic of "default apps."

5. **Choose a sound from the list.**

You hear a sound preview, but nothing is set until you:

6. **Tap OK.**

To use the phone's standard notification ringtone, choose Default Notification Sound in Step 5.

The Tweet Life

Twitter is a social networking site, similar to Facebook but far briefer. On Twitter, you write short spurts of text that express your thoughts or observations, or you share links. Or you can just use Twitter to follow the thoughts or *tweets* of other people.

>> A message posted on Twitter is a tweet.

>> A tweet can be no more than 140 characters long, including spaces and punctuation.

>> You can post messages on Twitter and follow others who post messages. It's a good way to get updates and information quickly, from not only individuals but also news outlets, corporations, various organizations, and evil robots.

Setting up Twitter

Your Android tablet most likely didn't come with the Twitter app installed. So your first step into the twitterverse involves getting the app: Visit Google Play and search for the Twitter app from Twitter, Inc. Install that app; use the directions in Chapter 15 if you need assistance.

After the Twitter app is installed, open it.

You can use your Google (Gmail) account to sign in to Twitter, create a new account, or use an existing account. These options are presented when the Twitter app first runs.

Figure 9-4 shows the Twitter app's main screen, which shows the current news-feed. The Twitter app is updated frequently, so its exact appearance may change after this book has gone to press.

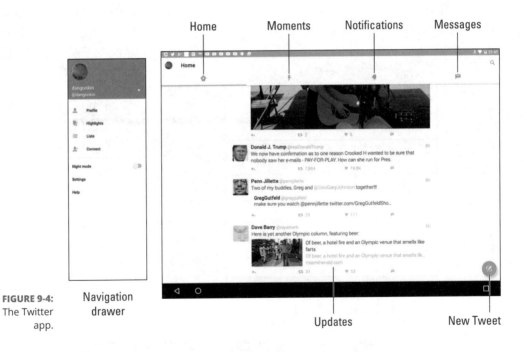

Home   Moments   Notifications   Messages

FIGURE 9-4:
The Twitter
app.

Navigation
drawer

Updates   New Tweet

>> To access the Twitter app's navigation drawer, swipe in from the far left side of the tablet's touchscreen.

>> The Twitter app doesn't automatically update. To refresh, swipe down the screen, starting just below the status bar, or tap the Home icon.

>> The Twitter app comes with companion widgets you can affix to the Home screen. Use the widgets to peruse recent tweets or compose a new tweet. Refer to Chapter 18 for information on affixing widgets to the Home screen.

Tweeting

The Twitter app provides an excellent interface to the many wonderful and interesting things that Twitter does. Of course, the two most basic tasks are reading and writing tweets.

To read tweets, choose the Home category, shown in Figure 9-4. Recent tweets are displayed in a list, with the most recent information at the top. To update the list, swipe from the middle of the screen downward.

To create a new tweet, tap the New Tweet icon, shown in the margin (and refer to Figure 9-4). Use the New Tweet screen, shown in Figure 9-5, to compose your tweet.

FIGURE 9-5: Creating a tweet.

Tap the Location item to add your current whereabouts to the tweet. Tap the Photo icon to add an image or a video stored on the tablet.

Touch the Tweet button to share your thoughts with the twitterverse. If you chicken out, tap the Back navigation icon and choose DELETE.

>> You have only 140 characters, including spaces, for creating your tweet. That includes spaces. The character counter, shown in Figure 9-5, lets you know how close you're getting to the 140-character limit.

>> The Twitter app appears on various Share menus in other apps. Use those Share menus to send to Twitter whatever you're looking at, such as a link to a video, web page, photo, and so on.

More Social Networking Opportunities

The Internet is brimming with social networking opportunities. Facebook may be the king, but lots of landed gentry are eager for that crown. It almost seems as though a new social networking site pops up every week. Beyond Facebook and Twitter, other social networking sites include, but are not limited to

>> Google+

>> LinkedIn

>> Meebo

>> Myspace

Apps for these services are obtained from Google Play. Use the app itself to sign up for an account or use an existing account.

>> See Chapter 15 for more information on Google Play.

>> Google+ is Google's social networking app, which is related to the Hangouts app. See Chapter 8 for information on using Hangouts.

>> If you find yourself overwhelmed with social networking sites and sources, consider obtaining the HootSuite app. Use that single app to share your thoughts on a multitude of social networking platforms.

>> As with Facebook and Twitter, your social networking apps might appear on various Share menus on the Android tablet. That way, you can easily share your pictures and other types of media with your online social networking pals.

3
Omni Tablet

» **Adding layers to the map**

» **Saving a map for later**

» **Finding your location**

» **Sharing your location**

» **Searching for places**

» **Using your tablet as a navigator**

Chapter **10**

There's a Map for That

'm hoping that teleportation becomes a reality someday. It would be so convenient to travel instantly, to get where you're going without sitting in a cramped cabin. In fact, the only mystery will be whether teleportation has the same knack for losing your luggage as air travel.

One thing our fortunate descendants probably won't complain about is being lost. That's because their Android tablets will tell them exactly where they are, thanks to the Maps app. They'll be able to find all sorts of things, from tacos in pill form to used flying cars to Hello Kitty light sabers. Because it's the future, they might even be able to use the futuristic version of an Android tablet to find their lost luggage.

Map 101

To find your location, as well as the location of things near and far, summon the Maps app on your Android tablet. Good news: You run no risk of improperly folding the Maps app. Better news: The Maps app charts the entire country, including freeways, highways, roads, streets, avenues, drives, bike paths, addresses, businesses, and various points of interest.

Unfolding the Maps app

To start the Maps app, tap its launcher on the tablet's Home screen. You might find the launcher inside a Google folder. And, as with all apps on the tablet, you tap the Apps icon to locate the Maps app in the Apps drawer.

If you're starting the app for the first time or it has been recently updated, you can read the What's New screen; tap the OK or GOT IT button to continue.

Your tablet communicates with Global Positioning System (GPS) satellites to hone in on your current location. The position is accurate to within a given range, referenced by a blue circle around your location shown on the screen, as illustrated in Figure 10-1. If the circle doesn't appear, either your location is pretty darn accurate or you need to zoom in.

Search for stuff | Points of interest

FIGURE 10-1:
Your location on a map.

Your location on the map | Directions | Location

Here are some fun things you can do when viewing the basic street map:

Zoom in: To make the map larger (to move it closer), double-tap the screen. You can also spread your fingers on the touchscreen to zoom in.

Zoom out: To make the map smaller (to see more), pinch your fingers on the touchscreen.

Pan and scroll: To see what's to the left or right or at the top or bottom of the map, swipe your finger on the touchscreen. The map scrolls in the direction you swipe.

Rotate: Using two fingers, rotate the map clockwise or counterclockwise. Tap the Compass Pointer icon, shown in the margin, to reorient the map with north at the top of the screen.

Perspective: Touch the screen with two fingers and swipe up or down to view the map in perspective. You can also tap the Location icon to switch to Perspective view, though that trick works only for your current location. To return to Flat-Map view, tap the Compass Pointer icon.

The closer you zoom in on the map, the more detail you see, such as street names, address block numbers, businesses, and other sites — but no tiny people.

>> See the nearby sidebar "Activate location technology!" to confirm that the tablet presents your location accurately.

>> The blue triangle (shown in the center of Figure 10-1, inside a faint blue circle) shows in which general direction the tablet is pointing.

>> When the tablet's direction is unavailable, you see a blue dot as your location on the map.

>> When the Location icon is blue, you're viewing your current location on the map. Tap the icon to enter Perspective view. Tap the Perspective icon, shown in the margin, to return to Flat-Map view.

>> When all you want is a virtual compass, similar to the one you lost as a kid, get a compass app from Google Play. See Chapter 15 for more information about Google Play.

ACTIVATE LOCATION TECHNOLOGY!

The Maps app works best when you activate all the tablet's location technologies, including both GPS and Wi-Fi. To ensure that these technologies are in use, open the Settings app and choose the Location item. On Samsung tablets, this item might be located in the Privacy area. Ensure that the master control is in the On position. Further, if a Mode item or Locating Method item is available, choose it and select either the High Accuracy item or the GPS and Wi-Fi option.

Applying layers

You add details to the map by applying layers: A layer can enhance the map's visual appearance, provide more information, or add other fun features to the basic street map, such as the Satellite layer, shown in Figure 10-2.

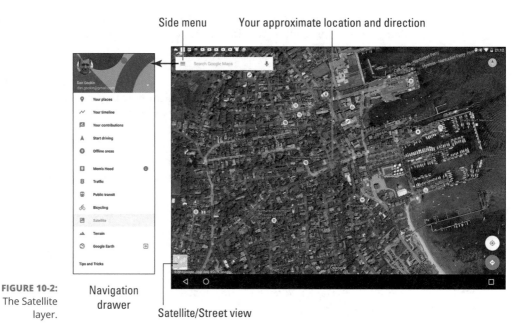

FIGURE 10-2:
The Satellite
layer.

The key to accessing layers is to tap the Side Menu icon to view the navigation drawer. It lists layers you can add to the map, such as the Satellite layer, shown in Figure 10-2. Another popular layer is Traffic, which shows updated travel conditions.

To remove a layer, choose it again from the navigation drawer; any active layer appears highlighted. When a layer isn't applied, Street view appears.

TIP

Tap the Satellite/Street icon in the lower left corner of the screen to quickly switch between those two layers.

Saving an offline map

For times when an Internet connection isn't available (which is frequent for a Wi-Fi–only tablet), you can still use the Maps app, though only in a limited capacity. The secret is to save the portion of the map you need to reference. Obey these steps:

1. **View the map chunk you desire to save.**

   Zoom. Pan. Square in the area to save on the screen. It can be as large or as small as you need. Obviously, smaller maps occupy less storage.

2. **Tap the Side Menu icon.**

3. **Choose Offline Areas from the navigation drawer.**

   Any maps you've previously saved appear in the list.

4. **Tap the Add icon.**

5. **Tap the DOWNLOAD button.**

6. **Type a title for the map.**

7. **Tap the SAVE button.**

   The map appears in the list of offline maps.

To use an offline map, display the navigation drawer and choose Offline Areas. Tap the offline map to view, and it shows up on the screen whether an Internet connection is active or not.

>> Offline maps remain valid for 30 days. After that time, you must update the map to keep it current. A notification reminds you to update.

>> To update an offline map, choose it from the Offline Areas screen and tap the UPDATE button.

>> Offline maps don't display traffic information.

>> You can zoom and pan to peruse an offline map, but you cannot search the map. Searching works only when an Internet connection is active.

>> If you're out traveling and the tablet's Wi-Fi is on, the offline map may display updated location information. Don't count on this feature to work properly for navigation.

TIP

It Knows Where You Are

It was common to use a map to find out where you were going. New is the concept of using a map to find out where you are. You no longer need to worry about being lost. The Maps app can instantly disclose where you are and what's nearby.

You can even send a message to someone in the tablet's address book to have that person join you — or rescue you.

Finding a location

The Maps app shows your location as a blue dot on the screen. But where is that? I mean, if you need to contact a tow truck, you can't just say, "I'm the blue dot on the gray slab by the green thing."

Well, you can say that, but it probably won't do any good.

To view your current location, tap the Location icon, shown in the margin. If you desire more information, or you want more info about any random place, long-press the Maps screen. Up pops a card, similar to the one shown in Figure 10-3. The card gives your approximate address.

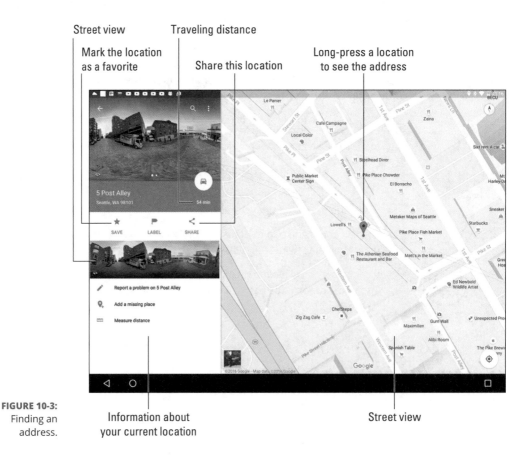

Street view

Mark the location as a favorite

Traveling distance

Share this location

Long-press a location to see the address

FIGURE 10-3:
Finding an address.

Information about your current location

Street view

Tap the card to see a screen with more details and additional information, shown on the right in Figure 10-3.

>> This trick works only when the tablet has Internet access. When Internet access isn't available, the Maps app can't communicate with the Google map servers.

>> The time display under the Travel icon (the car shown in the upper left corner of Figure 10-3) indicates how far away the address is from your current location. You might also see the Route icon, shown in the margin.

TIP

>> When you have way too much time on your hands, play with the Street View command. Choosing this option displays the location from a 360-degree perspective. In Street view, you can browse a locale, pan and tilt, or zoom in on details to familiarize yourself with an area, for example — whether you're familiarizing yourself with a location or planning a burglary.

Helping others find your location

TIP

It's possible to use the Maps app to send your current location to a friend. If your pal has a mobile device (phone or tablet) with smarts similar to your Android tablet, he can use the coordinates to get directions to your location. Maybe he'll even bring some tacos in pill form!

To send your current location in an email message, obey these steps:

1. **Long-press your current location on the map.**

REMEMBER

To see your current location, first tap the Location icon in the lower right corner of the Maps app screen.

After long-pressing your location (or any location), you see a card displayed, showing the approximate address, similar to the card shown on the right in Figure 10-3.

2. **Tap the card's Share icon.**

3. **Choose the app to share the location.**

For example, choose Gmail to send the location data in an email message, choose Hangouts to instantly chat with someone, or choose another, appropriate app from among those listed.

4. **Continue using the selected app to complete the process of sending your location to someone else.**

When the recipients receive the message, they can tap the link to open your location in the Maps app — if they have an Android device. When the location appears, they can follow my advice in the later section "Getting from here to there" for getting to your location. And don't loan them this book, either; have them purchase their own copy. Thanks.

Find Things

The Maps app can help you find places in the real world, just like the Google Search app helps you find places on the Internet. Both operations work basically the same: Open the Maps app and type something to find in the Search box. (Refer to Figure 10-1.) The variety of terms you can type in the Search box is explained in this section.

Looking for a specific address

To locate an address, type it in the Search box. For example:

```
1313 N. Harbor Blvd., Anaheim, CA 92803
```

You may not need to type the entire address: As you tap the keys, suggestions appear onscreen. Tap a matching suggestion to view that location. Otherwise, tap the onscreen keyboard's Search key, and that location is shown on the map.

After finding a specific address, the next step is to get directions. See the later section "Getting from here to there."

>> You don't need to type the entire address. Oftentimes, all you need is the street number and street name and then either the city name or zip code.

>> If you omit the city name or zip code, the Maps app looks for the closest matching address near your current location.

>> Tap the X button in the Search box to clear the previous search.

Finding a business, restaurant, or point of interest

You may not know an address, but you know when you crave sushi or perhaps the exotic flavors of Manitoba. Maybe you need a hotel or a gas station or you must find a place that buys old dentures. To find a business entity or a point of interest, type its name in the Search box. For example:

```
Movie theater
```

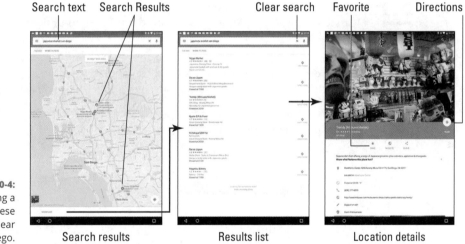

This search text locates movie theaters on the current Maps screen. Or, to find locations near you, first tap the Location icon (shown in the margin) and then type the search text.

To look for points of interest at a specific location, add the city name, district, or zip code to the search text. For example:

```
Japanese Market San Diego
```

After typing this command and tapping the onscreen keyboard's Search key, you see the assortment of Japanese (or Asian) markets located in the San Diego metropolitan area, similar to the results shown on the left in Figure 10-4.

Search text   Search Results   Clear search   Favorite   Directions

FIGURE 10-4:
Finding a
Japanese
market near
San Diego.

Search results   Results list   Location details

To see a list of the results, tap the SHOW LIST button at the bottom of the screen. Tap an item in the results list to view more details — including the exact address, hours of operation, phone number, and website — similar to what's shown on the far right in Figure 10-4.

To get to the location, tap the Route icon on the location's card. See the later section "Getting from here to there."

>> Every letter or dot on the search results screen represents a matching location. For each dot, a card is available, as shown in the center in Figure 10-4.

>> Spread your fingers on the touchscreen to zoom in on the map.

>> If you really like the location, tap the Save (Star) icon. The location is added to your list of favorite places. A star also appears on the map, indicating that one of your favorite places is nearby. See the next section.

Searching for favorite or recent places

Just as you can bookmark favorite websites on the Internet, you can use the Maps app to mark favorite places in the real world. The feature is called Your Places.

To review your favorite places or browse your recent map searches, tap the Side Menu icon and choose Your Places from the navigation drawer. The Your Places screen features four tabs:

>> **Labeled** lists locations related to your contacts, as well as your home and work locations. (See the later section "Setting your Home and Work locations.")

>> **Saved** lists any locations you've flagged as favorites. Tap the Save (Star) icon on the location's details card to save a location.

>> **Visited** refers to any locations you've been to recently.

>> **Maps** lets you view custom maps you've created. It's a feature not yet fully implemented as this book goes to press.

Select a tab, and then swipe through the list to see recent searches, saved places, and any offline maps you've saved. To revisit a location or view an item, tap its entry in the list.

Android the Navigator

The Maps app not only shows you where you want to go but also helps you get there. You can start from your current location, or special home and work locations, or just get directions from two random points.

Setting your Home and Work locations

Two places that you frequent the most in the real world are where you live and where you work. The Maps app lets you create shortcuts for these locations. They're called, logically enough, Home and Work.

To set the Home and Work locations, follow these steps in the Maps app:

1. **Tap the Side Menu icon to display the navigation drawer.**

2. **Choose Your Places.**

3. **On the LABELED tab, choose Home.**

4. **Type your home address.**

5. **Tap Work.**

6. **Type your work address.**

You can use the Home and Work shortcuts when searching for a location or getting directions. For example, type **Home** into the Search box to instantly see where you live, or whichever place you call home. To get directions from your current location to work, type **Work** as the destination. Keep reading in the next section.

>> If you choose Home or Work from the Your Places menu, you see that location displayed on the map.

>> To reset your home or work locations, display the Your Places screen (refer to Steps 1 and 2), but tap the Action Overflow icon and choose Edit Home or Edit Work, respectively.

Getting from here to there

One command associated with locations found in the Maps app deals with getting directions. The command is called Route, and it shows either the Route icon (see the margin) or a mode of transportation, such as a car, bike, or bus. Here's how it works:

1. **Tap the Route icon on a location's card.**

   After tapping the Route icon, you see a screen similar to the one shown in Figure 10-5. (When the tablet is held vertically, the information is displayed on two screens instead of one.)

2. Set a starting point.

The starting point is listed as Your Location, which is the tablet's current location. You can type another location or use the Home or Work shortcuts, as described in the preceding section.

TIP

If the starting point and destination are reversed, tap the Action Overflow and choose Reverse.

Destination

Starting location   Mode of transportation

Alternative routes (gray)

Best route (in blue)

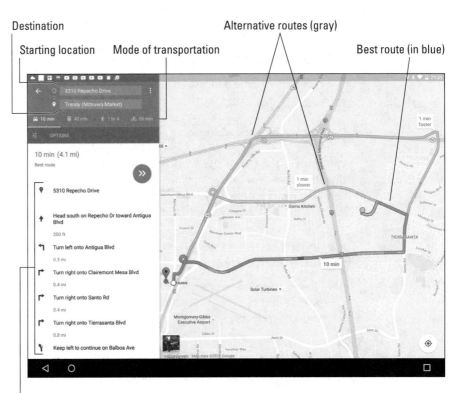

FIGURE 10-5:
Planning a trip.

Directions

3. Choose a method of transportation.

The available options vary, depending on your location. In Figure 10-5, the items are (from left to right) Car, Public Transportation, On Foot, and Bicycle. If ride services, such as Uber or Lyft, are available, they might appear as well.

4. Ensure that the starting location and destination are what you want.

If they're backward, tap the Swap icon. (Refer to Figure 10-5.)

5. **To select another route, tap it on the screen.**

Alternate routes appear in gray. (Refer to Figure 10-5.) When you choose one, check the route card to observe time and distance differences. You can also drag the route lines on the map to set your own directions.

The map shows your route, highlighted as a blue line on the screen. Detailed directions also appear. Traffic jams show up in red, with slow traffic in yellow.

 To use the Maps app navigation feature, tap the navigation icon, shown in the margin. The voice guides you as well as interactive feedback on the tablet's screen. If you tire of hearing the voice, tap the Speaker icon on the screen and set the Mute option.

 To exit from Navigation mode, tap the Close icon on the screen.

>> The Maps app alerts you to any toll roads on the specified route. As you travel, you can choose alternative, non-toll routes, if available. You're prompted to switch routes during navigation; see the next section.

>> If you're navigating in a car, I recommend that you connect the tablet to the car's 12-volt power source. Navigation consumes a lot of power.

TIP

>> Navigation works best on LTE tablets. Wi-Fi–only tablets can't use navigation without Internet access. See the earlier section "Saving an offline map," though even with a saved map, navigation may not be possible.

>> You may not get perfect directions from the Maps app, but it's a useful tool for places you've never visited.

>> The tablet stays in Navigation mode until you exit. A navigation notification can be seen atop the touchscreen while you're in Navigation mode.

REMEMBER

Chapter **11**

Everyone Say "Cheese!"

I have no idea why people say "Cheese" when they get their pictures taken. Supposedly, it's to make them smile. Even in other countries, where the native word for *cheese* can't possibly influence the face's smile muscles, they still say their word for cheese whenever a picture is taken. Apparently, it's a tradition that's present everywhere. Well, except for maybe on the moon, where it's rumored that Buzz Aldrin said "Green cheese."

Whenever you hear folks say "Cheese" around your Android tablet, it's most likely because you're taking advantage of the tablet's photographic and video capabilities. Or I suppose that you could use the tablet as a festive cheese platter. But whenever you opt to take pictures or shoot video, turn to this chapter for helpful words of advice.

Android Tablet Camera 101

An Android tablet isn't the world's best camera. And I'm sure that Mr. Spock's tricorder wasn't the best camera in the *Star Trek* universe, either, but it could take pictures. That comparison is kind of the whole point: Your Android tablet is an incredible gizmo that does many things. One of those things is to take pictures, which is the responsibility of the Camera app.

Introducing the Camera app

Google makes a standard Camera app, which is called Google Camera. Not every tablet uses that app, however. In fact, of all the apps on various Android tablets, the Camera app is the one that differs the most.

Generally speaking, the Camera app features at least two shooting modes: Still Shot and Video. Additional modes may offer features like a panorama and even special-effects shots. All these shooting modes are handled by the single Camera app.

The Camera app also controls both the tablet's cameras: the main camera, which is on the tablet's backside, and the front-facing camera, which is on the tablet's front above the touchscreen.

Figure 11-1 shows the Google Camera app's main interface in Still Shot mode. To switch to Video mode, swipe the screen from right to left, as indicated in the figure.

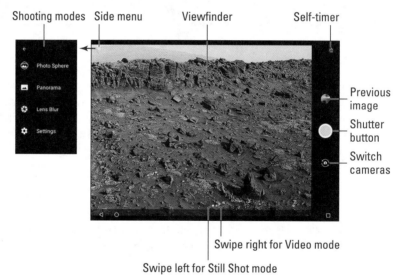

FIGURE 11-1: The Google Camera app, Still Shot mode.

Just to show you how different things can be, Figure 11-2 shows the Camera app on a Samsung Galaxy Tab S2. This isn't even the same app you'd find on all Samsung Galactic tablets; nope, each one can be unique.

Similar items are present in both Figures 11-1 and 11-2, which is probably true for your tablet's camera app as well. Refer to the next section for details on what's important when it comes to taking pictures or recording video.

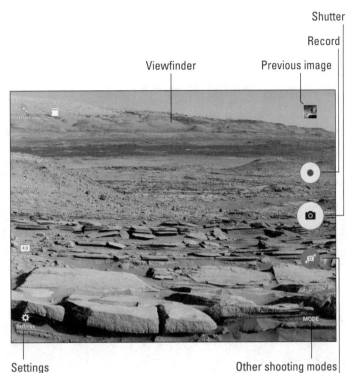

Shutter

Record

Viewfinder   Previous image

FIGURE 11-2:
The Galaxy
Tab S
Camera app.

Settings   Other shooting modes

Switch cameras

>> You can take as many pictures or record as much video with your tablet as you like, as long as you don't run out of space in the tablet's internal storage or external storage.

>> A tablet with a microSD card installed automatically saves images to that location. Otherwise, images are saved internally.

>> See Chapter 12 for information on previewing and managing pictures and videos.

Using basic camera controls

Here are some pointers to consider when using your tablet to take a still shot or record a video:

>> The tablet can be used as a camera in either landscape or portrait orientation. Don't worry either way: The image is always saved with the proper side up.

» If you're recording a video, please-o-please use the tablet in a horizontal orientation. That's the way people expect to see video, and your fans on YouTube will appreciate the proper orientation.

» The tablet's touchscreen serves as the viewfinder; what you see on the screen is exactly what appears in the final photo or video.

» Tap the screen to focus on a specific object. You see a focus ring or square that confirms how the camera lens is focusing. Not every tablet has a camera that can focus; I've not seen any front-facing camera that can focus.

» Spread your fingers on the touchscreen to zoom.

» Pinch your fingers on the touchscreen to zoom out.

» Some tablets let you use the volume key to zoom in or out: Volume Up zooms in, Volume Down zooms out. On other cameras, press the volume key to take a still shot, a function that works even while you record video.

» Hold the tablet steady! I recommend using two hands for taking a still shot and for shooting video.

» The phone stores pictures and videos in the DCIM/Camera folder. Still images are stored in the JPEG or PNG file format; video is stored in the MPEG-4 format.

Capturing a still shot

Taking a still image requires only two steps. First, ensure that the Camera app is in Single-Shot mode. Second, tap the Shutter icon to snap the photo.

In the Google Camera app, to ensure that you're in Single-Shot mode, check for the Shutter icon, shown in the margin. (Also refer to Figure 11-2 for what the Shutter icon looks like on a Galaxy Tab.)

» The image you see in the Camera app's viewfinder is exactly what you see for the final photo.

» Most Camera apps play a shutter sound when a still-shot image is taken.

» Set the resolution before you shoot. See the later section "Choosing resolution and quality."

Recording video

To record video, switch the Camera app to Video mode. The Shutter icon becomes the Record icon, similar to the one shown in the margin and in Figure 11-3. Tap that icon to start recording. The elapsed time, and maybe even storage consumed, appears on the touchscreen as video is being recorded.

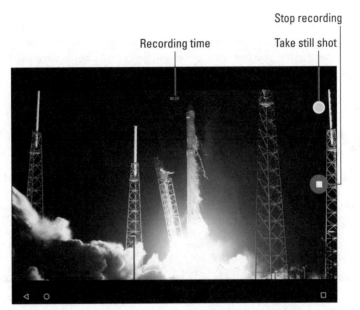

Stop recording

Recording time   Take still shot

FIGURE 11-3:
Recording
video.

Tap the Stop icon to end the recording.

>> In the stock Android Camera app, shown in Figure 11-3, swipe the screen from right to left to enter Video-Recording mode.

>> On some Samsung tablets, you tap the Record button on the Camera app's screen. (Refer to Figure 11-2.) Some tablets may feature a Still/Video toggle that switches the Camera app between Still Shot and Video modes.

>> Some Camera apps feature the Pause icon. Tap that icon to temporarily suspend recording. Tap the Record icon to resume. The video you record is saved as a single video as opposed to multiple videos.

>> Some versions of the Camera app may allow you to grab a still image while the tablet is recording: Tap the screen or press the volume key to snap and save a still shot.

>> Hold the tablet horizontally when you record video.

REMEMBER

Using the self-timer

One common feature found on just about every Android tablet's Camera app is the self-timer. Though it's normally disabled, you can enable this feature to delay taking a still image for a given number of seconds after you tap the Single-Shot Shutter icon. Supposedly, that gives you enough time to run in front of the tablet so that you, too, can be in the photo.

To activate the self-timer feature, tap its icon. On the Google Camera app, tap once to set a 3-second delay, tap again to set a 10-second delay. Tap a third time to disable the feature. The icons on the Camera app's screen are similar to those shown in Table 11-1.

TABLE 11-1   ## Self-Timer Icon Round-Up

Icon	Setting
⌀	The self-timer function is disabled; photos snap instantly.
3s	The photo snaps 3 seconds after you tap the icon.
10s	The photo snaps 10 seconds after you tap the icon.

After you set the timer, tap the Still-Shot Shutter icon. Then dash out in front of the tablet so that it can take your photo.

Oh: You probably want to prop up the tablet on something stable, or even get a tablet tripod mount. The self-timer is pretty useless without one.

» On some Samsung tablets, you tap the Self-Timer icon, similar to the one shown in the margin, and choose a delay from the pop-up menu.

» Turn off the self-timer when you want to return to standard, Still Shot mode, or when you're exhausted from running around.

REMEMBER

Reviewing what you just shot

To preview the image you just shot, or to watch the video you just recorded, tap the previous image thumbnail on the Camera app's screen. You might be able to swipe the previous image left or right to view other recently taken images. Tap the Back navigation icon to return to the Camera app.

>> With some versions of the Android Camera app, where the previous image thumbnail may not appear, swipe the screen from right to left to view the previous image.

>> One reason to review an image you just shot is to delete it. To do so, view the image or video and tap the Delete (Trash) icon. The image is removed immediately, although some tablets may prompt you for confirmation; tap the OK button to delete the image or video.

>> To manage all images taken by or stored in the tablet, use the Photos app. See Chapter 12.

TIP

>> If your pictures or videos appear blurry, ensure that the camera lens on the back of the tablet isn't dirty. Or, you may have neglected to remove the plastic cover from the rear camera when you first set up your tablet.

Camera Settings and Options

Some tablets feature a Camera app laden with features, controls, and more special effects than you'll find in a Hollywood movie. Perhaps I'm exaggerating, but even the most basic Camera app sports options necessary for any amateur photographer.

Switching cameras

You can do more with the tablet's front-facing camera than take those infamous selfie shots. What more exactly you can do I can't think of right now, but the key is to be able to switch between front and rear cameras while using the Camera app.

The Switch Cameras icon is usually found right on the main Camera app screen, which is illustrated in Figures 11-1 and 11-2. Variations on these icons appear in Figure 11-4. If you don't see such an icon on your tablet's Camera app screen, tap the Action Overflow or Settings icon to look for the Switch Cameras icon or action.

FIGURE 11-4:
Switch Camera
icons.

When you see yourself on the touchscreen, you know that you've successfully switched cameras. Take a picture, record a video, ask yourself whether that's a zit on your chin.

Setting the flash

Not all Android tablets feature a flash on the rear camera. None features a flash for the front camera, which is a good thing.

If your tablet has a flash, you can set its behavior: Tap the Flash icon that appears on the Camera app screen. As you tap the icon, it cycles through various flash options, all of which are shown in Table 11-2.

TABLE 11-2   **Android Tablet Camera Flash Settings**

Setting	Icon	When the Flash Activates
Auto	⚡A	During low-light situations but not when it's bright out
On	⚡	Always
Off	⚡̸	Never, even in low-light situations

When you can't find the Flash icon on the screen, tap the Action Overflow or Settings icon. I've also seen Camera apps that feature a sliding drawer on which you'll find the Flash icon. Look for a triangle or chevron near the edge of the screen, which could be one of those slide-in drawers.

TIP

>> A good time to turn on the flash is when taking pictures of people or objects in front of something bright, such as Aunt Ellen showing off her prized peach cobbler in front of a burning munitions factory.

> » A "flash" setting is also available for shooting video in low-light situations. In that case, the flash LED is on the entire time. This setting is made similarly to setting the flash, though the options are only On and Off. It must be set before you shoot video, and, yes, it devours a lot of battery power.

Choosing resolution and quality

You don't always have to set the highest resolution or top quality for images and videos. Especially when you're shooting for the web or uploading pictures to Facebook, top quality is a waste of storage space and upload time because the image is shown on a relatively low-resolution computer monitor.

As you may suspect, setting the image resolution or video quality is done differently by the various tablet Camera apps. No matter what, you must set the new still-shot resolution or video quality *before* you shoot.

In the Google Camera app, follow these steps to access still-shot resolution and video-quality settings:

1. **Tap the Side Menu icon to display the Camera app's shooting modes.**

    The Side Menu icon is shown in the margin. It's also illustrated earlier, in Figure 11-1, which also shows the shooting modes.

2. **Tap the Settings icon.**

3. **Choose Resolution & Quality.**

    The Resolution & Quality screen is organized by shooting mode: Camera (still image) and Video. It's further organized by back or front camera.

4. **Choose a mode and a camera (back or front).**

    For example, tap Back Camera Photo to set the still-image resolution for the tablet's rear camera.

5. **Choose a resolution or video-quality setting from the list.**

    Options are presented in aspect ratio and in megapixels.

For other Camera apps, tap the Action Overflow or Settings icon to view resolution and video-quality options. The item may be titled Resolution, Picture Size, or Photo Size. You may also have to switch cameras (back or front) before setting the resolution.

>> Set the resolution or video quality before you shoot!

>> A picture's resolution describes how many *pixels,* or dots, are in the image. The more dots, the better the image looks when enlarged.

>> The resolution and video-quality choices are more limited on the front-facing camera because it's not as sophisticated as the rear camera.

>> The *aspect ratio* describes the image's overall dimensions horizontally by vertically. A 4:3 ratio is pretty much standard for photographs and is similar in proportion to the tablet's screen. The 16:9 ratio is the widescreen format.

>> The video quality settings HD and SD refer to High Definition and Standard Definition, respectively. The *p* value represents vertical resolution, with higher values indicating higher quality.

>> *Megapixel* is a measurement of the amount of information stored in an image. One megapixel is approximately 1 million pixels, or individual dots that comprise an image. It's often abbreviated MP.

Checking the location tag feature

Your Android tablet not only takes pictures but also keeps track of where you're located when you take the picture — if you've activated that option. The feature is called location tag, geotag, or GPS-tag.

To confirm the location-tag setting in the Google Camera app, follow these steps:

1. **Tap the Side Menu icon and choose Settings.**

2. **Enable or disable the Save Location feature.**

   The master control by the Save Location item is either on or off, reflecting the location-tag setting.

For the Camera app on some Samsung tablets, obey these steps to check the location-tag feature:

1. **Tap the Settings icon on the main Camera app screen.**

   Refer to Figure 11-2, though on your Galactic tablet the icon's location may be different.

2. **Set the master control by the Location Tags item on or off.**

Other Camera apps may require you to jump through various hoops, such as wade through an Action Overflow or Settings icon menu, to locate the Location Tag item.

>> Deactivating the location-tag feature doesn't remove that information from photos you've already taken.

>> The location-tag information is stored in the picture itself. This means that other devices, apps, and computer programs can read the GPS information to determine where the image was taken.

>> See Chapter 12 for information on reviewing a photograph's location.

Selecting the storage device

When you place a microSD card into your Android tablet's removable storage slot, the Camera app automatically chooses that location to save new photos and videos. To confirm or change this setting, follow these steps in the Camera app:

1. **Tap the Action Overflow or Settings icon.**

2. **Choose Storage Location.**

The option may have a name different from but similar to Storage Location.

3. **Set the location.**

The options are Device or Internal for the tablet's internal storage; or microSD, Memory Card, or External Storage for the removable media card.

REMEMBER

Not every tablet features removable storage.

Chapter **12**

Image Management

What's the point of an Android tablet having a camera unless you can eventually review, peruse, browse, and chortle at those various images and videos? To solve that problem, your tablet features a digital photo album. You use it to view, manage, and manipulate the images stored in the tablet. Further, you can export your images, sharing them with friends farflung and wide, as well as enjoy images shared on Google and from other Android devices you might own.

The Digital Gallery

The stock Android app for viewing pictures and videos is called Photos. It's the natural companion to the Camera app, covered in Chapter 11. To start the app, tap its icon, which may be lurking on the Home screen or, like all the tablet's apps, found on the Apps drawer.

>> The Photos app not only lets you look at pictures and watch videos, but you can also manage that media, edit, and share your visual creations online.

TECHNICAL STUFF

>> The traditional Android tablet photo-management/album app is Gallery. You may still find the Gallery app on your tablet, though this chapter is specific to the Photos app.

Viewing pics and vids

The Photos app organizes your photos and videos in several ways. The Photos screen, shown in the center of Figure 12-1, lists photos by date. Tap the Photos icon at the bottom of the screen to ensure that this view is active.

To behold your photo albums, tap the Albums icon at the bottom of the screen. Albums are closely associated with the online photos accessed from your Google account, covered elsewhere in this chapter.

To view an image, tap its thumbnail. You see the image appear full-screen, as shown on the right in Figure 12-1. Swipe the screen left or right to peruse other images.

Videos thumbnails feature the Play icon, which is shown in Figure 12-1, though it might not be easy to see. Tap that icon to play the video. As the video is playing, tap the screen again to view onscreen controls.

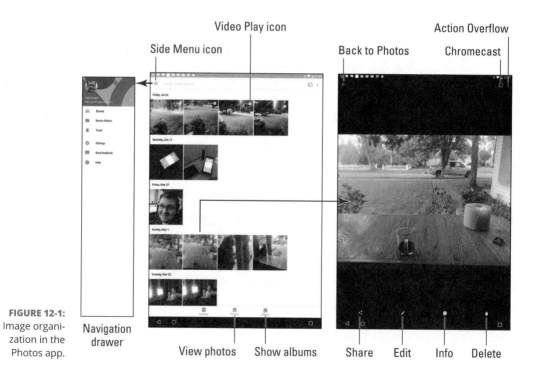

FIGURE 12-1: Image organization in the Photos app.

» While you're viewing an image or a video full-screen, the navigation icons may disappear. Tap the screen to view them.

 » Tap the Back navigation icon to return to an album after viewing an image or a video.

Visiting Google Photos

The Photos app is linked to your Android account and a location on the Internet called Google Photos. To visit that site on a computer, go to photos.google.com and sign in to your Google account.

Your Android tablet automatically synchronizes your tablet's photos and videos, so don't be surprised when you see them online. The process is called *image backup,* and you can disable it, if you prefer. Follow these steps:

1. **In the Photos app, tap the Side Menu icon.**

2. **On the navigation drawer, choose Settings.**

3. **Choose Back Up & Sync.**

4. **Slide the master control by Back Up & Sync to the Off position.**

Changing this setting doesn't affect any images already backed up to Google Photos, though any new images you snap or record will not be shared online. Likewise, you won't be able to access those images on other Android devices.

Creating an album

If you prefer to organize your tablet's images by album instead of by date, the Photos app is glad to oblige. Follow these steps:

1. **View the image you want to add to an album.**

   Ensure that the image is shown full-screen, similar to the picture on the far right in Figure 12-1.

2. **Tap the Action Overflow and choose Add to Album.**

3. **Select an existing album from the list, or tap Album under the Create New heading.**

   The image is added to an album, or you're prompted to type a name for a new album.

Repeat these steps to add more images to the album, choosing the existing album in Step 3.

REMEMBER

To switch between Album and Photos mode, tap the proper icon at the bottom of the Photo app's main screen, as shown in Figure 12-1.

Starting a slideshow

The Photos app can display a slideshow of your images, but without the darkened room and sheet hanging over the mantle. To view a slideshow, follow these steps:

1. **View an image full-screen.**

2. **Tap the Action Overflow icon.**

3. **Choose Slideshow.**

    Images from that particular album or date appear one after the other on the screen.

Tap the Back navigation icon to exit the slideshow.

Slideshows don't have to remain in your tablet. If a nearby HDMI TV or monitor features a Chromecast dongle, tap the Chromecast icon, shown in the margin. Choose a specific Chromecast gizmo from the list to view the slideshow on a larger screen. See Chapter 17 for more details on using Chromecast to stream media.

Finding a picture's location

In addition to snapping a picture, your tablet records the specific spot on Planet Earth where the picture was taken. Depending on the tablet, this feature is called location tag, GPS-tag, or geotag. To view the information, heed these steps:

1. **View the image in the Photos app.**

2. **Tap the Info icon.**

    The icon is found below the image, as shown in the margin. On some tablets, you may have to tap the Action Overflow and choose Details.

The Info card that's displayed shows details about when, how, and where the image was taken, similar to what's shown in Figure 12-2. Map information, if available, appears on the card.

See Chapter 11 for more information on the location-tag feature, including steps to take to enable or disable it.

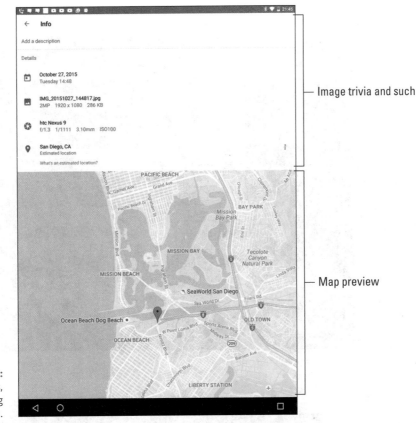

— Image trivia and such

— Map preview

FIGURE 12-2:
Image details,
including
location.

Edit and Manage Images

The best tool for image editing is a computer amply equipped with photo editing software, such as Photoshop or a similar program that's also referred to as "Photoshop" because the term is pretty much generic. Regardless, you can use the Photos app to perform some minor photo and video surgery.

Editing an image

To enter Image Editing mode in the Photos app, view the image you want to modify and tap the Edit icon, similar to what's shown in the margin. If you don't see the icon, tap the screen and it shows up.

Editing tools are presented in three categories, shown at the bottom of the screen and illustrated in Figure 12-3: basic settings, image effects, and crop/rotate.

Cancel edits

Action Overflow

Basic settings   Crop/Rotate

Image effects

FIGURE 12-3:
Image editing
in the
Photos app.

The basic settings are shown in the figure, just below the image. These include an auto-adjustment tool, brightness and contrast, color, and so on. To use a tool, tap its icon, and then adjust a slider on the screen to change the effect. Tap the Done icon when you're satisfied, or Cancel if you change your mind.

The center category, shown in Figure 12-3, is image effects. Tap an effect to instantly apply its changes to the image.

Using the crop/rotate tool is covered in a later section.

Changes are applied immediately to the image. To peel them away, tap the Action Overflow and choose Undo Edits. Otherwise, tape the SAVE button to keep the modified image.

Unediting an image

The changes you make are directly applied to the image; an original copy isn't retained. To remove any previously applied edits, crops, or rotation effects, view the image in the Photos app and follow these steps:

1. **Tap the Edit icon to edit the image.**

2. **Tap the Action Overflow.**

3. **Choose Undo Edits.**

4. **Tap the SAVE button.**

The original image is restored.

Cropping

To *crop* an image is to snip away parts you don't want or need, similar to taking a pair of scissors to a photograph of you and your old girlfriend, though the process is far less cathartic. To crop an image, obey these steps:

1. **View the image in the Photos app.**

2. **Tap the Edit icon.**

3. **Tap the Crop / Rotate icon.**

    The icon is shown in the margin. The screen changes as illustrated in Figure 12-4. The tools presented crop and rotate the image.

4. **Drag any of the four corners to crop the image.**

    As you drag, portions of the image are removed. You can also drag the image within the cropping rectangle to modify the crop action.

5. **Tap the Done button.**

    The image is cropped. You can continue to edit, or tap the SAVE button to make the changes permanent.

If you're unhappy with the changes after tapping the Done button, tap the Action Overflow and choose Undo Edits.

Use the Aspect Ratio icon (refer to Figure 12-4) to adjust the cropping box for the image to a new presentation, such as square or widescreen.

Cropping corners   Cropping rectangle

FIGURE 12-4:
Rotating and
cropping an
image.

Cancel   Set rotation angle   Done

Set aspect ratio   90° Tool

Rotating pictures

Showing someone else an image on your phone can be frustrating, especially
when the image is a vertical picture that refuses to fill the screen when the tablet
is in a vertical orientation. To fix this issue, rotate the picture in the Photos app.
Follow these steps:

1. **Display the cockeyed image and tap the Edit icon.**

2. **Choose the Crop / Rotate tool.**

3. **Tap the 90° icon to rotate the image in 90-degree increments, or drag the
   sliders to set a specific angle.**

   Refer to Figure 12-4 for the location of these buttons on the editing screen.

4. **Tap the Done icon to save the changes.**

   You can continue editing, or tap the SAVE button to make the changes
   permanent.

Rotating an image to a specific angle also crops the image. This step is necessary to maintain the image's aspect ratio.

Deleting images and videos

It's entirely possible, and often desirable, to remove unwanted, embarrassing, or questionably legal images and videos from the Photos app.

 To banish something to the big dumpster, tap the Delete (Trash) icon on the screen when viewing an image or a video. It's not really gone; no, it's moved to the Trash album. You might even see a MOVE TO TRASH button after you tap the Delete icon.

>> If you don't see the Delete icon, the item cannot be deleted. It's most likely a copy pulled in from a web photo-sharing service or a social networking site.

>> To view the Trash album, tap the Side Menu icon and choose Trash from the navigation drawer.

>> Items held in the Trash album are automatically deleted after 60 days. To hasten the departure, long-press items in the Trash album and then tap the Delete icon atop the screen.

Selecting multiple pictures and videos

Three commands can be applied to groups of images and videos in the Photos app: Share, Copy to Album, and Delete. To select a group, follow these steps:

1. **Long-press an image or a video to select it.**

Instantly, Image-Selection mode is activated. The thumbnail you long-pressed grows a check mark.

2. **Continue tapping images and videos to select them.**

3. **Perform an action on the group of images or videos.**

The actions you can perform in Step 3 are

Share: Choose an app to use for sharing the images, such as Gmail to send the lot as an email attachment.

Copy to Album: Select an album to copy the images to, or create a new album.

Delete: The items are banished to the Trash album. See the preceding section.

To deselect items, tap them again. To deselect everything, tap the Back navigation icon.

Set Your Pictures and Videos Free

Keeping your precious moments and memories in your tablet is an elegant solution to the problem of lugging around photo albums. But when you want to show your pictures to the widest possible audience, you need a much larger stage. That stage is the Internet, and you have many ways to send and save your pictures.

Posting a video to YouTube

The best way to share a video is to upload it to YouTube. As a Google account holder, you also have a YouTube account. Why not populate that account with your latest, bestest videos? Who knows what may go viral next!

To upload a video you've recorded, follow these steps:

1. **Ensure that the Wi-Fi connection is activated.**

   The best way to upload a video is to turn on the Wi-Fi connection, which (unlike the mobile cellular network) doesn't incur data surcharges. In fact, if you opt to use the 4G LTE network for uploading a YouTube video, you see a reminder about the data surcharges.

2. **Open the Photos app.**

3. **View the video you want to upload.**

   You do not need to play the video; just have it on the screen.

4. **Tap the Share icon.**

   If you don't see the Share icon, tap the screen.

5. **Choose YouTube.**

   The Add Details screen appears. You may first see a tutorial on trimming the video, which is the next step.

6. **Trim the video, if necessary, resetting the starting and ending points.**

   If you opt to trim, drag the starting and ending points for the video left or right. As you drag, the video is scrubbed, allowing you to preview the start and end points.

7. **Type the video's title.**

8. **Set other options.**

   Type a description, set the privacy level, add descriptive tags, and so on.

9. **Tap the Upload button.**

    You return to the Photos app, and the video is uploaded. It continues to upload even if the tablet locks or you do other things on the tablet.

The Uploading notification appears while the video is being sent to YouTube. When the upload has completed, the notification stops animating and becomes the Uploads Finished icon. You also receive a Gmail message announcing your movie's publication.

To view your video, open the YouTube app. See Chapter 14 for details on using that app.

Sharing images with other apps

Just about every app wants to get in on the sharing bit, especially when it comes to pictures and videos. The key is to view an item full-screen in the Photos app and then tap the Share icon, shown in the margin. Choose an app to share the image or video, and that item is instantly sent to that app.

What happens next?

That depends on the app. For Facebook, Twitter, and other social networking apps, the item is attached to a new post. For Gmail, the item becomes an attachment. Other apps treat images and videos in a similar manner, somehow incorporating the item(s) into whatever wonderful thing that app does. The key is to look for that Share icon.

Chapter **13**

Music, Music, Music

Your Android tablet's amazing arsenal of features includes the capability to play music. So it effectively replaces any gramophone that you've been lugging around, which is the whole idea behind an all-in-one gizmo like an Android tablet. And beyond all your Eddie Cantor and Bing Crosby cylinders, you can add new tunes to the tablet's music library. I hear this new guy Elvis is really something.

Listen Here

Music is just a tap away on your Android tablet. Plug in some headphones, summon a music-playing app, and choose tunes to match your mood. The stock Android app is called Play Music. It's one of Google's arsenal of "play" apps that entertain and inform you.

Browsing your music library

The Play Music app opens the door to music on your tablet. You can choose to listen to a preprogrammed slate of music, purchase a music subscription service, or examine any music you've purchased or transferred to the device.

That last category is referred to as your *music library.* To view it, heed these directions:

1. **Start the Play Music app.**

2. **Tap the Side Menu icon to display the navigation drawer.**

The Side Menu icon is found in the upper left corner of the screen, similar to what's shown in the margin. If you see a left-pointing arrow instead, tap that arrow until the Side Menu icon appears.

3. **Choose Music Library.**

Figure 13-1 shows the Play Music app with the Music Library screen selected. Your music is organized by categories, shown as tabs on the screen. Tap a tab to switch categories, or swipe the screen left or right to browse your music library.

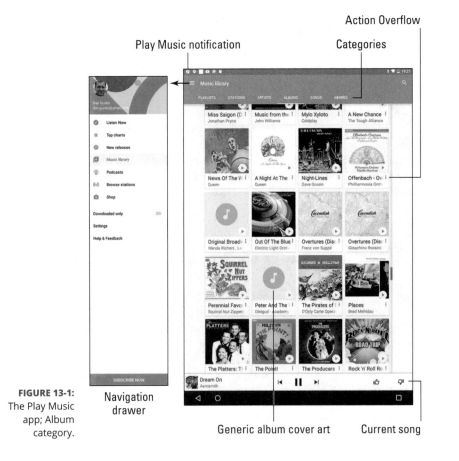

Action Overflow

Play Music notification   Categories

FIGURE 13-1:
The Play Music
app; Album
category.

Navigation
drawer

Generic album cover art   Current song

The categories make your music easier to find, because you don't always remember song, artist, or album names. The Genres category is for those times when you're in the mood for a certain type of music but don't know, or don't mind, who recorded it.

TIP

>> Choose the Listen Now category from the navigation drawer to browse songs you frequently listen to or to discover tunes that the tablet guesses you'll like. The more you use the Play Music app, the more you'll appreciate the results shown in the Listen Now category.

>> Songs and albums feature the Action Overflow icon, shown in the margin. Use that icon to view actions associated with the album or artist.

>> Two types of album artwork are used by the Play Music app. For purchased music, or music recognized by the app, original album artwork appears. Otherwise, the app shows a generic album cover.

>> When the tablet can't recognize an artist, it uses the title Unknown Artist. This usually happens with music you copy manually to your tablet, but it can also apply to audio recordings you make.

>> Music you obtain from Google Play is available on not only your tablet but also all other Android devices you have as well as the Internet. Visit:

`play.google.com/music`

Playing a tune

When you've found the proper tune to enhance your mood, play it! Tap on a song to play that song. Tap on an album to view songs in the album, or tap the album's large Play button, shown in the margin, to listen to the entire album.

While a song plays, controls appear at the bottom of the screen, as shown in the lower right corner in Figure 13-1. Tap that strip to view the song full-screen, as shown in Figure 13-2.

While the song plays, you're free to do anything else on the tablet. In fact, the song continues to play even when the tablet is locked. Choose the Play Music notification, shown in the margin, to return to the Play Music app, or you can use the controls in the notifications drawer or on the Lock screen to pause the song or skip to the next or previous tune.

After the song is over, the next song in the list plays. The order depends on how you start the song. For example, if you start a song from Album view, all songs in that album play in the order listed.

Song queue

Album cover
artwork

Previous song

Play/Pause

Next song

FIGURE 13-2: Repeat
A song is
playing. Shuffle

The next song doesn't play when you have the Shuffle button activated. (Refer to Figure 13-2). In that case, the Play Music app randomly chooses another song from the same list. Who knows which one is next?

The next song also might not play when you have the Repeat option on: The three repeat settings, along with the Shuffle settings, are illustrated in Table 13-1. To change settings, tap the Shuffle icon or Repeat icon.

TABLE 13-1   **Shuffle and Repeat Icons**

Icon	Setting	What Happens When You Touch the Icon
⤴	Shuffle Is Off	Songs play one after the other.
⤴	Shuffle Is On	Songs are played in random order.
🔁	Repeat Is Off	Songs don't repeat.
🔂	Repeat Current Song	The same song plays over and over.
🔁	Repeat All Songs	All songs in the list play over and over.

To stop the song from playing, tap the Pause icon, labeled in Figure 13-2.

>> Use the volume key on the side of the tablet to set the volume.

>> Music on your Android tablet is played by streaming it from the cloud. That means music won't play when an Internet connection is unavailable.

>> You can download music to store on your tablet all the time, regardless of an active Internet connection. See Chapter 15 for details.

>> To change the song order, tap the Song Queue icon, shown in Figure 13-2. Use the tab to the left of each song in the list to change the order; drag the song up or down. Also see the section "Organize Your Music," later in this chapter.

>> Use the Play Music app's search command to locate tunes in your music library. You can search by artist name, song title, or album: Tap the Search icon, illustrated in the margin. Type a song name, artist, or album, and then tap the Search icon on the onscreen keyboard. Choose the song you want to hear from the list that's displayed.

>> When a song is playing or paused, its album artwork might appear as the Lock screen wallpaper. Don't let the change alarm you.

"WHAT'S THIS SONG?"

Ever hear a song playing and you want to know what it is? Google is happy to oblige, but with a reason: The Sound Search for Google Play widget uses the tablet's microphone to listen to music. It matches what's playing with Google's song library and eventually gives you the song's name and artist — plus a chance to purchase the music from Google Play. (That's the reason for the app.)

The Sound Search widget works best (exclusively, I would argue) with recorded music. Try as you might, you cannot sing into the thing and have it recognize a song. Humming doesn't work, either. I've tried playing the guitar and piano and — nope — that doesn't work either. But it's a great tool for discovering details about the music you're listening to.

You can obtain the Sound Search for Google Play widget from the Play Store app, as described in Chapter 15. Directions for adding widgets to the Home screen are offered in Chapter 18.

Queuing up the next song

It's fun to randomly listen to your music library, plucking out tunes like a mad DJ. Oftentimes, however, you don't have patience to wait for the current song to finish before choosing the next tune. The solution is to add songs to the queue. Follow these steps:

1. **Browse your music library for the next song (or album) you want to play.**

2. **Tap the song's Action Overflow.**

3. **Choose Add to Queue.**

   The Play Music app adds the song to the list of tunes to play next.

Songs are added to the queue in the order you tap them. That is, unless you instead choose the command Play Next in Step 3, in which case the tune is inserted at the top of the queue.

 To review the queue, tap the Song Queue icon, shown in the margin as well as in Figure 13-2. Songs in the queue play in order, top down. To change the order, drag a song card up or down. To remove a song from the queue, swipe its card left or right.

If you like your queue, consider making a playlist of those same songs. See the section "Saving the song queue as a playlist," later in this chapter.

TIP

Add Some Music to Your Life

Consider yourself fortunate if your Android tablet came with music preinstalled. Otherwise, your music library may be a little light. To pack it full of those songs you adore, you have two options:

» Buy lots of music from Google Play, which is what Google wants you to do.

» Borrow music from your computer, which Google also wants you to do, just not as enthusiastically as the first option.

For information on buying music at Google Play, see Chapter 15. The next section covers borrowing music from your computer.

Getting music into the Google cloud

Realizing that you probably don't want to buy yet another copy of the Beatles' White Album, you can take songs from your computer and transfer them to your Google Play Music library on the Internet. Here's how that procedure works:

1. **On your computer, locate the music you want to upload to your Play Music library.**

   You can open a music jukebox program, such as Windows Media Player, or just have a folder window open that lists the tunes you want to copy.

2. **Open the computer's web browser and visit** `music.google.com`

   You see a copy of your Play Music library, including your playlists and any recent songs. You can even listen to your music right there on the computer, but no: You have music to upload.

3. **On the web page, click the Side Menu button.**

   It's located in the upper left corner of the window.

4. **Scroll down the list of commands and choose Upload Music.**

5. **Drag music into the web browser window.**

Google may prompt you to configure your PC, so work through those gyrations described on the web page. Follow the steps to continue uploading music.

>> You can repeat these steps to upload tens of thousands of songs. The limit was once 25,000, but I believe Google increased that number recently.

>> The songs you upload are available to your Android tablet, just like any other songs in your music library.

Synchronizing music directly

Some tablets may let you copy music from the computer directly. Use the USB cable to connect the tablet to the computer. Use a music jukebox program on the computer, such as Windows Media Player, to synchronize music with your Android tablet, just as you would any portable music player. Follow these steps:

1. **Connect the Android tablet to your PC.**

   See Chapter 17 for details on making the connection.

2. **On the PC, choose Windows Media Player from the AutoPlay notification or dialog box.**

   If the AutoPlay dialog box doesn't appear, start the Windows Media Player program.

3. **Choose your Android tablet from the Sync List, as illustrated in Figure 13-3.**

   Click the Next Device link until you see your gizmo, such as the Galaxy Tab S2 shown in Figure 13-3.

4. **Drag music to the Sync area.**

   Drag an individual song or an entire album.

5. **Click the Start Sync button to transfer the music from the PC to your tablet.**

The Start Sync button may be located atop the list, as shown in Figure 13-3, or it might be found on the bottom.

6. **Close Windows Media Player and disconnect the tablet.**

Sync tab

Android tablet

Android tablet

Click to sync

Drag music to here

Music to sync

FIGURE 13-3:
Windows Media Player meets Android tablet.

This technique may not work for all tablets. If not, try the steps for uploading music to Google Play in the preceding section.

WARNING

>> You cannot use iTunes to synchronize music with Android devices. Duh.

>> The Android tablet can store only so much music! Don't be overzealous when copying your tunes. In Windows Media Player (refer to Figure 13-3), a capacity-thermometer thing shows you how much storage space is used and how much is available on your tablet. Pay heed to the indicator!

Organize Your Music

The Play Music app categorizes your music by album, artist, song, and so forth, but unless you have only one album and enjoy all the songs on it, this organization probably won't do. To better manage your music, you can create playlists. That way, you can hear the music you want to hear, in the order you want, for whatever mood hits you.

Reviewing your playlists

To view any playlists that you've already created, or that have been preset on the tablet, tap the Playlists tab on the Music Library screen. Available playlists are displayed on the screen, similar to what's shown in Figure 13-4.

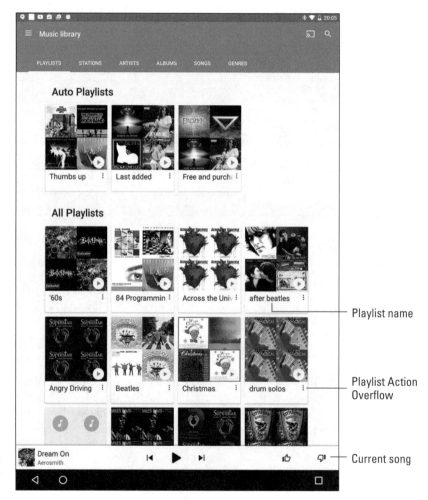

Playlist name

Playlist Action Overflow

Current song

FIGURE 13-4: Playlists in the Play Music app.

To see which songs are in a playlist, tap the playlist's card. To play the songs in the playlist, tap the first song in the list.

TIP

A *playlist* is a helpful way to organize music when a song's information may not have been completely imported into your Android tablet. For example, if you're like me, you probably have a lot of songs labeled Unknown. A quick way to remedy this situation is to name a playlist after the artist and then add those unknown songs to the playlist.

Creating your own playlists

The Play Music app features "auto" playlists, three of which are shown in Figure 13-4. Beyond those few, the playlists you see are those you create. Here's how it works:

1. **Locate some music you want to add to a playlist.**

2. **Tap the Action Overflow icon by the album or song.**

3. **Choose Add to Playlist.**

   Ensure that you're viewing a song or an album; otherwise, the Add to Playlist action doesn't show up.

4. **Choose an existing playlist or, to create a new playlist, tap NEW PLAYLIST.**

   If you choose to create a new playlist, type a name for the playlist and tap the CREATE PLAYLIST button.

The song or album is added to the playlist you selected, or it's placed into a new playlist you created. You can continue to add songs to the playlist by repeating these steps.

>> You can have tons of playlists on your tablet and stick as many songs into them as you like. Adding songs to a playlist doesn't noticeably affect the tablet's storage capacity.

>> To remove a song from a playlist, open the playlist and tap the Action Overflow by the song and choose Remove from Playlist.

>> Removing a song from a playlist doesn't delete the song from the music library; see the later section "Removing unwanted music."

>> Songs in a playlist can be rearranged: While viewing the playlist, use the tab on the far left end of a song title to drag that song up or down in the list.

>> To delete a playlist, tap the Action Overflow icon in the Playlist icon's lower right corner. (Refer to Figure 13-4.) Choose Delete and tap OK to confirm.

Saving the song queue as a playlist

If you've created a song queue, and it's a memorable one, consider saving that queue as a playlist that you can listen to over and over. Obey these directions:

1. **Tap the Song Queue icon to view the song queue.**

   Refer to the earlier section "Queuing up the next song" for details on the song queue.

2. **Tap the Action Overflow icon and choose Save Queue.**

   The Action Overflow icon appears to the right of the Song Queue.

3. **Choose NEW PLAYLIST.**

   Or you can add the songs to an existing playlist, as described in the preceding section.

4. **Fill in the New Playlist card.**

   Refer to the earlier section "Creating your own playlists."

5. **Tap the CREATE PLAYLIST button.**

The songs in the current queue now dwell in their own playlist, always accessible.

Removing unwanted music

To remove a song or an album, tap its Action Overflow icon. Choose the Delete action. Tap the OK button to remove the song. Bye-bye, music.

I don't recommend removing music. Most music on your Android tablet is actually stored on the cloud, Google's Play Music service. Therefore, removing the music doesn't affect the tablet's storage, so unless you totally despise the song or artist, removing the music has no effect.

Music from the Stream

Though they're not broadcast radio stations, some sources on the Internet — Internet radio sites — play music. These Internet radio apps are available from Google Play. Some free services that I can recommend are

>> Pandora Radio

>> Spotify

>> TuneIn Radio

Pandora Radio and Spotify let you select music based on your mood and preferences. The more feedback you give the apps, the better the music selections.

The TuneIn Radio app gives you access to hundreds of Internet radio stations located around the world. They're organized by category, so you can find just about whatever you want. Many of the radio stations are also broadcast radio stations, so odds are good that you can find a local station or two, which you can listen to on your Android tablet.

These apps, as well as other, similar apps, are available for free. Paid versions might also be found on Google Play. The paid versions generally provide unlimited music with no advertising.

» Google offers an unlimited music listening service. You can tap the item SUBSCRIBE NOW in the navigation drawer to sign up. (Refer to Figure 13-1.) The service is free for 30 days, and then a nominal fee, currently $9.99, is charged monthly.

» It's best to listen to Internet radio when your tablet is connected to the Internet via a Wi-Fi connection. Streaming music consumes mobile data at a slow but steady clip.

WARNING

» Be wary of music subscription services offered through your tablet's manufacturer or cellular provider. I've subscribed to such services only to find them terminated for various reasons. To avoid that disappointment, stick with the services described in this section until you feel comfortable enough to buy into another service.

» See Chapter 15 for more information about Google Play.

TECHNICAL STUFF

» Music provided over the Internet is referred to as *streaming*. That's because the music arrives on your Android tablet as a continuous download from the source. Unlike music you download and save, streaming music is played as it comes in and isn't stored long-term.

Chapter **14**

Amazing Tablet Feats

E ven given the variety of things your Android tablet can do, you will find some limitations. For example, you cannot use an Android tablet as a yoga block. It makes a poor kitchen cutting board. And despite efforts by European physicists, the Android tablet simply cannot compete with the Large Hadron Collider. Still, for more everyday purposes, I believe you'll find your tablet more than up to the task.

Clock

Your Android tablet keeps constant, accurate track of the time, which is displayed at the top of the Home screen as well as on the Lock screen. That's handy, but it just isn't enough, so the tablet ships with an app that tells the time and also may double as an alarm clock.

The app may be called Clock or Alarm. If it's called Alarm, it's probably nothing more than a basic alarm clock. The Clock app, on the other hand, is more of a chronometric app, featuring a timer, stopwatch, alarm, and world clock functions. Of these activities, setting an alarm is pretty useful: In that mode, your tablet becomes your nightstand companion.

Here's how to set a wake-up alarm in the stock Android Clock app:

1. **Tap the Alarm icon or tab atop the Clock app's screen.**

2. **Tap the Add icon.**

   Some Clock apps may simply present a new alarm card, so you don't have to add anything.

3. **Set the alarm time.**

   Tap hours, then minutes. Tap OK when you're done. The new alarm appears on the screen, but you can add more details.

4. **Fill in details about the alarm.**

   Set the alarm's ringtone and assign a label such as "Wake up for the airport." On Samsung tablets, you may have to tap the OPTIONS button to set details.

The alarms you create are set active. Use the master control near the alarm, or tap the Alarm icon, to set or reset the alarm. Only a set alarm triggers. And you can confirm that an alarm is set when you see the Alarm Set status icon atop the touchscreen, similar to what's shown in the margin.

When the alarm triggers, tap the Dismiss icon to tell the tablet, "Okay! I'm up!" Or you can tap the Snooze icon to be annoyed again after a few minutes.

>> Your tablet keeps its clock accurate by accessing an Internet time server. You never have to set the time.

>> Information about a set alarm appears on the Clock app's screen and on the tablet's Lock screen.

>> Unsetting an alarm doesn't delete the alarm. To remove an alarm, tap the alarm to select it and then tap the Delete (Trash) or Close (X) icon.

>> To make the alarm sound on specific days of the week, tap the Repeat check box. Choose the days of the week when you want the alarm to sound. Otherwise, the alarm sounds only when you set it.

>> The alarm doesn't work when you turn off the Android tablet. However, the alarm triggers when the tablet is locked.

Calculator

The next time you do math, don't bother whipping out your brain. Instead, whip out your Android tablet and summon the Calculator app. The stock Android

Calculator app appears in Figure 14-1. Most Android tablet manufacturers mess with this app, so what you see on your tablet might look subtly different, although the basic operation remains the same.

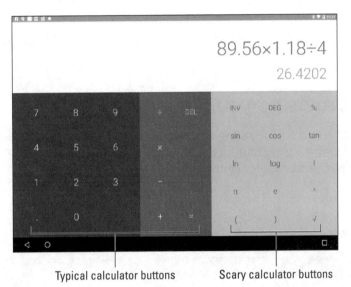

89.56×1.18÷4

26.4202

FIGURE 14-1:
The Calculator
app.

Typical calculator buttons   Scary calculator buttons

Tap various buttons on the Calculator app screen to input your equations. Parentheses buttons can help you determine which part of a long equation gets calculated first. Use the DEL, CLR, or C keys to clear input.

TIP

>> Long-press the calculator's text (or results) to copy the results. This trick may not work in every Calculator app.

>> When the Clear All button isn't available, long-press the DEL, CLR, or C buttons.

>> I use the Calculator app most often to determine my tip at a restaurant. In Figure 14-1, a calculation is being made for an 18 percent tip on an $89.56 tab split evenly between four people even though Jeremiah didn't drink any beer.

Calendar

Your Android tablet is the 21st century version of the old ball-and-chain of the busy person's world: the date book. Thanks to the Calendar app and the Google Calendar service on the Internet, you can toss out your date book.

>> Well, before you toss out the date book, consider copying into the Calendar app any future appointments and recurring info, such as birthdays and anniversaries

>> Google Calendar works with your Google account to keep track of your schedule and appointments. You can visit Google Calendar on the web at

```
calendar.google.com
```

Browsing your schedule

To see what's happening next, to peruse upcoming important events, or simply to know which day of the month it is, summon the Calendar app. Figure 14-2 shows the Calendar app's Month and Week views.

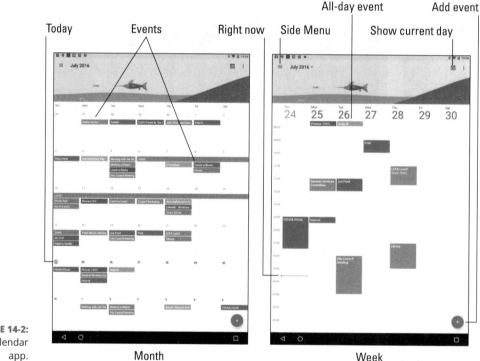

FIGURE 14-2:
The Calendar
app.

To choose a view in the stock Android Calendar app, tap the Side Bar icon and select Choose a View from the navigation drawer. In addition to Month and Week, the Calendar app offers Schedule view and Day view. Schedule view lists only upcoming appointments.

Variations of the Calendar app may let you tap a view tab to present the calendar in Year, Month, Week, Day, and Tasks views.

To return to the current day, tap the Show Current Day icon, illustrated in the figure. If that icon isn't visible, tap the TODAY button.

TIP

>> Schedule view might be called Agenda or Tasks in some versions of the Calendar app.

>> Some Calendar apps feature 4-Day view as well.

>> Use Month view to see an overview of what's going on, and use Week view or Day view to see your appointments.

>> I check Week view at the start of the week to remind me of what's coming up.

>> Swipe the screen left or right to change the view from month to month, week to week, or day to day.

>> Different colors flag your events, as shown in Figure 14-2. The colors represent a calendar category to which events are assigned. See the later section "Creating an event" for information on calendar categories.

Reviewing appointments

To see more detail about an event, tap it. When you're using Month view, tap the date to see a card displaying events for that day. Tap a specific event to see its details, similar to what's shown in Figure 14-3.

Edit event

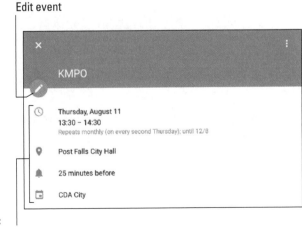

FIGURE 14-3:
Event details.

Event details

The details you see depend on how much information was recorded when the event was created. Some events have only a minimum of information; others may have details, such as a location for the event, the time, and with whom you're meeting.

 Tap the Close icon to dismiss the event's details, or touch the Back navigation icon.

>> Birthdays and a few other events on the calendar may be pulled in from the tablet's address book or from social networking apps. That probably explains why some events are listed twice — they're pulled in from two sources.

>> When the event's location is listed, you can tap that item to open the Maps app. See where the event is being held and get directions, as covered in Chapter 10.

TIP

>> The best way to review upcoming appointments is to choose the Schedule view from the navigation drawer.

>> The Calendar widget also provides a great way to see upcoming events from right on the Home screen. See Chapter 18 for information on applying widgets to the tablet's Home screen.

>> The Google Now feature lists any immediate appointments or events. See the later section "Google Now."

Creating an event

To make the calendar useful, add events: appointments, things to do, meetings, or full-day events such as birthdays or colonoscopies. To create an event, follow these steps in the Calendar app:

1. **Go to the event's day and tap the approximate time when the event starts.**

   It's easier to work in Week view when you want to tap a specific time on a specific day.

2. **Touch the Add Event icon (refer to Figure 14-2) or the Add box that appears where you tapped in Step 1.**

   The Create Event card appears. Your job now is to fill in the blanks to create the new event.

3. Add information about the event.

The more information you supply, the more detailed the event and the more you can do with it on your Android tablet and on Google Calendar on the Internet. Here are some of the many items you can set when creating an event:

- *Title:* The name of the event, person you're going to meet, or place you're headed.

- *Calendar Category:* Choose a specific calendar to help organize and color-code your events. The Calendar app may by default choose the Events calendar.

- *Time/Duration:* If you followed Step 1 in this section, you don't have to set a starting time. Otherwise, specify the time the event starts and stops, or choose to set an all-day event such as a birthday or your mother-in-law's visit that was supposed to last for an hour.

- *Location:* Type the location just as though you're searching for a location in the Maps app.

- *Repeat:* Tap the More Options button if you don't see this item. Use the Repeat setting to configure events on a recurring schedule.

- *Notification/Reminder:* Set an email, SMS, or Calendar notification to signal an upcoming event.

4. Tap the SAVE button to create the new event.

The new event appears on the calendar, reminding you that you need to do something on such-and-such a day with what's-his-face.

- » Tap an existing event to modify it. Tap the Edit icon (refer to Figure 14-3) to make any changes.

- » For events that repeat twice a week or twice a month, create two repeating events. For example, when you have meetings on the first and third Mondays, you create two separate events: one for the first Monday and another for the third. Then have each event repeat monthly.

- » To remove an event, tap the event to bring up its card. Look for the DELETE button or icon. If it's not found, tap the Action Overflow icon on the card and choose Delete. Tap OK to confirm. For a repeating event, choose whether to delete only the current event or all future events.

- » Setting an event's time zone is necessary only when the event takes place in another time zone or spans time zones, such as an airline flight. In that case, the Calendar app automatically adjusts the starting and stopping times for events, depending on where you are.

WARNING

>> If you forget to set the time zone and you end up hopping around the world, your events are set according to the time zone in which they were created, not the local time.

>> An event reminder appears as a notification (shown in the margin), a text (SMS) message, or a Gmail message. I prefer notifications, which also display an alert on the tablet's Lock screen.

eBook Reader

Printed books are O so 14th century. These days, reading material is presented electronically in the form of an eBook. The great Googly way to read eBooks is to employ the Play Books app.

Open the Play Books app to begin your reading experience. If you've been reading a book, the app opens to the last page you read. Otherwise, you view your entire book library, as shown in Figure 14-4.

 To view the library at any time, tap the Side Menu icon (shown in the margin) and choose the My Library command from the navigation drawer. Books listed in the library are those titles you've obtained for your Google Books account. Swipe the screen to scroll through the selection.

Tap a book's cover to open it. If you've opened the book previously, you return to the page you last read. Otherwise, you see the book's first page.

Figure 14-5 illustrates the basic book-reading operation in the Play Books app. Swipe the screen from right to left to turn the "pages," assuming that you're reading English or other languages that read in that direction.

The Play Books app works in both vertical and horizontal orientations. To lock the screen orientation, choose Settings from the navigation drawer and tap the Auto-Rotate Screen item. Choose how you want the screen locked or not.

>> If you don't see a book in the library, tap the Action Overflow icon and choose Refresh.

>> Books in your Play Books library are stored on the Internet and available to read only when an Internet connection is active. It's possible to keep a book on your tablet by downloading it to the device. Refer to Chapter 15 for details on downloading books.

Downloaded book

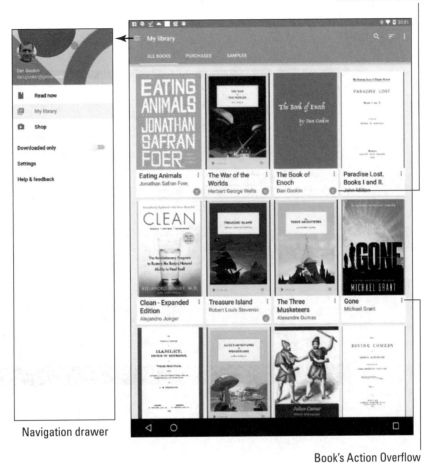

FIGURE 14-4:
The Play Books
library.

Navigation drawer

Book's Action Overflow

>> To remove a book from the library, tap the Action Overflow icon on the book's cover and then choose the Delete from Library command. Tap the DELETE button to confirm.

>> If the onscreen controls (refer to Figure 14-5) disappear, tap the screen to see them again.

>> Tap the Aa icon to display a menu of options for adjusting the text on the screen and the brightness.

>> Unlike dead-tree books, eBooks lack an index. That's because text on digital pages can change based on the book's presentation. Therefore, use the Search command (refer to Figure 14-5) to look for items in the text.

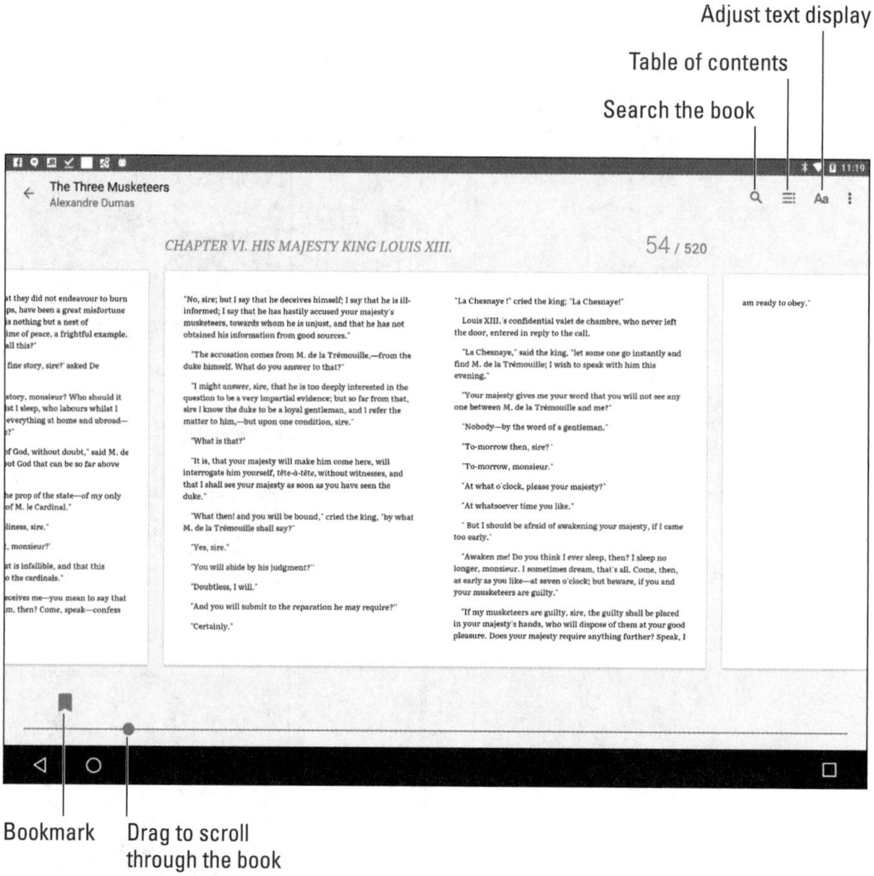
Adjust text display
Table of contents
Search the book
The Three Musketeers
Alexandre Dumas
CHAPTER VI. HIS MAJESTY KING LOUIS XIII.
54 / 520
Bookmark
Drag to scroll through the book

FIGURE 14-5: Reading an eBook in the Play Books app.

- A copy of your eBook library is available on all your Android devices and on the Play Books website:

  ```
  play.google.com/books
  ```

- Refer to Chapter 15 for information on obtaining books from Google Play.

Game Machine

Nothing justifies your expensive, high-tech investment in electronics like playing games. Don't even sweat the thought that you have too much "business" or "work" or other important stuff you can do on an Android tablet. The more advanced the mind, the more the need for play, right? So indulge yourself.

Your tablet's manufacturer may have tossed in a few sample games to whet your gaming appetite. If not, visit Google Play and choose the Apps & Games category. Chapter 15 has more details.

>> Look for the "lite" versions of games, which are free. If you like the game, you can fork over the pocket change that the full version costs.

>> Refer to Chapter 25 for some specific game suggestions.

Google Now

Don't worry about your tablet controlling too much of your life: It harbors no insidious intelligence, and the Robot Uprising is still years away. Until then, you can use the tablet's listening abilities to enjoy the feature called Google Now. It's not quite like having your own personal Jeeves, but it's close.

Google Now is often found dwelling on the far left Home screen page: Swipe the Home screen from left to right until you see it. This feature isn't available on every tablet, so you can instead find the Google app in the Apps drawer.

The main Google Now screen looks similar to what's shown in Figure 14-6. Below the Search text box, you'll find cards. The variety and number of cards depend on how often you use Google Now. Though you can't manually add cards, the more the app learns about you, the more cards appear.

BARKING ORDERS TO GOOGLE NOW

One way to have a lot of fun is to use the Google Now app verbally: Say "Okay, Google." Say it out loud. Any time you see the Google Now app, the tablet is listening to you. Or, when the tablet is being stubborn, touch the Microphone icon.

You can speak simple search terms, such as "Find pictures of Megan Fox." Or you can give more complex orders, among them:

- Will it rain tomorrow?

- What time is it in Oslo?

- How many euros equals $25?

- What is 103 divided by 6?

(continued)

(continued)

- What are the directions to Epcot?

- Where is the nearest Canadian restaurant?

- What's the score of the Lakers–Celtics game?

- What is the answer to life, the universe, and everything?

When asked such questions, Google Now responds with a card and a verbal reply. When a verbal reply isn't available, you see Google search results.

You can also use Google Now to verbally control your tablet. To use the camera, say "Okay, Google, take a picture" or "Okay, Google, record a video." Future versions of Google Now may offer additional spoken commands.

Search for something   Ask a question

FIGURE 14-6:
Google Now
is ready
for business.
Or play.

Cards

You can use Google Now to search the Internet, just as you would use Google's main web page. More interestingly than that, you can ask Google Now questions; see the nearby sidebar "Barking orders to Google Now."

Video Entertainment

Someday, it may be possible to watch "real" TV on an Android tablet, but why bother? You'll find plenty of video apps available on your tablet to sate your video watching desires. Two of the most common are YouTube and Play Movies & TV. So though you may not be able to pick up and enjoy the local Action News Team every day at 5 p.m., you're not bereft of video enjoyment on your tablet.

Enjoying YouTube

YouTube is the Internet phenomenon that proves that real life is indeed too boring and random for television. Or is it the other way around? Regardless, you can use the YouTube app on your Android tablet to view the latest YouTube videos.

 Tap the Search icon to find the video you want. Type the video's name, a topic, or any search terms to locate videos. Zillions of videos are available.

The YouTube app displays suggestions for any channels you're subscribed to, which allows you to follow favorite topics or YouTube content providers.

To view a video, touch its name or icon in the list.

>> Because you have a Google account, you also have a YouTube account. I recommend that you log in to your YouTube account when using YouTube on your Android tablet: Tap the Action Overflow icon and choose the Sign In command. Log in if you haven't already. Otherwise, you see your account information, your videos, and any video subscriptions.

>> Refer to Chapter 12 for information on uploading a video you've recorded on your Android tablet to your account on YouTube.

 >> To view the video in a larger size, rotate the tablet to its horizontal orientation. You can also tap the Expand icon, shown in the margin, to view a video full-screen.

REMEMBER

>> Use the YouTube app to view YouTube videos, rather than use the tablet's web browser app to visit the YouTube website.

>> Not all YouTube videos are available for viewing on mobile devices.

Buying and renting movies

You can use the Play Movies & TV app to watch videos you've rented or purchased from Google Play. Open the app and choose the video from the main screen. Items you've purchased show up in the app's library.

The actual renting or purchasing is done in the Play Store app. Check that app often for freebies and discounts. More details for renting and purchasing movies and shows is found in Chapter 15.

TIP

» Movies and shows rented at the Play Store are available for viewing for up to 30 days after you pay the rental fee. After you start the movie, you can pause and watch it again and again during a 24-hour period.

» Not every film or TV show is available for purchase. Some are rentals only.

» Any videos you've purchased from Google Play are available on the Internet for anytime viewing. Visit:

```
play.google.com/movies
```

» Also see Chapter 17 for information on streaming video from your phone to a large-screen monitor or HDTV.

Chapter **15**

Google Play Shopping

The place to find more apps, books, music, and video for your Android tablet is a digital marketplace called Google Play. The good news is that most of the stuff available is free. Better news is that the nonfree stuff is cheap. For little or no cost, you can add new apps and media to expand your Android tablet's capabilities.

Hello, Google Play

Although it sounds like a kid's clothing store, Google Play is where you obtain new apps, books, movies, music, and other goodies for your Android tablet. The Google Play app's name is Play Store.

>> You obtain goodies from Google Play over an Internet connection. Therefore:

>> I highly recommend that you connect your tablet to a Wi-Fi network when you shop at Google Play. Wi-Fi not only gives you speed but also helps avoid data surcharges. See Chapter 16 for details on connecting your tablet to a Wi-Fi network.

TIP

» The Play Store app is frequently updated, so its look may change from what you see in this chapter. Refer to my website for updated info and tips:

```
wambooli.com/help/android
```

TECHNICAL
STUFF

» Google Play was once known as Android Market, and you may still see it referred to as the Market. You may also see the term Play Store used, though that's the app's name and not the store's name. My guess is that the app will be rechristened as Google Play in a future Android update.

Browsing Google Play

To access Google Play, open the Play Store app. You may find a Launcher icon on the tablet's Home screen, or it can be located on the Apps screen with the rest of your tablet's apps.

After opening the Play Store app, you see the main screen, similar to what's shown in Figure 15-1. The store has two parts: one for Apps & Games and the other for Entertainment — music, books, movies, and so on.

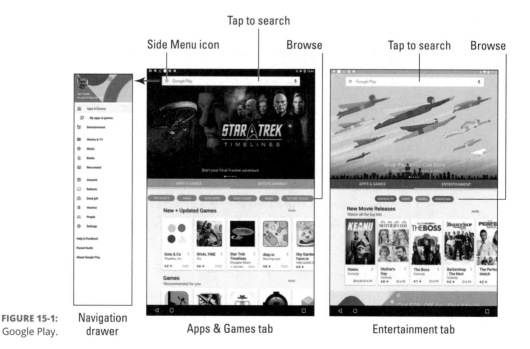

FIGURE 15-1: Google Play.

Navigation drawer

Apps & Games tab

Entertainment tab

If you don't see the main screen, similar to what's shown in Figure 15-1, tap the Side Menu icon (shown in the margin) to display the navigation drawer. Choose Apps & Games to view the apps portion of the store or choose Entertainment to view media items.

To browse each top-level category, choose a category. For Apps & Games, you can choose Top Charts, Games, and so on, as illustrated in Figure 15-1. For Entertainment, choose Movies & TV, Music, Books, and so on.

After you browse to a specific item, further categories help you browse. These categories include top sellers, new items, free items, and so on. Eventually, you see a list of suggestions, similar to what's shown on the left in Figure 15-2. Swipe the suggestions up and down to peruse the lot.

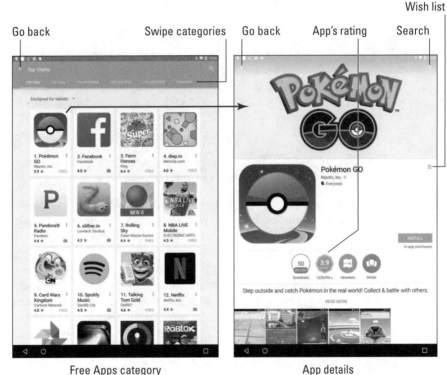

FIGURE 15-2: App details.

Free Apps category

App details

To see more information about an item, tap its card. You see a more detailed description, screen shots, or perhaps a video preview, as shown on the right in Figure 15-2.

>> The first time you enter the Play Store app, or after the app is updated, you must accept the terms of service. To do so, tap the ACCEPT button.

>> When you have an idea of what you want, tap the Search icon at the top of the Play Store screen, shown in Figure 15-2. At the main Play Store screen, tap the Google Play bar to search. (Refer to Figure 15-1.) Type all or part of the item's title, such as an app name, album name, book author, or perhaps a description.

>> You can be assured that all apps available on Google Play are compatible with your Android tablet. You cannot download or buy an app that's incompatible.

>> Pay attention to an app's ratings. Ratings are added by people who use the apps — people like you and me. Having more stars is better.

>> Another good indicator of an app's success is how many times it's been downloaded. Some apps have been downloaded more than 100 million times. That's a good sign.

TECHNICAL
STUFF

>> In Figure 15-2, the app's description (on the right) shows the Install button. Other buttons that may appear on an app's description screen include Open, Update, Refund, and Uninstall. The Open button opens an app that's already installed on your tablet. The Refund option is available just after you purchase something. See Chapter 18 for information on using the Update and Uninstall buttons.

Obtaining an item

After you locate the item you've always wanted — an app, some music, or a book — the next step is to download it. The item is copied from Google Play on the Internet to your tablet. Apps are installed. Entertainment items are made available at once.

Good news: Most apps are free. Classic books are available at no cost. And occasionally, Google offers movies and music *gratis.* Even the items you pay for don't cost that much. In fact, it seems odd to sit and stew over whether paying 99 cents for a game is "worth it."

TIP

I recommend that you download a free app or book first, to familiarize yourself with the process. Then try downloading a paid item.

Free or not, the process of obtaining something from Google Play works pretty much the same. Follow these steps:

1. **If possible, activate the Wi-Fi connection to avoid incurring data overages.**

   See Chapter 16 for information on connecting your Android tablet to a Wi-Fi network.

2. **Open the Play Store app.**

3. **Find the item you want and open its description.**

   All items in the Play Store app feature a description screen. It looks similar to the app description screen, shown on the right in Figure 15-2.

4. **Tap the button to obtain the item.**

   A free app features the INSTALL button. A free book features the ADD TO LIBRARY button. For a free movie, TV show, or music, look for the FREE button. You might also see the Free Trial button for some items. In that case, tap the button to view or listen to a free sample of the media.

   Paid items feature a button that shows the price. For movies and TV shows, you may see a Rent or Purchase button. See the later section "Renting or purchasing videos."

5. **Tap the Accept button.**

   The Accept button appears for some apps that access various tablet features. The card isn't a warning; it simply lists which features the app wants to use. If you're concerned about viruses, see the later sidebar, "Avoiding Android viruses."

6. **For a paid item, tap the BUY button.**

   See the next section for further details on purchasing items at Google Play.

7. **Wait for the item to become available.**

   Media items are available instantly. Apps are downloaded and installed, which may take some time. The Downloading notification appears as the app is transferred. Feel free to do something else on your tablet while the app downloads. Installation takes place automatically.

8. **Tap the Open, Play, Listen, Read, or similar button to run the app, watch a video, listen to music, or read a book, respectively.**

Media is available instantly because it's not actually copied to your tablet. Instead, the item is *streamed*, or made available only when you request it. This process works as long as an Internet connection is available. See the later section "Keeping stuff on the device" for information on accessing media when an Internet connection isn't available.

>> The Play Store app prompts you for payment information if you haven't yet supplied it. This prompt appears even for free items, in which case you can skip the prompt: Tap the SKIP button. You can always supply payment information the first time you actually buy something.

>> If you choose to do something else while an app downloads, refer to the status bar to check for the Successfully Installed notification, shown in the margin. Choose that notification to open the recently obtained app.

>> Apps you download are added to the Apps drawer, made available like any other app on your tablet.

>> Some apps may install Launcher icons on the Home screen after they're installed. See Chapter 18 for information on removing the icon from the Home screen, if that is your desire.

>> Many apps prompt for permissions when they're first opened. Tap ALLOW or DENY. Generally speaking, it's okay to tap ALLOW, but also refer to the nearby sidebar, "Avoiding Android viruses."

>> Media you've obtained from Google Play is accessed from a specific app: Play Music for music, Play Books for books, and Play Movies & TV for video. Other chapters in this part of the book offer details.

>> After obtaining an item from Google Play, you receive a Gmail message confirming your purchase, paid or free.

>> Be quick on that refund: For a purchased app, you have only two hours to get your money back. You know when the time limit is up because the Refund button on the app's description screen changes to Uninstall.

>> Also see Chapter 18 for information on uninstalling apps.

>> Google Play doesn't currently offer refunds on purchased media, which includes music, books, and movies.

TIP

>> Keep an eye out for special offers from Google Play. These offer a great way to pick up some free songs, movies, and books.

AVOIDING ANDROID VIRUSES

How can you tell which apps are legitimate and which might be viruses or evil apps that do odd things to your Android tablet? Well, you can't. In fact, most people can't, because most evil apps don't advertise themselves as such.

The key to knowing whether an app is evil is to look at what it does, as described in this chapter. The key to knowing whether an app is malicious is to look at its access card: Open the app's description in the Play Store app, and see which permissions it's granted. If a simple grocery list app uses the tablet's microphone and the app doesn't need to use the microphone, it's suspect.

In the history of the Android operating system, only a handful of malicious apps have been distributed, and most of them were found on devices used in Asia. Google routinely removes malicious apps from its inventory. Google is also capable of remotely uninstalling malicious apps from your tablet. So you're pretty safe.

Generally speaking, avoid "hacker" apps, porn apps, and apps that use social engineering to make you do things on your tablet that you wouldn't otherwise do, such as visit an unknown website to see racy pictures of politicians or celebrities.

Making a purchase at Google Play

To purchase an app or media on Google Play, you tap the BUY button. A card appears, listing your preferred payment method, such as the example shown in Figure 15-3.

In the figure, the album *Brothers in Arms* is listed for $9.49. The chosen payment method is a VISA card ending in 4870. To use that payment method, follow these steps:

1. **Tap the BUY button.**

   For security, you're prompted to type your Google password.

2. **Type your Google password.**

   I strongly recommend that you *do not* choose the option Never Ask Me Again. You want to be prompted every time for your password.

3. **Tap the Confirm button.**

Current payment method

Chevron

Brothers In Arms $9.49
Visa-4870 ˅

Google Play   BUY

Brothers In Arms $9.49
Visa-4870 ˄

Payment methods

Redeem

dan.gookin@gmail.com

Google Play   BUY

Cash in a gift card

FIGURE 15-3:
The Buy card. Choose another form of payment

4. **Type the credit card's security code.**

   This is the CVC code, found on the back of the card.

5. **Tap the VERIFY button.**

   The app is downloaded or the media made available to your phone.

To select another payment method, tap the chevron by the current payment method, as shown in Figure 15-3. The Buy card expands, illustrated at the bottom of the figure. Choose Payment Methods and select another credit or debit card, or use your Google Play balance. After another payment method is selected, continue with Step 1 in this section.

If you've not yet set up a payment method, the chevron appears by the item's price, not below the item purchased. (Refer to Figure 15-3.) Tap the chevron, and then choose a payment method. You can add a credit or debit card, bill via your cellular provider, use PayPal, or redeem a Google Play gift card.

NEVER BUY ANYTHING TWICE

Any apps or media you obtain from Google Play are available to all your Android devices as well as from your Google account on the Internet. These items include apps, books, music, videos, and anything else.

For example, if you have an Android phone and you've already paid for a slew of apps, you can get those same apps for your Android tablet: Open the Play Store app and install the apps. You'll also find your purchased music, books, and videos in the Play Music, Play Books, and Play Movies & TV apps.

To review any already purchased apps, display the Play Store app's navigation drawer. (Refer to the left side of Figure 15-1.) Choose Apps & Games, and then display the navigation drawer again and choose My Apps & Games. Tap the All tab on the My Apps & Games screen to see all the apps you've ever obtained from Google Play, including apps you've previously paid for. Those apps are flagged with the text *PURCHASED*. Choose that item from the list to reinstall the paid app.

>> Media you purchase is available instantly. Apps are downloaded after the purchase method is verified.

>> Information about any potential refund is provided in the Gmail message you receive after the purchase. Review the message for refund details.

>> Be quick on that refund: For a purchased app, you have only two hours to get your money back. You know when the time limit is up, because the Refund button on the app's description screen changes to Uninstall.

>> The credit or debit cards listed in Google Play are those you've used before. Don't worry: Your information is safe.

>> All music sales are final. Don't blame me; I'm just writing down Google's current policy for music purchases.

Renting or purchasing videos

When it comes to movies and TV shows available at the Google Play Store, you have two options: rent or purchase.

When you choose to rent a video, the rental is available to view for the next 30 days. Once you start watching, however, you have only 24 hours to finish — you can also watch the video over and over again during that time span.

Purchasing a video is more expensive than renting it, but you can view the movie or TV show at any time, on any Android device. You can also download the movie so that you can watch it even when an Internet connection isn't available.

One choice you must make when buying a movie is whether to purchase the SD or HD version. The SD version is cheaper, and the HD version plays at high definition only on certain output devices.

>> See Chapter 14 for information on the Play Movies & TV app.

>> Also see Chapter 18 for information on streaming videos from your phone to a large-screen device, such as an HDTV.

Google Play Tricks

I don't want you to be a Google Play expert. If you're like me, you just want to get the app, music, movie, or whatever you want and get on with your life. Yet more exists to the Play Store app than simply obtaining new stuff.

Using the wish list

While you dither over getting a paid app, some music, a book, or any other purchase at Google Play, consider adding it to your wish list: Tap the Wish List icon, shown in the margin. (Refer to Figure 15-2.)

To review your wish list, tap the Side Menu icon in the Play Store app. (Refer to Figure 15-1.) Choose the Wish List item from the navigation drawer. You see all the items you've flagged. When you're ready to buy, choose one and buy it!

Sharing a Google Play item

Sometimes you love your Google Play purchase so much that you just can't contain your glee. When that happens, consider sharing the item. Obey these steps:

1. **Open the Play Store app.**

2. **Browse or search for the app, music, book, or other item you want to share.**

3. **When you find the item, tap it to view its description screen.**

4. **Tap the Share icon.**

You may have to swipe down the screen to locate the Share icon, shown in the margin. After tapping the Share icon, you see a menu listing various apps.

5. **Choose an app.**

For example, choose Gmail to send a Google Play link in an email message.

6. **Use the chosen app to share the link.**

What happens next depends on which sharing method you've chosen.

The result of following these steps is that your friend receives a link. That person can tap the link on his Android device and be whisked instantly to the Play Store app, where the item can be obtained.

Keeping stuff on the device

Books, music, movies, and TV shows you obtain from Google Play aren't copied to your Android tablet. Instead, they're stored on the Internet. When you access the media, it's streamed into your device as needed. This setup works well, and it keeps your tablet from running out of storage space, but it works only when an Internet connection is available.

When you plan on being away from an Internet connection, such as when you are flying across the country and are too cheap to pay for in-flight Wi-Fi, you can download Play Store music, eBook, and movie purchases and save them on your tablet.

To see which media is on your tablet and which isn't, open the Play Books, Play Music, or Play Movies & TV app. Follow these steps, which work identically in each app:

1. **Tap the Side Menu icon.**

2. **In the navigation drawer, choose the Downloaded Only item.**

To view items that are *downloaded* (saved on your tablet), ensure that the master control is set to the On position.

3. **Choose the Library item from the navigation drawer.**

You see only those items on your tablet. The rest of your library is held on the Internet.

To see your entire library again, repeat these steps, but in Step 3 slide the master control to the Off position.

Items downloaded to your tablet feature the On Device icon, similar to the one shown in the margin. The icon's color differs between Play Music, Play Books, and Play Movies & TV apps.

To keep an item on your tablet, look for the Download icon, shown in the margin. Tap that icon, and the item is fetched from the Internet and stored on your tablet.

WARNING

Movies and music consume storage space on your Android tablet, especially feature-length films. Downloading these items is fine for short trips and such, but for the long term, consider purging some of your downloaded media.

To remove an item from the tablet, tap the On Device icon. Choose the Remove Download action and then tap the REMOVE button to confirm.

Don't worry about removing downloaded media. You can always access items you've purchased (or obtained for free) when an Internet connection is active. And you can download items over and over without having to pay again.

4
Nuts & Bolts

Chapter **16**

It's a Wireless Life

At one time, truly advanced technology was easily identified by its nest of tangled cables. Today, the opposite is true. Your Android tablet lives an untethered existence, thanks to its beefy battery and wireless Internet access. Welcome to the carefree digital lifestyle. Well, of course, with occasional stops to charge that beefy battery.

The Wonderful World of Wireless

An Android tablet demands an Internet connection. To sate that desire, the tablet communicates with the information superhighway in a wireless way. Given how wireless networking has proliferated around the globe, finding an available wireless network is no longer a big deal. No, the issue is how to coax the tablet into making the connection happen.

Using the mobile data network

LTE Android tablets use the mobile data network to connect to the Internet. That's the same digital cellular network used by smartphones. Several types of this network are available, based on the network's speed:

4G LTE: The fourth generation of wide-area data network and the fastest.

3G: The third-generation network, which is the fastest network used when a 4G signal isn't available.

1X: Several types of the original, slower cellular data signals are still available. They all fall under the 1X banner. It's slow.

Your tablet always uses the best network available. So, when the 4G LTE network is within reach, it's used for Internet communications. Otherwise, the 3G network is chosen, and then 1X networking in an act of last-ditch desperation.

>> A status icon representing the network connection type appears atop the touchscreen, right next to the Signal Strength icon.

>> The H or H+ status icons used by some cellular providers refer to the LTE (fast) network.

WARNING

>> Accessing the digital cellular network isn't free. You likely signed up for some form of subscription plan for a certain quantity of data. When you exceed that quantity, the costs can become prohibitive.

>> See Chapter 21 for information on how to avoid cellular data overcharges when taking your Android tablet out and about.

>> Also see Chapter 23 for information on monitoring your mobile data usage as well as tips on sharing the tablet's mobile data connection.

Understanding Wi-Fi

The mobile data connection is nice, and it's available pretty much all over, but it costs you money every month. A better option is Wi-Fi, the same wireless networking standard used by computers to communicate with each other and the Internet.

To make Wi-Fi work on an Android tablet requires two steps. First, you must activate the tablet's Wi-Fi radio. The second step is connecting to a specific wireless network. The next two sections cover these steps in detail.

>> When your tablet is connected to a Wi-Fi network, it uses that network rather than the mobile data network.

>> Wi-Fi stands for wireless fidelity. It's brought to you by the numbers 802.11 and various letter suffixes too many to mention.

Activating Wi-Fi

Follow these steps to activate your Android tablet's Wi-Fi radio:

1. Open the Settings app.

2. Choose Wi-Fi.

On some Samsung tablets, tap the Connections tab to locate the Wi-Fi item.

3. Ensure that the Wi-Fi master control is set to the On position.

To deactivate the Wi-Fi radio, which also disconnects the tablet from the Wi-Fi network, set the master control to the Off position in Step 3.

>> Use the Wi-Fi Quick Settings to instantly activate or deactivate the Wi-Fi connection. See Chapter 3 for information on accessing the Quick Settings.

>> Once Wi-Fi is activated, the tablet connects automatically to any memorized Wi-Fi networks. See the next section.

>> It's perfectly okay to keep the tablet's Wi-Fi radio on all the time. It does drain the battery, but you really need that Internet access to get the most from your Android tablet.

>> Using Wi-Fi to connect to the Internet doesn't incur data usage charges — unless you're accessing a metered network. See the later section "Setting a metered Wi-Fi connection."

Connecting to a Wi-Fi network

After you've activated the Wi-Fi radio, you can connect your tablet to an available wireless network. If you've previously connected to an available network, the connection is made automatically — as long as the network's Wi-Fi password is still valid.

To connect to a new Wi-Fi network, obey these steps:

1. **Open the Settings app and choose Wi-Fi.**

On some Samsung tablets, you find the Wi-Fi item on the Connections tab.

2. **Choose a wireless network from the list.**

Available Wi-Fi networks appear on the screen, similar to what's shown in Figure 16-1. When no wireless networks are listed, you're sort of out of luck regarding wireless access from your current location.

Signal strength

Password-protected network   Wi-Fi master control

Available
Wi-Fi
networks

FIGURE 16-1:
Hunting down
a wireless
network.

3. **If prompted, type the network password.**

Tap the Show Password check box so that you can see what you're typing; some of those network passwords can be long.

TIP

4. **Tap the CONNECT button.**

The network is connected immediately. If not, try the password again.

When the tablet is connected to a wireless network, you see the Wi-Fi Connected status icon, similar to the one shown in the margin. This icon indicates that the tablet's Wi-Fi is on, connected, and communicating with a Wi-Fi network.

» Some public networks are open to anyone, but you must use the tablet's web browser app to find a login web page. Heed that page's directions to get network access. To find the page, browse to any page on the Internet, and the login web page shows up.

» Your tablet memorizes all previously connected Wi-Fi networks. To view the list, tap the Settings icon or Action Overflow and choose Saved Networks. To remove a saved network, tap the entry and then tap the FORGET button. Also see the next section for details on manipulating the saved networks list.

WARNING

» Not every wireless network has a password. Its absence makes the connection faster, but use caution when connecting to such a network. It's possible that the Bad Guys can monitor your connection, stealing passwords and other information.

» To disconnect from a Wi-Fi network, turn off the tablet's Wi-Fi. Refer to the preceding section.

TIP

» Use Wi-Fi whenever you plan to remain in one location for a while. Unlike a mobile data network, a Wi-Fi network's broadcast signal has a limited range. If you wander too far away, your tablet loses the signal and is disconnected.

Updating a Wi-Fi network's password

Some locations follow good computer security and change their Wi-Fi passwords. When you revisit that one charming café and find that your tablet doesn't reconnect to the network, follow these steps:

1. **Obtain the new password.**

    Demand the new password from someone in charge, like the confused young woman who keeps asking whether you want "room" in your black coffee.

2. **Open the Settings app and choose Wi-Fi.**

3. **If the given network doesn't appear in the list (refer to Figure 16-1), tap the Action Overflow or MORE button and choose Saved Networks.**

    The list of saved network appears — if any networks have been saved.

4. **Choose the Wi-Fi network from the list.**

    For example, Café Wambooli has changed its Wi-Fi password. Choose the Wambooli network from the list.

5. **Tap the FORGET button.**

6. **Tap the Back navigation icon, and then repeat the steps in the preceding section to establish a new connection to the network.**

If these steps don't work, and you're certain that you typed the proper password, disable the tablet's Wi-Fi radio (turn off the master control), and then enable it again (turn on the master control).

Connecting to a hidden Wi-Fi network

Some wireless networks don't broadcast their names, which adds security but also makes connecting more difficult. In these cases, follow these steps to make the Wi-Fi network connection:

1. **Open the Settings app and choose Wi-Fi.**

For some Samsung tablets, locate the Wi-Fi item on the Connections tab in the Settings app.

2. **Tap the Action Overflow or MORE button, and choose Add Network.**

The action might be titled Add Wi-Fi Network, or it may appear as the Add (Plus) icon on the screen.

3. **Type the network name.**

The network name text box might be labeled SSID.

4. **Choose the security setting.**

5. **Type a password.**

The password may be optional, though heed my advice from the earlier section "Connecting to a Wi-Fi network" regarding password-less networks.

6. **Tap the SAVE button or Connect button.**

Details such as the security setting and password are obtained from the same cheerful individual who provided you with the network name or SSID.

SSID stands for Service Set Identifier. Any further information on this acronym would needlessly lower your blood pressure, so I'll leave it at that.

TECHNICAL
STUFF

Connecting to a WPS router

TIP

Many Wi-Fi routers feature WPS, which stands for Wi-Fi Protected Setup. It's a network authorization system that's simple and secure. If the wireless router features WPS, follow these steps to quickly connect your Android tablet to the network:

1. **Tap the WPS connection button on the router.**

   The button either is labeled WPS or uses the WPS icon, shown in the margin.

2. **On your tablet, open the Settings app and choose Wi-Fi.**

   On some Samsung tablets, look on the Connections tab to locate the Wi-Fi item.

3. **If you see no WPS options on the screen, tap the Action Overflow icon or MORE button and choose Advanced.**

4. **Choose WPS Push Button or WPS Pin Entry, depending on how the router does its WPS thing.**

   If the router is a WPS push-button router, push the WPS button on the router.

   If the router is a WPS PIN router, look on your tablet's screen for a PIN. Type that number on the Wi-Fi router.

Connection with the router may take a few minutes, so be patient. The good news is that, as on all Wi-Fi networks, once the initial connection is established, the tablet automatically connects in the future.

Setting a metered Wi-Fi connection

Not every Wi-Fi network provides free, unlimited access. Some connections are metered. That means the provider may charge you per minute or per megabyte for accessing the Internet, similar to the limitations placed on the mobile data network.

To configure the Wi-Fi connection as metered, and to ensure that you don't exceed your data quota, follow these steps:

1. **Connect to the network as you normally would.**

   Directions are found earlier in this chapter.

2. **Open the Settings app and choose Data Usage.**

   This item is located in the Wireless & Networks area, or on the Connections tab on some Samsung tablets.

3. **Tap the Action Overflow icon or MORE button.**

4. **Choose Network Restrictions.**

   This action might be titled Restrict Networks.

5. **Locate the current connection in the list and set its master control to the On position.**

When a Wi-Fi connection is set as metered, your tablet monitors and restricts data access. You are warned when a large download or upload is attempted.

The Bluetooth World

Bluetooth has nothing to do with the color blue or dental hygiene. No, it's a wireless protocol for communication between two or more Bluetooth-equipped devices. Your Android tablet just happens to have a Bluetooth wireless radio in its belly, so it can chat it up with Bluetooth devices, such as keyboards, headphones, printers, and robotic mice armed with deadly lasers.

Understanding Bluetooth

To make Bluetooth work, you need a Bluetooth peripheral, such as a wireless keyboard. The goal is to pair that peripheral with your tablet. The operation works like this:

1. **Turn on the Bluetooth wireless radio on both your tablet and the peripheral.**

2. **Make the peripheral discoverable.**

   The peripheral must announce that it's available and willing to go steady with other electronics in the vicinity.

3. **On your tablet, choose the peripheral from the list of Bluetooth devices.**

4. **If required, confirm the connection.**

   For example, you may be asked to input a code on the tablet, confirm a code on a printer, or press a button on peripherals that have buttons.

5. **Use the Bluetooth peripheral.**

You can use the Bluetooth peripheral as much as you like. Turn off the tablet. Turn off the peripheral. When you turn both on again, they're automatically reconnected.

 Bluetooth devices are branded with the Bluetooth logo, shown in the margin. It's your assurance that the gizmo works with other Bluetooth devices.

Activating Bluetooth on your tablet

You must turn on the tablet's Bluetooth radio before you can enjoy using any Bluetoothy peripherals. Here's how to activate Bluetooth on an Android tablet:

1. **Open the Settings app.**

2. **Choose Bluetooth.**

   On some Samsung tablets, tap the Connections tab to locate the Bluetooth item.

3. **Ensure that the Bluetooth master control is set to the On position.**

Slide the icon to the right to activate.

When Bluetooth is on, the Bluetooth status icon appears. It uses the Bluetooth logo, shown in the margin.

To turn off Bluetooth, repeat the steps in this section but slide the master control to the Off position in Step 3.

TIP

You'll also find a Bluetooth activation button in the tablet's Quick Settings, as foretold in Chapter 3.

Pairing with a Bluetooth peripheral

To make the Bluetooth connection between your tablet and some other gizmo, such as a Bluetooth keyboard, follow these steps:

1. **Ensure that the tablet's Bluetooth radio is on.**

Refer to the preceding section.

2. **Make the Bluetooth peripheral discoverable.**

Turn on the gizmo and ensure that its Bluetooth radio is on. Keep in mind that some Bluetooth peripherals have separate power and Bluetooth switches. If so, press the Bluetooth button or take whatever action is necessary to make the peripheral discoverable.

3. **On the Android tablet, open the Settings app.**

4. **Choose Bluetooth.**

On some Samsung tablets, tap the Connections tab in the Settings app to locate the Bluetooth item.

The Bluetooth screen shows already paired and available peripherals, similar to what's shown in Figure 16-2. If not, tap the Action Overflow and choose Refresh. Some tablets may use the Scan button or show the Refresh icon, illustrated in the margin.

5. **Choose the Bluetooth peripheral from the list.**

6. **If necessary, type the device's passcode or otherwise acknowledge the connection.**

For example, with a Bluetooth keyboard, you may see a prompt on the tablet showing a series of numbers. Type those numbers on the keyboard and then press the Enter or Return key. That action completes the pairing.

Keyboard   Headphones

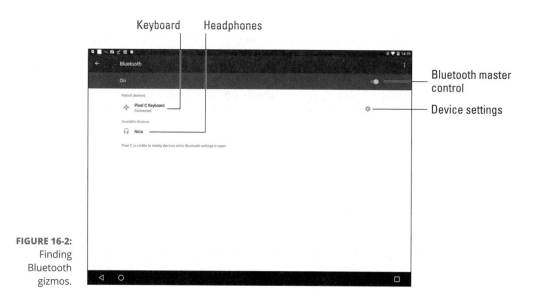

Bluetooth master
control

Device settings

FIGURE 16-2:
Finding
Bluetooth
gizmos.

After the device is paired, you can begin using it.

Connected devices appear in the Bluetooth Settings window, under the heading Paired Devices, such as the Pixel C Keyboard, shown in Figure 16-2.

» Bluetooth peripherals stay paired whether you turn off the tablet, turn off the device, or disable the Bluetooth radio. The connection is reestablished automatically when you turn things on again.

» To stop using a device long-term, you unpair it. To do so, visit the Bluetooth screen (refer to Figure 16-2) and tap the Settings icon by the device's entry. Tap the FORGET button or the Unpair action. The device is unpaired.

» Unpair only the devices that you plan never to use again. Otherwise, simply turn off the Bluetooth device when you're done using it.

REMEMBER

» The Bluetooth radio consumes a modicum of power. It's not a lot of juice for the tablet, but could be for the peripheral. If you don't plan on using the peripheral for a while, turn it off.

Android, Beam It to Me

A handful of Android tablets feature an NFC radio, where NFC stands for Near Field Communications and radio is a type of vegetable. NFC allows your tablet to communicate wirelessly with other NFC devices. That connection is used for the quick transfer of information. The technology is called Android Beam.

To play with the Android Beam feature, ensure that the tablet's NFC radio has been activated. Follow these steps:

1. **Open the Settings app.**

2. **Locate the NFC item.**

   On a stock Android device, choose the More item in the Wireless & Networks area. On Samsung tablets with this feature, tap the Connections heading to find the NFC item.

   If you can't find an NFC item, your tablet lacks this technology.

3. **Ensure that the NFC item is activated.**

   Either place a check mark next to the NFC item or ensure that its master control icon is in the On position.

With NFC activated, you can use your tablet to communicate with other NFC devices, such as tablets, phones, and payment systems for various merchants.

To make the Android Beam feature work, touch your tablet to another NFC device, usually back-to-back. As long as both devices have an NFC radio and the Android Beam feature is active, they can share information. You can beam items such as a contact, map location, web page, YouTube video, or just about anything you're viewing on the tablet's touchscreen.

>> When two Android Beam devices touch, you see a prompt appear on the screen: Touch to Beam. Tap the screen, and the item you're viewing is immediately sent to the other device. That's pretty much it.

>> Generally speaking, if an app features the Share icon, you can use Android Beam to share an item between two NFC gizmos.

>> Both devices present the Touch to Beam prompt when they get close. If the other person touches his screen at the same time you do, information is swapped between both devices.

>> The NFC field is most frequently found on the tablet's rump. The pitiful documentation that came with your Android tablet may illustrate the exact spot.

TECHNICAL STUFF

>> NFC is not the same as the Nearby Devices feature found on some Samsung tablets. The Nearby Devices feature is used for sharing media over a network.

Chapter **17**

Connect, Share, and Store

Your Android tablet is no island. True, it's wireless, but it does need to communicate with other devices. You can use those avenues of communications to share photos, transfer files, print items, or beam movies and music to another technology gizmo. That way, the tablet remains an island, just not a lonely island.

The USB Connection

The most direct way to connect an Android tablet to a computer is to use a wire — specifically, the wire nestled at the core of a USB cable. Conveniently, such a cable came with the tablet. It's for more than giving the device's battery a charge.

Configuring the USB connection

The USB connection is configured automatically whenever you connect your Android tablet to a computer. Everything should work peachy. When it doesn't, you can try manually configuring the USB connection. Follow these steps:

1. **Swipe down the notifications drawer.**

2. **Choose the USB notification.**

   The USB icon is shown in the margin.

3. **Choose a connection option.**

   The USB Computer Connection screen lists several options for configuring the USB connection:

   Charging: The USB connection charges the tablet.

   File Transfers: Also called Transferring Media Files, MTP, or CTP, this connection is ideal for transferring files. The computer views the tablet as a thumb drive or similar storage device.

   Photo Transfers (PTP): In this mode, which might also be labeled Transferring Image, the computer sees the tablet as a digital camera, which is best for importing photos and videos.

   MIDI: Choose this mode to use the tablet as a keyboard or similar device for musical input.

After choosing the mode, you may see a notification on the computer, prompting you to do something with the tablet. Your choices are based on which option you choose in Step 3.

TIP

>> If the computer fails to recognize the tablet, select another USB connection option.

>> If you're using a Macintosh, see the later section "Connecting your tablet to a Mac."

>> The computer might not access the tablet when it's locked. Work the Lock screen on the tablet to address this issue.

>> Some tablets may use their own file transfer software, which is annoying but you must deal with it. For example, some Samsung tablets require you to use the Samsung Kies utility to transfer files.

>> Most tablets charge while connected to the computer's USB port. Some tablets, however, may not charge. If they don't, try connecting the tablet to a USB port on the PC's console (as opposed to an external USB hub).

» If your Android tablet has a microSD card, its storage is also mounted to the computer as well as to the tablet's internal storage. You do not need to configure that storage separately to make the USB connection.

» Tablets with a USB 3.0 jack come with a USB 3.0 cable. You can still use the old-style, USB 2.0 micro-USB cables on such devices: Connect the micro-USB plug to the larger side of the USB 3.0 jack on the tablet's edge.

» For data transfer to take place at top speeds over the USB 3.0 cable, you must connect the tablet's USB 3.0 cable into the USB 3.0 port on a computer. These ports are color-coded blue.

» Android tablets lack the capability to use the USB connection to add peripherals, such as a mouse or thumb drive, to the device. Some tablets may come with a multimedia dock that offers this connectivity, but it can't happen with a direct USB connection.

» MTP stands for Media Transfer Protocol. This setting persuades the computer to believe that the tablet is a portable media player or thumb drive. The PTP, or Picture Transfer Protocol, setting misleads the computer into thinking that the tablet is a digital camera.

Connecting your tablet to a PC

Upon making the USB connection between an Android tablet and a PC, a number of things happen. Don't let the flurry of activity frighten you.

You may see drivers install. That's normal Windows behavior when a new USB gizmo is connected.

You may also see a notification, such as the Windows 10 notification, shown in Figure 17-1. Click or tap that notification to see how to deal with the new connection.

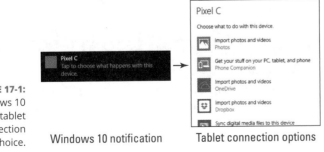

FIGURE 17-1:
Windows 10 tablet connection choice.

Windows 10 notification   Tablet connection options

For example, choose Open Devices to View Files (not shown in Figure 17-1, but it's on the scrolling list of options). This choice opens a File Explorer window listing files and folders on the Android tablet. Or you can choose Import Photos and Videos to quickly copy over the tablet's pictures and movies.

>> The choice you make from the list of items is remembered by Windows 10. The next time you connect your tablet, that option is chosen automatically.

>> Other versions of Windows also display a list of actions, though they appear in the AutoPlay dialog box. As with Windows 10, if you select a specific item, that choice is always selected for you when the tablet is connected.

>> See the later section "Files Back and Forth" for details on transferring files between your tablet and a computer.

Connecting your tablet to a Mac

You need special software to deal with the Android-to-Macintosh connection. That's because the Mac doesn't natively recognize Android devices. Weird, huh? It's like Apple wants you to buy some other type of tablet. I just don't get it.

To help deal with the USB connection on a Mac, obtain the Android File Transfer program. On your Mac, download that program from this website:

```
android.com/filetransfer
```

Install the software. Run it. From that point on, whenever you connect your Android tablet to the Mac, you see a special window appear, similar to the one shown in Figure 17-2. It lists the tablet's folders and files. Use that window for file management, as covered later in this chapter.

If the tablet has a microSD card inserted, you see two buttons on the Android File Transfer program window: Tablet and Card, as shown in Figure 17-2. Click one or the other to see files and folders in that storage location.

Disconnecting the tablet from a computer

The process is cinchy: When you're done transferring files, music, or other media between a computer and your tablet, close all programs and folders you have opened on the computer — specifically, those you've used to work with the tablet's storage. Then you can disconnect the USB cable. That's it.

Internal storage

The microSD card storage

SM-T813

< > Tablet Card

Name	^ Last Modified	Size
▶ Alarms	--	--
▶ Android	--	--
▶ DCIM	--	--
▶ Download	--	--
▶ Movies	--	--
▶ Music	--	--
▶ Notifications	--	--
▶ Pictures	--	--
▶ Playlists	--	--
▶ Podcasts	--	--
▶ Ringtones	--	--
▶ Samsung	--	--

12 items, 19.63 GB available

FIGURE 17-2:
The Android
File Transfer
program.

WARNING

» It's a Bad Idea to unplug the tablet while you're transferring information or while a folder window is open on your computer. Doing so can damage the tablet's internal storage, rendering unreadable some of the information that's kept there. To be safe, close those programs and folder windows you've opened before disconnecting.

» Unlike other external storage on the Macintosh, you don't need to eject the tablet's storage when you're done accessing it. Quit the Android File Transfer program on the Mac, and then unplug the tablet — or vice versa. The Mac doesn't get angry, either way.

Files Back and Forth

The USB connection provides only one way to transfer files between your tablet and another device. Files can also flee to and fro on cloud storage. And when the need arises, the tablet can connect to a printer and generate a hard copy of a file, photo, or other item shown on the touchscreen.

» Transferring a file from a computer to the tablet is no guarantee that you can do productive things with it. Specifically, don't copy an eBook from your computer to the tablet and expect to be able to read it. See Chapter 14 for information on eBooks.

>> You can use a web browser on a computer to access your Google Play Music, Play Books, and Play Movies & TV content. See Chapters 13 and 14 for details.

>> Pictures and movies can be synchronized between devices. See Chapter 12.

Sharing files on the cloud

Perhaps the best and easiest way to swap files between your Android tablet and just about any other device is to use *cloud storage.* That's just fancy talk for storing files on the Internet.

All Android tablets come with Google cloud storage called Google Drive. Use the Drive app to access that storage. On a computer, visit `drive.google.com` to view the storage. From that site, you can also obtain the Google Drive program for your computer, which I recommend.

All files saved to Google Drive are synchronized instantly with all devices that access that storage. Change a file in a Google Drive folder on a computer, and that file is instantly updated on your tablet.

To move an item from your Android tablet to your computer, first view that item. Follow these steps:

1. **Locate the item you want to send to the computer.**

   It can be a picture, movie, web page, YouTube video, or just about anything.

2. **Tap the Share icon.**

   If you don't see the Share icon, the item you're viewing cannot be copied to Google Drive.

3. **Choose Save to Drive.**

   If you prefer to use other cloud storage, choose that app icon instead.

4. **Fill in the Save to Drive card, changing information if necessary.**

   I typically change the name to something memorable. Also, because I'm organized, I tap the Folder action bar to choose a specific Google Drive folder on which to save the item.

5. **Tap the SAVE button.**

Likewise, to make a file available to the tablet, copy that file to the Google Drive folder on your computer. When you next access the Drive app on the tablet, open the proper folder and find the file.

>> Other cloud storage apps include the popular Dropbox, Microsoft's OneDrive, the Amazon Cloud, and more. Each of these works similarly to Google Drive; just choose the proper app in Step 3.

>> You can obtain the Dropbox app from Google Play, but you also need to get a Dropbox account and probably get the Dropbox program for the computer. Visit dropbox.com to get started.

>> Cloud storage apps are free, and you can use a modicum of storage at no cost. Beyond that amount, you must pay a monthly fee.

REMEMBER

Using the USB cable to transfer files

After you make the USB connection between your tablet and a computer (covered earlier in this chapter), you can transfer files back and forth.

To best transfer files between the two devices, ensure that folder windows for both the tablet and the destination or source are open. Figure 17-3 illustrates such an arrangement.

Tablet's Camera folder

Tablet device

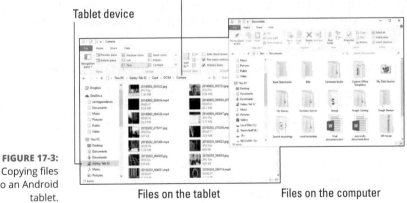

Files on the tablet   Files on the computer

FIGURE 17-3: Copying files to an Android tablet.

Drag file icons between the two windows to copy between tablet and computer, or vice versa.

When you're done copying files, close both windows and detach the tablet as described earlier in this chapter.

REMEMBER

>> On the PC, choose the action that opens the tablet's storage for viewing.

>> On a Macintosh, you use the Android File Transfer window and a Finder window to transfer the files.

>> When an Android tablet has a microSD card installed, two storage locations are available for file transfer. One is named Card for the microSD card storage; the other, Device or Tablet for the tablet's main storage.

>> The best way to synchronize music with your Android tablet is to use a music jukebox program in Windows. See Chapter 13.

TIP

>> If you don't know where to copy files to your Android tablet, place the files into the Download folder. They may not show up in the Downloads app (covered in Chapter 7), but they can be read from that location by other apps.

>> Tablets that feature a microSD card can use that card to transfer files: Remove the microSD card from the tablet and insert it into a computer. From that point, the computer can read the files just as they can be read from any media card. See the later section "Unmounting the microSD card," for details.

Adding a print service

Android tablets have the capability to print information, which is another form of file transfer. To get printing to work properly, you must have printers available on the same Wi-Fi network as the tablet; plus, you must install a print service that's compatible with those network printers.

Heed these directions to confirm or add a print service to your tablet:

1. Open the Settings app and choose the Printing category.

On some Samsung tablets, choose More Connection Settings to locate the Printing category.

You see a list of print services. You're looking for a service that matches the printer models on the Wi-Fi network; for example, the HP Print Service Plugin, which lets you print to any networked HP printer.

2. If a print service is off, choose it and switch its master control to the On position.

You're done. Otherwise, if you don't see a print service for the network printer, continue with Step 3:

3. **Choose Add Service or Download Plug-In.**

   The Play Store app opens, listing available printing services.

4. **Select and install a print service.**

   For example, if you use Canon printers, choose and install the Canon print service. Refer to Chapter 18 for details on installing apps.

After the service is installed, or if you confirm that the service is available, you can print from your Android tablet. Keep reading in the next section.

Printing

Printing on an Android tablet is not only possible, it's actually kind of cinchy. If the tablet uses a Wi-Fi network with an available printer and if that printer's printing service is installed, printing works like this:

1. **View the material you want to print.**

   You can print a web page, photo, map, or any number of items.

2. **Tap the Action Overflow or MORE button and choose the Print action.**

   If you don't see the Print action, your tablet lacks this feature.

3. **Choose a printer.**

   The current printer is shown on the Action Bar, shown in Figure 17-4. To view additional printers, tap the Action Bar, illustrated in the figure. You see a list of all printers available on the Wi-Fi network.

4. **To change any print settings, tap the Show More Details chevron.**

   The items presented let you set which pages you want to print, change the number of copies, and make other common printer settings.

5. **Tap the Print button.**

   The item prints.

Not every app supports printing. The only way to know is to work Steps 1 and 2 in this section. If you don't see the Print action, you can't print.

Streaming your own media

Your tablet may have a nice, big screen. Your HDTV or computer monitor may have a larger screen. And if that larger screen has a Chromecast dongle attached to one of its HDMI ports, you can stream video and music from your tablet to that large-format device.

Select printer action bar   Show more details

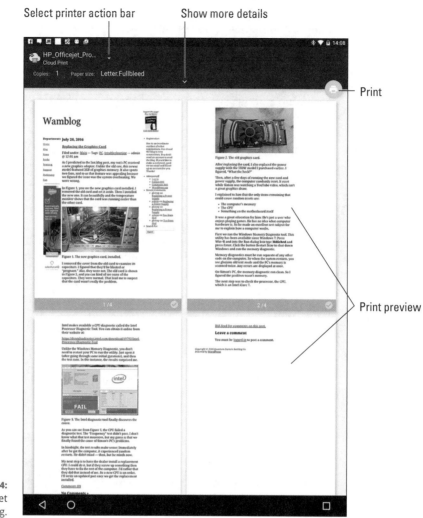

Print

Print preview

FIGURE 17-4:
Android tablet
printing.

After the Chromecast dongle is installed and configured, follow these steps to stream media from the tablet:

1. **Open the app that plays the media you want to watch or listen to.**

   Compatible apps include Play Music, Play Movies & TV, YouTube, Netflix, and so on.

2. **Tune the HDTV or monitor to the proper HDMI input.**

   For example, if a Chromecast dongle is installed on HDMI Input 4, switch the TV to that input. The casting dongle must be awake and active.

3. **Tap the Chromecast icon.**

The icon appears similar to the one shown in the margin. If you don't see this icon, either the Chromecast dongle isn't awake or the media cannot be cast to another device.

4. **Choose the TV or monitor's Chromecast from the list.**

5. **Play the media.**

The media appears or is heard from the other device.

You can still use your tablet while it's casting. The app on the screen may offer you controls, such as Play and Pause, or it might display additional information about the media.

To stop streaming, tap the Chromecast icon, then tap the DISCONNECT button.

Android Tablet Storage

Somewhere, nestled in your Android tablet's bosom, lies a storage device. That storage works like the hard drive in a computer, and for the same purpose: to keep apps, music, videos, pictures, and a host of other information for the long term.

» Android tablets come with a given quantity of internal storage. The amount is preset by the manufacturer, usually given as an option at purchase time.

» Typical quantities of internal storage include 16GB, 32GB, 64GB, and more.

» Removable storage in the form of a microSD card is available on some Android tablets.

TECHNICAL STUFF

» GB stands for gigabyte, or 1 billion bytes (characters) of storage. A typical 2-hour movie occupies about 4GB of storage, but most items that you store on the tablet — music and pictures, for example — take up only a sliver of storage.

Reviewing storage stats

You can see how much storage space is available on your Android tablet; follow these steps:

1. **Open the Settings app.**

2. **Choose the Storage & USB item.**

On some Samsung tablets, this item is called Storage, and it might be found on the General tab in the Settings app.

You see a screen similar to the one shown in Figure 17-5. It details information about storage space on the tablet's internal storage and, if available, the microSD card.

Unmount microSD card

FIGURE 17-5:
Android tablet
storage
information.

Tap the storage item or tap a storage category, if listed, to view details on how the storage is used or to launch an associated app. For example, tap the Apps item to see a list of running apps. Choose Videos to view videos stored on the tablet.

REMEMBER

TECHNICAL
STUFF

>> Things that consume the most storage space are videos, music, and pictures, in that order.

>> To see how much storage space is unoccupied, refer to the Available item.

>> Don't feel gypped if the Total Space value is far less than the stated capacity of your Android tablet. For example, your tablet may have 32GB of storage but the Storage screen reports on 29.85GB of total space. The missing space is considered overhead, as are several gigabytes taken by the government for tax purposes.

Managing files

You probably didn't get an Android tablet because you enjoy managing files on a computer and you wanted another gizmo to hone your skills. Even so, you can practice the same type of file manipulation on the Android tablet as you would on a computer. Is there a need to do so? Of course not! But if you want to get dirty with files, you can.

To view files and folders, attempt these steps:

1. Open the Settings app and choose Storage & USB.

This item might be titled Storage.

2. Swipe to the bottom of the screen and choose Explore.

You may have to tap the storage item to view the Explore action. Upon success, you see folders and files stored on your tablet.

Some Android tablets come with a file management app. It's called Files or My Files, and it's a traditional type of file manager, which means that if you detest managing files on your computer, you'll experience the same delightful frustration on your tablet.

>> If you simply want to peruse files you've downloaded from the Internet, open the Downloads app, found in the Apps drawer. Refer to Chapter 7.

>> If your tablet lacks a file management app, you can swiftly obtain one. An abundance of file management apps are available from Google Play. See Chapter 15.

Unmounting the microSD card

The microSD card provides removable storage on some Android tablets. When the tablet is turned off, you can insert or remove the microSD card at will; directions are provided in Chapter 1. The microSD card can also be removed when the tablet is turned on, but you must first unmount the card. Obey these steps:

1. Open the Settings app and choose Storage & USB.

On some Samsung tablets, tap the General tab to locate the Storage item.

2. Choose Unmount SD Card or press the Eject button.

Refer to Figure 17-5 for the location of the Eject button. Otherwise, the Unmount SD Card action is found near the bottom of the screen.

3. **Ignore the warning and tap the OK button.**

4. **Remove the microSD card.**

It's important that you follow these steps to safely remove the microSD card. If you don't and you just pop out the card, it could damage the card and lose information.

REMEMBER

You can insert a microSD card at any time. See Chapter 1 for details.

Formatting microSD storage

Your Android tablet should instantly recognize a microSD card after it's inserted. If not, you can try formatting the card to see if that fixes the problem.

WARNING

All data on the microSD card is erased by the formatting process.

To format a microSD card, follow these steps:

1. **Open the Settings app and choose Storage or Storage & USB.**

   On some Samsung tablets, you find the Storage item on the General tab.

2. **Choose the action Format SD Card.**

   If necessary, tap the microSD card's item on the Storage screen to locate the Format action.

3. **Tap the Format or Format SD Card button.**

4. **If prompted, tap the DELETE ALL button to confirm.**

   The microSD card is unmounted, formatted, and then mounted again and made ready for use.

After the card is formatted, you can use it to store information, music, apps, photos, and stuff like that.

Chapter **18**

Apps and Widgets

O f the more than 2 million apps available for your Android tablet, you probably want to keep a handful of your favorites ready and available. The best way to keep them accessible, neat, and tidy is to place their Launcher icons on the Home screen. Indeed, the whole point of having a Home screen is to keep handy apps and widgets.

Apps and Widgets on the Home Screen

You can be an idle observer, frustrated that the apps you need don't occupy their own postage stamp of real estate on the Home screen, or you can customize the Home screen to show those apps you use all the time.

REMEMBER

The app icons on the Home screen are called *launchers,* or *launcher icons.*

Adding apps to the Home screen

As you find yourself using an app frequently, consider slapping a launcher icon for the app on the Home screen. Here's how that works:

1. Visit the Home screen page on which you want to stick the launcher icon.

The page must have room for the launcher icon. If it doesn't, swipe the screen left or right to hunt down a page with room. Or, if you're organizing pages by app type, visit the proper page. For example, on my tablet, the second Home page is just for games.

2. Tap the Apps icon to display the Apps drawer.

3. Long-press the app icon you want to add to the Home screen.

After a moment, the Home screen page you chose in Step 1 appears, similar to the one shown in Figure 18-1.

Drag the icon to a position on the Home screen

Favorites tray

FIGURE 18-1: Placing an app icon on the Home screen.

4. Drag the app to a position on the Home screen page.

Launcher icons on the Home screen are aligned to a grid. Other launchers may wiggle and jiggle as you find a spot. That's okay.

5. Lift your finger to place the app.

Don't worry if the launcher isn't in the exact spot you want. The later section "Moving launchers and widgets" describes how to rearrange items on the Home screen.

The app hasn't moved: What you see is a launcher, which is like a copy or shortcut. You can still find the app in the Apps drawer, but now the app is available — more conveniently — on the Home screen.

TIP

>> Newly installed apps often automatically affix a launcher icon to the Home screen.

>> Not every app needs a launcher icon on the Home screen. I recommend placing only those apps you use most frequently.

>> Some tablets use the top row of the Apps drawer to list frequently accessed apps. Review the Apps drawer to peruse your frequent apps, and consider adding them to the Home screen if they're not there already.

>> You can't cram more launchers on the Home screen than will fit in the grid. As an alternative, consider rearranging launchers by moving some to another Home screen page, as covered in the later section "Moving launchers and widgets." Also see the later section "Working with folders" for another solution. Finally, if your tablet allows you to add more Home screen pages, you can solve the problem that way; see Chapter 19.

Placing an app on the favorites tray

The row of launcher icons at the bottom of the Home screen remains the same no matter which Home screen page you're viewing. It's called the *favorites tray*, and it's an ideal spot for apps you use most frequently.

Launchers are added to the favorites tray in one of two ways:

>> **Drag a launcher off the favorites tray**, to either the Home screen page or the Remove or Delete icon. This step makes room for a new icon on the favorites tray.

>> **Drag a launcher from the Home screen to the favorites tray**, in which case any existing icon swaps places with the icon that's already there.

Of these two methods, the second one may not work on all tablets. In fact, the second method may create an app folder on the favorites tray, which is probably not what you want. (See the later section "Working with folders.")

The best apps to place on the Home screen are those that show launcher notifications, similar to the icon shown in the margin. The apps include Facebook, Twitter, the Email app, and others.

Slapping down widgets

Beyond app launchers, the Home screen is also where you find widgets. A *widget* works like a tiny, interactive or informative window, often providing a gateway into another app on the tablet. Widgets may display the time, the weather, tweets, or new videos or serve as placeholders for the eBook you're reading or represent a contact, a location on the map, and a host of other goodies.

To add widgets to the Home screen, obey these steps:

1. **Switch to a Home screen page that has enough room for the new widget.**

   Widgets come in a variety of sizes. The size is measured by launcher dimensions: A 1x1 widget occupies the same space as a launcher icon. A 2x2 widget is twice as tall and twice as wide as a launcher icon.

2. **Long-press a blank part of the Home screen.**

   You see a Home screen overview, along with icons at the bottom of the screen.

3. **Tap the Widgets icon.**

   A list of widgets appears.

4. **Long-press the widget you want to add.**

   Swipe through the pages to find widgets, which are listed alphabetically and show preview images just like apps. Also shown are the widget's dimensions.

5. **Drag the widget to the Home screen.**

   As you drag the widget, existing launcher icons and widgets jiggle to make room.

6. **Lift your finger.**

   If the widget grows a border, it can be resized. See the next section.

After adding widgets, you may be prompted for additional information — for example, a location for a weather widget, a contact name for a contact widget, and so on.

>> The variety of available widgets depends on the apps installed. Some apps come with widgets; some don't. Some widgets are independent of any app.

>> Fret not if you change your mind about the widget's location. See the later section "Moving launchers and widgets" for obtaining the proper feng shui.

>> To remove a widget, see the later section "Removing an item from the Home screen."

Resizing a widget

Some widgets are resizable. You can change a widget's size right after plopping it down on the Home screen — or at any time, really: The secret is to long-press the widget. If it grows a box, as shown in Figure 18-2, you can change the widget's dimensions.

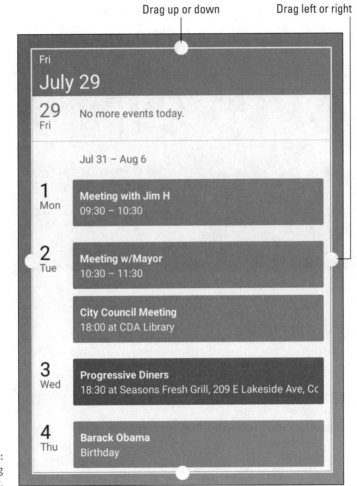

Drag up or down   Drag left or right

FIGURE 18-2:
Resizing
a widget.

To resize, drag one of the orange dots in or out. Tap elsewhere on the touchscreen when you're done resizing.

Moving launchers and widgets

Launcher icons and widgets aren't fastened to the Home screen with anything stronger than masking tape. That's obvious because it's quite easy to pick up and move a launcher or widget, relocating it to a new position or removing it completely. To start, long-press an item, as illustrated in Figure 18-3.

Delete item   Long-press to "lift"

Drag to another page

FIGURE 18-3:
Moving a
launcher icon.

Drag the item to another position on the Home screen. If you drag to the far left or far right of the screen, the icon or widget is sent to another Home screen page.

Removing an item from the Home screen

To banish a launcher or widget from the Home screen, move the launcher or widget to the Remove icon located atop the Home screen. The Remove icon may be an X, the word *Remove* (refer to Figure 18-3), or the Delete icon, similar to what's shown in the margin.

Removing an app or widget from the Home screen doesn't uninstall the app or widget. See the later section "Uninstalling an app."

REMEMBER

Working with folders

For further organization of the Home screen, consider gathering similar apps into folders. For example, I have a Listen folder that contains all my streaming music apps. Your tablet may have come with a Google folder, which contains all the various apps provided by Google. These folders can not only help organize your apps but also help solve the problem of an overly crowded Home screen.

Folders are created in different ways, depending on the tablet. The stock Android method to create a folder is to drag one launcher icon on top of another. When the two launchers get close, a circle encloses them, which provides visual feedback that a folder is created.

Another technique is to look for a Folder creation icon: Drag the launcher icon up to that icon, which creates a new folder. Or, perhaps, you long-press the Home screen and choose the Create Folder action. Drag icons into the new folder.

Examples of various folder icons are shown in Figure 18-4.

FIGURE 18-4:
Folder icon
varieties.

Stock Android
folder

Samsung
folder

To use a folder, tap its icon. The folder opens, displaying its contents. Tap a launcher to start the associated app. Or, if you don't find what you want, tap the Back navigation icon to close the folder.

» To add more app launchers to the folder, drag in their icons. Some folders may feature a Plus (+) or Add icon. In that case, tap the icon to add more launchers.

» Folders are managed just like other icons on the Home screen. You drag folder icons around or delete them. When you delete a folder, you remove the launcher icons from the folder; deleting the folder doesn't uninstall the apps.

» To change a folder's name, open the folder and tap the folder's name. Use the onscreen keyboard to type a new name.

» To remove a launcher icon from a folder, open the folder and drag out the icon. When the second-to-last icon is dragged out of a folder, the folder is removed. If not, drag the last icon out, and then remove the folder as you would any other item on the Home screen, as described in the preceding section.

App Management

When I think of managing apps on my Android tablet, I say, "Oh, pish!" That's because, first of all, I enjoy saying the word *pish*. But more importantly, I don't really need to manage apps. The Android operating system deftly handles that task for you. Still, you have a few duties you can perform.

Reviewing your apps

To peruse the apps you've downloaded from Google Play, follow these steps:

1. **Open the Play Store app.**

2. **Ensure that you're at the top level in the app.**

   Tap the Back navigation icon until you see the main screen.

3. **Tap the Side Menu icon.**

4. **Choose My Apps & Games from the navigation drawer.**

   If you don't see the My Apps & Games item, choose Apps & Games and repeat Steps 3 and 4.

5. **Peruse your apps.**

Your apps are presented in three categories: SUBSCRIPTIONS, INSTALLED, and ALL, as shown in Figure 18-5.

The SUBSCRIPTIONS tab lists recurring items, such as a video subscription app, magazine, and so on.

Apps listed on the INSTALLED tab are found on your tablet.

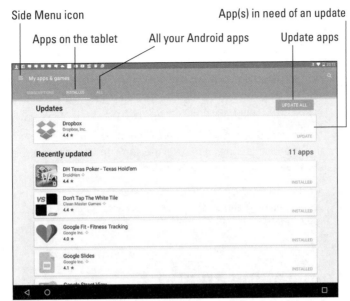

Side Menu icon

Apps on the tablet

All your Android apps

App(s) in need of an update

Update apps

FIGURE 18-5:
Locating
all your
tablet's apps.

Apps on the ALL tab include all apps on your tablet, as well as any apps you've downloaded but that may not currently be installed.

>> Tap an app in the list to view its details. Some of the options and settings on the app's details screen are discussed elsewhere in this chapter.

>> Uninstalled apps remain on the ALL list because you did, at one time, download the app. To reinstall them (and without paying a second time for paid apps), choose the app from the ALL list and tap the INSTALL button.

Updating apps

New versions, or updates, of apps happen all the time. They're automatic. Occasionally, you're called upon to perform a manual update. How can you tell? The App Update notification appears, looking similar to what's shown in the margin.

To deal with a manual update, open the Play Store app to view all installed apps; details for viewing your apps are presented in the preceding section. What you're looking for is the UPDATE ALL button, shown in Figure 18-5. Tap that button to apply necessary app updates. If prompted to accept the app's permissions, tap the Accept button.

You can view the app update process in the Play Store app or go off and do something else with your tablet.

> » Yes, you do need an Internet connection to update apps. If possible, try to use Wi-Fi so that you don't incur data surcharges on your cellular bill. Android apps aren't superhuge, but why take the risk?

> » Unlike updating a major computer operating system, if the Internet connection is broken during an update, the app's update automatically continues after the connection is reestablished.

 > » Most apps automatically update; you need not do a thing. The updates do generate a notification icon, shown in the margin. Feel free to dismiss that notification.

Uninstalling an app

I can think of a few reasons to remove an app. It's with eager relish that I remove apps that don't work or that somehow annoy me. It's also perfectly okay to remove redundant apps, such as when you're trying to find a decent music-listening app and you end up with a dozen or so that you never use.

Whatever the reason, remove an app by following these directions:

1. **Open the Play Store app.**

2. **Choose My Apps & Games from the navigation drawer.**

   If you don't see that item, choose Apps & Games and then repeat Steps 1 and 2.

3. **Tap the INSTALLED tab.**

4. **Choose the app that offends you.**

5. **Tap the UNINSTALL button.**

6. **Tap the OK button to confirm.**

   The app is removed.

The app continues to appear on the ALL list even after it's been removed. That's because you downloaded it once. That doesn't mean, however, that the app is still installed.

>> You can always reinstall paid apps that you've uninstalled. You aren't charged twice for doing so.

>> It's possible to remove an app from the Home screen *and* uninstall the app. Refer to Figure 18-3: When you drag an icon off the Home screen, drag it to the Uninstall icon instead of Remove. The app is then uninstalled.

WARNING

>> You can't remove apps that are preinstalled on the tablet by either the manufacturer or cellular provider. I'm sure there's a technical way to uninstall such apps, but seriously: Just don't use the apps if you want to remove them and discover that you can't.

Choosing a default app

Every so often, you may see the Complete Action Using prompt, which may look similar to the one shown in Figure 18-6. Regardless of its appearance, you're prompted to choose from one or more apps to complete an action, and given the choice of JUST ONCE or ALWAYS.

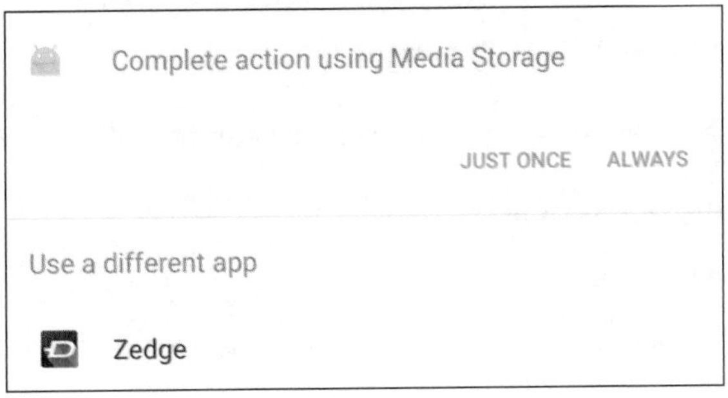

Complete action using Media Storage

JUST ONCE   ALWAYS

Use a different app

Zedge

FIGURE 18-6: The Complete Action Using question is posed.

When you choose ALWAYS, the same app is always used for whatever action took place: composing email, listening to music, cropping a photo, navigating, and so on.

When you choose JUST ONCE, you see the prompt again and again.

My advice is to choose JUST ONCE until you get sick of seeing the Complete Action Using prompt. At that point, choose ALWAYS.

The fear, of course, is that you'll make a mistake. Keep reading in the next section.

Some tablets may not offer the choice of always or just once. If so, the app you choose is always used to complete the action.

Clearing default apps

Fret not, gentle reader. The settings you chose for the Complete Action Using prompt can be undone. For example, if you select the Zedge app from Figure 18-6, you can undo that choice by following these steps:

1. **Open the Settings app.**

2. **Choose Apps.**

3. **Choose the app that always opens.**

   This is the tough step because you must remember which app you chose to "always" open.

4. **On the app's screen, choose Open by Default.**

   If the item shows the text *Some Defaults Set,* you're on the right track. Apps that haven't been chosen as the default show the text *No Defaults Set.*

5. **Tap the CLEAR DEFAULTS button.**

The steps on some Samsung tables work differently:

1. **Open the Settings app.**

2. **Choose Applications.**

   Some Samsung phones may feature an Applications tab, in which case you choose that tab to continue.

3. **Choose Default Applications.**

4. **Choose Set as Default.**

   You see a list of installed apps. If the text *Set As Default* appears below an app, it's been chosen as a default app.

5. **Tap to open the default app.**

6. **Tap the CLEAR DEFAULTS button.**

After you clear the defaults for an app, you see the Open With card again. The next time you see it, however, make a better choice.

Shutting down an app run amok

Sometimes an app goofs up or crashes. You may see a warning message on the touchscreen, informing you that the app has been shut down. That's good. What's better is that you too can shut down apps that misbehave or those you cannot otherwise stop. Follow these steps:

1. **Open the Settings app.**

2. **Tap the Apps item.**

   On Samsung tablets, choose Applications and then choose Application Manager. These items might be located on the Applications or General tab in the Settings app.

3. **Choose the errant app from the list.**

   For example, if the Annoying Sound app is bothering you, choose it from the list.

4. **Tap the FORCE STOP button.**

   The app is terminated.

WARNING

Use the FORCE STOP button only as a final act. Don't kill off any app or service unless the app is annoying or you are otherwise unable to stop it. Avoid killing off Google Services, which can change the tablet's behavior or make the Android operating system unstable.

MOVING AN APP TO THE MICROSD CARD

On Android tablets with removable storage, you may find an option that moves the app from internal storage to the microSD card. My advice: Don't.

First, apps don't occupy a lot of storage, so moving them to external storage isn't saving you anything. Second, you run the risk of losing the app should the storage vanish. Indeed, launcher icons for those apps disappear from the Home screen. Finally, the current trend is for Android tablets not to feature removable storage. So even if moving apps to the microSD card works for you, it's not a long-term solution.

Apps Drawer Organization

Some tablets offer tools for arranging apps in the Apps drawer. These tools allow you to present the apps in an order other than alphabetical, rearrange the apps, or even collect apps and place them into folders.

The key to organizing the Apps drawer is to look for the Action Overflow or other actions on the screen. For example, some Samsung tablets feature an EDIT command, which is used to arrange icons in the Apps drawer. The A–Z command arranges apps in alphabetical order.

You may find a FOLDER command that lets you build Apps drawer folders, or you might create folders by dragging icons over each other, similar to how folders work on the Home screen folder. Refer to the section "Working with folders," earlier in this chapter, for more details.

Chapter **19**

Customize Your Android Tablet

t's entirely possible to own an Android tablet for decades and never once customize it. It's not that customization is impossible; it's that most people just don't bother. Maybe they don't know how to customize it; maybe they don't try; or maybe they're deathly afraid that the tablet will seek revenge.

Poppycock!

It's your tablet! Great potential exists to make the device truly your own. You can change the way it looks to the way it sounds. Revenge is not part of the equation.

Home Screen and Display Settings

The Home screen is where the action happens on your Android tablet. To help hone the Home screen to meet your demands, several customization options are available. You can change the background image, control the automatic lock timeout, and even add or remove Home screen pages. This section uncovers the secrets.

Decorating the Home screen

To start your Home screen decoration project, long-press a blank part of the Home screen. Don't long-press on an icon or widget. Upon success, you see Home screen management icons, similar to what's shown in Figure 19-1.

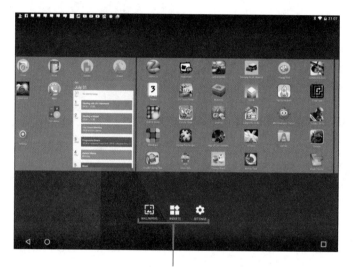

FIGURE 19-1:
The Home
screen menu.

Home screen management icons

The icons or options presented for Home screen management include some or all of the following:

Wallpaper: Change the background image on the Home screen.

Widgets: Add widgets to the Home screen.

Settings: Open the Settings app.

Folder: Create a Home screen folder.

Page: Add, remove, or manage Home screen pages.

These items might appear as icons (refer to Figure 19-1), or you may see a menu of options presented as a list. The most common items are the first three, as illustrated in Figure 19-1.

Hanging new wallpaper

The Home screen background can be draped with two types of wallpaper: traditional and live. *Traditional* wallpaper can be any image, such as a picture you've taken or an image provided by the tablet's manufacturer. *Live* wallpaper is animated or interactive.

To set a new wallpaper for the Home screen, obey these steps:

1. **Long-press the Home screen.**

2. **Choose Wallpapers.**

   The command might be Set Wallpapers on some tablets.

3. **Tap a wallpaper to see a preview.**

   Swipe the list left or right to peruse your options. You see the previous wallpaper images, plus those provided by the tablet manufacturer. On the far right, you'll find the live wallpapers.

   Some tablets may first prompt you to select a category, such as Wallpapers, Life Wallpapers, and Images.

4. **Tap the Set Wallpaper button to confirm your choice.**

   The new wallpaper takes over the Home screen.

If you prefer to use an image from the tablet's photo library, tap the My Photos or From Gallery button in Step 3. Choose an image. On some tablets, you're required to crop the image; manipulate the cropping rectangle to do so. Tap the Done button to set the wallpaper.

TIP

>> On some Samsung tablets, tabs atop the Wallpapers screen let you choose to set wallpaper for the Home screen, Lock screen, or both. See the later section "Setting the Lock screen background."

>> Be careful how you crop the wallpaper image when you choose one of your own photos. Zoom out (pinch your fingers on the touchscreen) to ensure that the entire image is cropped properly for both the tablet's horizontal and vertical orientations.

>> Live wallpapers can be obtained from Google Play. See Chapter 15.

>> The Zedge app is an über-repository of wallpaper images, collected from Android users all over the world. Zedge is a free app.

>> See Chapter 12 for more information on how to crop an image.

Managing Home screen pages

The number of pages on the Home screen isn't fixed. You can add pages. You can remove pages. You can even rearrange pages. This feature might not be available to all Android tablets and, sadly, it's not implemented in exactly the same way.

The stock Android method of adding a Home screen page is to drag an icon left or right, just as though you were positioning that icon on another Home screen page. When a page to the left or right doesn't exist, the tablet automatically adds a new, blank page.

Other tablets may be more specific in how pages are added. For example, you can choose a Page command from the Home screen menu.

The Home screen page overview for Samsung tablets is shown in Figure 19-2. To edit Home screen pages, pinch the Home screen: Touch the screen with two fingers and drag them together. You can then manage Home screen pages as illustrated in the figure.

Set primary Home screen page

Remove Home screen page

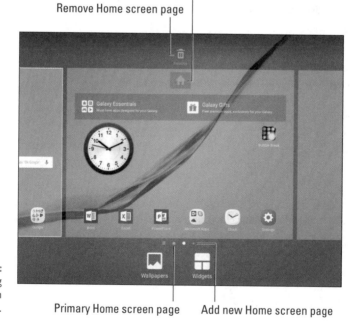

FIGURE 19-2: Manipulating Home screen pages.

Primary Home screen page   Add new Home screen page

Generally speaking, to rearrange the pages, long-press and drag it to a new spot. When you're done, tap the Back or Home navigation icon.

>> The maximum number of Home screen pages may be three, five, seven, or nine, depending on your tablet. The minimum is one.

>> On some tablets, the far left Home screen page is the Google Now app.

>> The trend is for Samsung tablets to feature some wacky Samsung app on the far left Home screen page.

>> Some tablets allow you to set the primary Home screen page, which doesn't necessarily have to be the center Home screen page. I've seen different ways to accomplish this task. The most common one is to tap the Home icon in a thumbnail's preview, which is illustrated in Figure 19-2.

Setting the screen lock timeout

You can manually lock your tablet at any time by pressing the Power/Lock key. That's probably why it's called the Power/Lock key, though I have my doubts. When you don't manually lock the tablet, it automatically locks after a given period of inactivity. Obey these steps to set that duration:

1. **Open the Settings app and choose Display.**

On some Samsung tablets, you need to first tap the Device tab before you can locate the Display item.

2. **Choose Sleep.**

This item is titled Screen Timeout on some tablets.

3. **Select a timeout value from the list.**

I prefer a value of ten minutes.

The lock timer measures inactivity; when you don't touch the screen, the timer starts ticking. About five seconds before the timeout kicks in, the touchscreen dims. Then the touchscreen turns off and the tablet locks. If you touch the screen before then, the timer is reset.

TECHNICAL
STUFF

The Lock screen has its own timeout. If you unlock the tablet but don't work the screen lock, the tablet locks itself automatically after about ten seconds. This timeout value cannot be adjusted.

Adjusting display brightness

You can set the screen brightness to very dim or very bright, or you can let the tablet determine the setting by using the ambient light in the room. Follow these steps:

1. **Open the Settings app and tap the Display item.**

On Samsung tablets, look for the Display item on the Device tab. This item might be titled Display and Wallpaper.

2. **Choose Brightness Level.**

3. **Adjust the slider to set the touchscreen's intensity.**

If you'd rather have the tablet adjust the brightness for you, set the master control by the Adaptive Brightness item to the On position, or tap to place a check mark in the Auto box. Not every tablet may feature this option.

TIP

>> The Adaptive Brightness setting might be called Automatic Brightness.

>> You might also find a Brightness setting in the tablet's Quick Settings area. See Chapter 3 for information on accessing the Quick Settings.

Lock Screen Settings

The Lock screen is different from the Home screen, although the two locations share similar traits. As with the Home screen, you can customize the Lock screen. You can change the background, add app launcher shortcuts, and perform all sorts of tricks.

>> Lock screen features might not be available for all Android tablets.

>> For information on setting screen locks, as well as controlling the Lock screen notifications, refer to Chapter 20.

Setting the Lock screen background

For most Android tablets, the Lock screen wallpaper is the same as the Home screen wallpaper. A few tablets, however, let you set a separate Lock screen wallpaper.

To determine whether your tablet provides for separate Lock screen wallpaper, follow the same steps as outlined in the earlier section "Hanging new wallpaper." If you see a prompt to set the Lock screen wallpaper, choose it. Then select a wallpaper for the Lock screen that's different from the Home screen.

>> Some tablets may feature a Lock Screen item in the Settings app. If so, choose that item to set the Lock screen background.

>> Samsung tablets may feature a Lock Screen tab atop the wallpaper selection screen. Refer to the earlier section "Hanging new wallpaper."

Adding Lock screen shortcuts

Some Android tablets feature the Camera icon in the lower right corner of the screen. Swipe that icon to run the Camera app without fully unlocking the tablet. It's a quick way to take a picture.

Some Samsung tablets allow for up to five launcher icons to appear on the Lock screen, but only when the Swipe screen lock is selected. You can use these Lock screen launchers to both unlock the tablet and immediately start the app: Swipe the App Launcher icon on the Lock screen.

To configure Lock screen shortcuts on some Samsung tablets, heed these steps:

1. **Open the Settings app and choose Lock Screen.**

    If you can't find the Lock Screen item, your tablet doesn't allow you to configure the Lock screen shortcuts.

    On some Samsung tablets, the item may be titled Lock Screen and Security. You might find this item on the Device tab.

2. **Choose the Info and Apps Shortcuts item.**

    If you don't see this item, set the Swipe screen lock for your tablet.

3. **Select App Shortcuts.**

4. **Choose the apps to place on the Lock screen.**

Other tablets use different steps to add the Lock screen shortcuts. Some tablets let you select from an array of apps to stick on the Lock screen. Others may let you select one or two, or simply enable or disable the Camera app shortcut on the Lock screen.

After activating the Lock screen shortcuts feature and choosing which apps to use, lock your tablet and then unlock it to review your choices.

Keyboard Settings

Quite a few options are available for the Google Keyboard, some of which enable special features and others that supposedly make the onscreen typing experience more enjoyable. I'll leave it up to you to determine whether that's true.

Generating keyboard feedback

The onscreen keyboard can help with your typing by generating haptic feedback. This is in the form of either a pleasing click sound or the tablet's vibration. To check these settings, follow these steps:

1. **Open the Settings app and choose Language & Input.**
2. **Choose Google Keyboard and then Preferences.**
3. **Set the Sound on Keypress master control to the On position.**

Samsung tablets follow a different set of steps:

1. **Open the Settings app and choose Language & Input.**

   On some Samsung tablets, look for this item on either the General or Controls tab.

2. **Choose Samsung Keyboard.**
3. **Choose Key-Tap Feedback.**
4. **Set the master control by the Sound item to the On position.**

Not every tablet features vibration.

Ensuring that predictive text is active

Predictive text is on all the time when you use the Google Keyboard. Not every Android tablet uses that keyboard, so to ensure that the feature is active, follow these steps:

1. **Open the Settings app and choose Language & Input.**
2. **Choose Google Keyboard and then Preferences.**

   On Samsung tablets, choose the Samsung Keyboard item.

3. **Choose Text Correction or Smart Typing.**

4. **Ensure that all the master controls on the Text Correction or Smart Typing screen are set to the On position.**

If your tablet doesn't show the Predictive Text item, it's most likely on all the time and can't be turned off.

See Chapter 4 for more information on using the predictive-text feature.

Activating keyboard gestures

Gesture typing allows you to swipe your finger over the onscreen keyboard to create text. Chapter 4 explains the details, although this feature may not be active on your tablet. To ensure that it is, follow these steps:

1. **Open the Settings app and choose Language & Input.**

2. **Choose Google Keyboard, and then choose Gesture Typing.**

3. **Ensure that the Master Control icons are all set to the On position.**

    Only the Enable Gesture Typing item needs to be enabled, although activating the other items does enhance the experience.

For some Samsung tablets, follow these steps:

1. **Open the Settings app and choose Language & Input.**

2. **Choose Samsung Keyboard.**

3. **Choose Smart Typing.**

4. **Choose Keyboard Swipe.**

5. **Ensure that the Continuous Input item is chosen.**

Turning on dictation

Voice input should be active on all Android tablets, but that's no guarantee. The secret is to find the Dictation (Microphone) icon on the keyboard. The icon looks similar to the one shown in the margin.

TIP

On some Samsung keyboards, long-press the multifunction key to locate the Dictation icon.

When you can find the Dictation key, and before you defenestrate the tablet in frustration, follow these steps to ensure that this feature is active:

1. **Open the Settings app and chose Language & Input.**

2. **Choose Google Voice Typing.**

3. **Ensure that the feature is enabled.**

   If you can't find a master control or check box, then Google Voice Typing is always active.

Information on disabling the voice-typing word filter is found in Chapter 23.

Audio Adjustments

The Sound & Notification screen in the Settings app is where you control the various ways your Android tablet can make noise. It's capable of more than beeping, and the volume can be set as well as the vibration options.

To witness the Sound screen for yourself, open the Settings app and tap the Sound & Notification item. On some tablets, the item is called Sound. On some Samsung tablets, the Sound item is found on the Settings app's Device tab.

Worthy options on the Sound screen include the following, although the specific titles used on your tablet may be slightly different from what's shown here:

Default Notification Ringtone: Choose which sound you want to hear for a notification alert. Choose a sound or select None or Silent (at the top of the list) for no sound.

Vibration: Choose the Vibration item to set whether the tablet vibrates during a notification and, potentially, how vigorously it vibrates. If you don't see this option, your Android tablet either doesn't let you control vibration or it lacks the vibration feature.

Volumes: Though you can use the Volume buttons on the side of the gizmo, the Volumes command on the Sound & Notification screen lets you set the volume for different types of sound events, such as music, games, and notifications.

Other items might also be available, controlling audio features specific to your tablet.

Chapter **20**

Android Tablet Security

In the last century, you didn't need to log in to your computer. Banking and shopping were done in person. And passwords were used only to keep the girls out of the boys' fort. Things today are different. Security is vital. Forts are gender–neutral. And passwords are necessary to secure your personal information for all your online personas.

Lock Your Tablet

If you keep anything important on your Android tablet or you have multiple users on the same tablet or you access a corporate email account, you need Lock screen security. I'm referring to more security than the simple Swipe screen lock.

Finding the screen locks

The keys to your Android tablet's screen locks are found within the Settings app. Here's how to get there:

1. Open the Settings app.

2. Choose Security.

This item may be titled Lock Screen and Security. On some Samsung tablets, tap the Device tab to locate the Lock Screen item.

3. **Choose Screen Lock or Screen Lock Type.**

   If you don't see the Screen Lock item, look for the item titled Set Up Screen Lock or Change Screen Lock.

4. **Work any existing screen lock to continue.**

   Eventually, you see the Choose Screen Lock screen, which may be instead called Screen Lock Type.

Several lock types are shown on the Choose Screen Lock screen. The stock Android screen locks are

None: The tablet has no screen lock. Press the Power/Lock key to instantly start using the tablet.

Swipe: Swipe your finger across the screen to unlock the tablet.

Pattern: Trace a pattern on the touchscreen to unlock the tablet.

PIN: Type a personal identification number (PIN) to unlock the tablet.

Password: Type a password to unlock the tablet.

Other locks may be available, including Fingerprint, Face Unlock, and Signature.

REMEMBER

» The most secure locks are the PIN and password. Using one or the other is required if the tablet has multiple users or a kid's account or it accesses a secure email server.

» If your tablet is encrypted, you may be prompted to require the screen lock (Pattern, PIN, or Password) to start the device. My recommendation is to require the screen lock; choose the option Require Lock to Start Device, where *lock* is the type of screen lock being applied.

WARNING

» I know of no recovery method available if you forget your tablet's PIN or password screen locks. If you use them, write them down somewhere inconspicuous, just in case.

» The Face Unlock uses the tablet's front camera to unlock the device. You stare at the screen and, as long as you haven't had any recent, major plastic surgery, the tablet unlocks.

» The signature lock is unique to the Samsung Galaxy Note tablets. Use the S Pen to scribble your John Hancock on the touchscreen. The tablet unlocks.

Removing the screen lock

You don't remove the screen lock on your Android tablet as much as you replace it. Specifically, to remove the Pattern, PIN, or Password screen lock, set the Swipe lock. Follow the directions in the preceding section to get to the Choose Screen Lock screen and change the existing screen lock to something else.

Assigning a password

The most secure way to lock an Android tablet is to apply a full-on password. The password can contain numbers, symbols, and both upper- and lowercase letters.

To set a password, choose Password from the Choose Screen Lock screen; refer to the earlier section "Finding the screen locks." The password you select must be at least four characters long. Longer passwords are more secure.

You're prompted to type the password whenever you unlock your Android tablet or whenever you try to change the screen lock. Tap the OK button to accept the password you've typed.

Setting a PIN

The PIN lock is second only to the Password lock as the most secure for your Android tablet. To access the tablet, you must type a PIN, or personal identification number. This type of screen lock is also employed as a backup for less secure screen locks, such as the Pattern lock.

The *PIN lock* is a code between 4 and 16 digits long. It contains only numbers, 0 through 9. To set the PIN lock for your Android tablet, follow the directions in the earlier section "Finding the screen locks" and choose PIN from the list of locks.

Use the onscreen keypad to type your PIN once and tap the CONTINUE button. Type the same PIN again to confirm that you know it. Tap OK. The next time you unlock the tablet, you need to type the PIN to gain access.

Creating an unlock pattern

One of the most popular screen locks is the Pattern. To unlock the tablet, a specific pattern must be traced exactly as it was created. To create an unlock pattern, follow these steps:

1. **Summon the Choose Screen Lock screen.**

   Refer to the earlier section "Finding the screen locks."

2. **Choose Pattern.**

   If you've not yet set a Pattern lock, you may see a tutorial describing the process; tap the Next button to skip over the dreary directions.

3. **If the Secure Start-Up screen is presented, choose the option Require Pattern to Start Device, and then tap CONTINUE.**

   Alternatively, you can choose No Thanks, which is less secure.

4. **Trace an unlock pattern.**

   Use Figure 20-1 as a guide. You can trace over the dots in any order, but you can trace over a dot only once. The pattern must cover at least four dots.

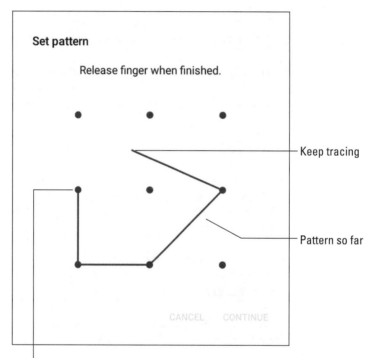

Set pattern

Release finger when finished.

Keep tracing

Pattern so far

CANCEL   CONTINUE

FIGURE 20-1: Set the unlock pattern.

I began the pattern here

5. **Tap the CONTINUE button.**

6. **Redraw the pattern.**

   You need to prove to the doubtful tablet that you know the pattern.

7. **Tap the CONFIRM button.**

   Your tablet may require you to type a PIN or password as a backup to the Pattern lock. If so, follow the onscreen directions to set that lock as well.

TIP

To ensure that the pattern appears on the Lock screen, place a check mark by the option Make Pattern Visible. For even more security, you can disable this option, but you must remember how — and where — the pattern goes.

Also: Clean the touchscreen! Smudge marks can betray your pattern.

Using a fingerprint lock

Though not as popular on an Android tablet as on an Android phone, some devices do come with fingerprint locks. Specifically, on some Samsung tablets the Home button doubles as a fingerprint scanner. After you configure the scanner to read one or more of your digits, and then add a Password or PIN lock as a backup, you can unlock your tablet with a touch of your finger.

Not all fingerprint locks are configured identically, but the concept is the same: You practice using the fingerprint reader until the tablet has a general idea of what your fingerprint looks like.

To unlock the tablet, tap or swipe the fingerprint-reading gizmo. On some Samsung tablets, tap or swipe the proper digit (or thumb) over the Home button. Upon success, the device unlocks, or you may have to type the PIN or password if you fail a given number of times.

WARNING

>> You choose the Fingerprint screen lock from the Choose Screen Lock screen, as described in this earlier section "Finding the screen locks."

>> The Fingerprint screen lock is *not* considered secure. Some tablets let you use it only in combination with a secure lock.

Other Tablet Security

The screen lock only keeps the Bad Guys at bay. Further tablet security is necessary if you truly want to protect your personal information or employ methods to locate a lost or stolen Android tablet.

Adding owner info text

If your Android tablet someday gets lost, it would be nice if a good Samaritan found it. What would be even more helpful is if you had some information on the Lock screen to help that kind person find you and return your gizmo. That info is called *owner info text.* Follow these steps to add that text to the tablet's Lock screen:

1. **Visit the Settings app and choose Security.**

2. **Choose Lock Screen Message.**

   This item might also be titled Owner Info or Owner Information.

3. **Type text in the box.**

   You can type more than one line of text, though the information is displayed on the Lock screen as a single line.

TIP

4. **Tap the SAVE button.**

On Samsung tablets, follow these steps:

1. **Open the Settings app and choose Lock Screen and Security.**

   This item might be located on the Device tab.

2. **Choose Info and App Shortcuts.**

3. **Choose Owner Information.**

4. **Type helpful text in the box and tap the DONE button.**

Whatever text you type in Step 3 appears on the Lock screen. Therefore, I recommend typing your name, address, phone number, email, and so on. That way, should you lose your tablet and an honest person finds it, he or she can get it back to you.

Showing Lock screen notifications

The Lock screen can list the tablet's notifications, just as they appear in the notifications drawer. You can double-tap a notification, unlock the tablet, and then use the app that generated the notification.

Then again, some notifications may pose a security risk. To limit those notifications, or suppress them altogether, follow these steps:

1. **Open the Settings app and choose Sound & Notification.**

2. **Choose When Device Is Locked.**

3. **Select a Lock screen notification level.**

   Three options shown are

   - Show All Notification Content

   - Hide Sensitive Notification Content

   - Don't Show Notifications at All

4. **Select a notification level.**

On Samsung tablets, try these steps instead:

1. **Open the Settings app and choose Lock Screen and Security.**

   On some tablets, tap the Device tab to locate the Lock Screen item.

2. **Choose Notifications on the Lock Screen.**

3. **Choose Content on the Lock Screen.**

   The options are

   - Show Content

   - Hide Content

   - Do Not Show Notifications

4. **Select a notification level.**

You can also use the list of apps that's presented (after Step 3) to determine which of those apps can generate Lock screen notifications. Set the app's master control to the Off position to suppress that specific app's Lock screen notifications.

Finding a lost tablet

Someday, you may lose your beloved Android tablet. It might be for a few panic-filled seconds, or it might be for forever. The hardware solution is to weld a heavy object to the tablet, such as a vending machine, yet that strategy kind of defeats the entire mobile/wireless paradigm. The software solution is to follow these steps:

1. **On a computer, open a web browser, such as Google Chrome.**

2. **Visit the main Google search page:** google.com

3. **Into the Search box, type** find my tablet **and press the Enter key.**

4. **If prompted, sign in to your Google (Gmail) account.**

   Your device's location appears on the screen.

This trick may not work when the tablet is turned off or it's been broken. Also, it may not work if you used a nonsecure screen lock and the Bad Guys have wiped clean the tablet's data.

Encrypting your tablet

When the information on your tablet must be really, really secure, you can take the drastic step of encrypting the internal and external storage. For most Android tablet users, this step is a bit much. However, if you're using your tablet to store the Colonel's secret recipe, you might want to consider it.

First, apply a secure screen lock, such as the PIN or password.

Second, ensure that the tablet is either plugged in or fully charged. Encryption takes a while, and you don't want your gizmo pooping out before the process is complete.

Third, follow these steps to encrypt your tablet's internal storage:

1. **Open the Settings app and choose Security.**

   On some Samsung tablets, choose Lock Screen and Security. This item might be located on the Settings app's General tab.

2. **Choose the item Encrypt Tablet, Encrypt Device, or Encrypt SD Card.**

   If you haven't followed my advice in this section, you'll need to charge the tablet or set a password or both.

3. **Tap the ENCRYPT button to proceed.**

4. **Wait.**

Once encrypted, only by unlocking the tablet will anyone be able to access its storage.

Performing a factory data reset

The most secure thing you can do with information on your Android tablet is to erase it all. The procedure is known as a *factory data reset.* It effectively restores the device to its original state, just like when you got it new.

WARNING

A factory data reset is a drastic thing. It not only removes all information from storage but also erases all your accounts. Don't take this step lightly! In fact, if you're using this procedure to cure an ill, I recommend first getting support.

When you're ready to erase all the tablet's data, follow these steps:

1. **Start the Settings app and choose Backup & Reset.**

On some Samsung tablets, tap the General tab to locate the Backup & Reset item.

2. **Choose Factory Data Reset.**

3. **Tap the RESET TABLET or RESET DEVICE button.**

4. **If prompted, work the screen lock.**

This level of security prevents others from idly messing with your tablet.

5. **Tap the ERASE EVERYTHING or DELETE ALL button to confirm.**

All the information you've set or stored on the tablet is purged, including all your accounts, any apps you've downloaded, music — everything.

TIP

Practical instances when this action is necessary include selling your tablet or giving it to someone else to use. That's the perfect time to perform a factory data reset.

It's Everyone's Tablet!

Computers have long featured the capability to allow multiple users on the same device. Each person has their own sign-in, with separate email and other online accounts, customizations, and features. It's a good idea for a computer, but for a tablet?

The best solution for multiple users is to get multiple Android tablets. When that's impractical, and you really do want to share your beloved gizmo, configure the device so that each human has their own user account. That includes accounts for the kiddies.

Adding another user

Your tablet already has one account — yours! It appears as a tiny circle on the Lock screen, located in the upper right corner, similar to the one shown on the left in Figure 20-2.

To add more accounts, first apply a secure screen lock to your account. See the earlier section "Lock Your Tablet." I strongly recommend a PIN or Password screen lock.

Second, grab the other person. Though you, as the Lord High User of your tablet, can create the new account, you need the other person to complete the job.

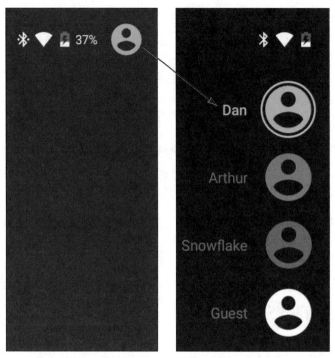

Current account   All accounts

FIGURE 20-2:
User accounts
on the Lock
screen.

Third, follow these steps:

1. **Open the Settings app and choose Users.**

   On some Samsung tablets, look on the Device tab or General tab for the Users item.

   If you're unable to find the Users category, your tablet doesn't support multiple users.

2. **Tap the Add User or Profile item.**

3. **Choose User.**

   See the later section "Configuring a kid's account" for information on the Restricted Profile account type.

4. **Tap the OK button.**

5. **Tap the SET UP NOW button.**

6. **Hand over the tablet to the other person so that they can continue configuring the device.**

At this point, the other person configures their account exactly as you did when you first set up your Android tablet. This process includes adding a Google/Gmail account, setting various options, and so on. Eventually, the account is created and the other user can start using the tablet.

» Settings, apps, email, and other options for each user are unique and separate. You cannot access another account unless you know how to work that user's screen lock. Oh, and:

» I recommend that each user have his account protected with a medium- to high-security screen lock.

» The tablet's first user (most likely you) is the main user, the one who has primary administrative control.

» To remove an account, open the Settings app and choose Users. Tap the Delete (Trash) icon next to the account you want to remove. Tap DELETE to confirm. Only the primary user can remove other accounts.

Switching users

To access another account, tap the account circle on the Lock screen, as shown in Figure 20-2. Tap an account bubble to switch to that account. Accounts are switched only from the Lock screen.

Configuring a kid's account

Don't just hand over your tablet to Snowflake! Craft her a kid's account. That way, you can set which apps she can or cannot use and prevent her from downloading millions of dollars of apps, music, and video.

To add a kid's account, follow the steps in the earlier section "Adding another user." Choose the Restricted Profile account type.

After creating the account, you see the Application/Content Restrictions screen, and you can configure it. Or you can configure it from your own account by tapping the Settings icon to the right of the account name. Here's what you can do:

>> Tap the account name to replace it with your child's name — or whatever name they choose.

>> Activate the master control by the Location Access item if you want their location tracked as they use the tablet. Most parents prefer to keep this item unchecked.

>> Swipe through the list of programs and set the master control to the On position for those apps you would allow your tiny tot to use. These would include various games or whatever other apps you deem appropriate.

>> Some apps feature the Settings icon, such as Google, Netflix, and Play Movies & TV. Tap that icon to make further adjustments, such as determining what level of entertainment would be appropriate for your child.

See the preceding section for information on switching to the kid's account.

Chapter **21**

On the Road

As a mobile device, your Android tablet is designed to go wherever you go. And if you give the tablet a good throw, it can go beyond where you go, but that's not my point. Because it is wireless and has a generous battery, the tablet is built to go on the road. Where can you take it? How can it survive? What if it runs off by itself? Does it need wheels? These are some of the issues regarding taking your tablet elsewhere.

You Can Take It with You

How far can you go with an Android tablet? As far as you desire to go. As long as you can carry the tablet with you, it goes where you do. How it functions may change depending on your environment, and you can do a few things to prepare before you go.

Preparing to leave

Unless you're being unexpectedly abducted, you should prepare several things before leaving on a trip with your Android tablet.

First and most important, of course, is to charge the thing. I plug in my Android tablet overnight before I leave the next day. The tablet's battery is nice and robust, so power should last until well after you reach your destination.

Second, consider loading up on some reading material, music, and a few new apps before you go.

Finally, don't forget your tickets! Many airlines offer apps. The apps may make traveling easy because they generate notifications for your schedule and provide timely gate changes or flight delays — plus, you can use the tablet as your e-ticket. Search Google Play to see whether your preferred airline offers an app.

>> For entertainment, consider getting some eBooks for the road. I prefer to sit and stew over Google Play's online library before I leave, as opposed to wandering aimlessly in some airport sundry store, trying hard to focus on the good books rather than on the salty snacks. Chapter 14 covers reading eBooks on your Android tablet.

>> Picking up some music might be a good idea as well. Visit Chapter 13.

>> I usually reward myself with a new game before I go on a trip with my tablet. Visit Google Play Store and see what's hot or recommended. A good puzzle game can make a nice, long international flight go by a lot quicker.

Going to the airport

I'm not a frequent flier, but I am a nerd. The most amount of junk I've carried with me on a flight is two laptop computers and three cell phones. I know that's not a record, but it's enough to warrant the following list of travel tips, all of which apply to taking an Android tablet with you on an extended journey:

>> Take the Android tablet's AC adapter and USB cable with you. Put them in your carry-on luggage.

>> Most airports feature USB chargers, so you can charge the tablet in an airport, if you need to. Even though you need only the cable to charge, bring along the AC adapter, anyway.

>> At the security checkpoint, place your Android tablet in a bin by itself or with other electronics. The exceptions are when you've been approved for pre-check or you're using a preapproved tablet carrying pouch.

TIP

>> Use the Calendar app to keep track of your flights. The event title serves as the airline and flight number. For the event time, use the take-off and landing schedules. For the location, list the origin and destination airport codes. And, in the Description field, put the flight reservation number. If you're using separate calendars (categories), specify the Travel calendar for your flight. See Chapter 14 for more information on the Calendar app.

>> Scan for the airport's Wi-Fi service. Most airports don't charge for the service, though you may have to agree to terms by using the tablet's web browser app to visit the airport's website.

Flying with an Android tablet

It truly is the trendiest of things to be aloft with the latest mobile gizmo. Like taking a cell phone on a plane, however, you have to follow some rules.

The good news is that because your Android tablet isn't a smartphone, you can leave it on for the duration of the flight. All you need to do is place the tablet into Airplane mode. Follow these steps just before take-off:

1. **Open the Settings app.**

2. **Tap the More item in the Wireless & Networks area.**

If you find an Airplane Mode item in the Wireless and Networks section, choose that item instead.

On some Samsung tablets, tap the Connections tab to locate the More or Airplane Mode item.

3. **Slide the master control by the Airplane Mode item to the On position.**

The tablet turns off its Wi-Fi, Bluetooth, and GPS radios.

When the Android tablet is in Airplane mode, a special icon appears in the status area, similar to the one shown in the margin.

To exit Airplane mode, repeat the steps mentioned in this section.

TIP

>> The Airplane Mode Quick Settings button is also available: Summon the Quick Settings and tap the Airplane Mode icon. See Chapter 3 for more information on the Quick Settings.

>> Some tablets feature the Airplane Mode action on the Device Options menu: Press and hold down the Power button and choose Airplane Mode.

>> If the airline features onboard wireless networking and you're not skittish about overpaying for dreadfully slow Internet access, you can reactivate the tablet's Wi-Fi radio after you place the device into Airplane mode. After doing so, use the web browser app to display any web page. What you see instead is the inflight Wi-Fi access screen. Heed the directions, pay the hefty fees, and you're online.

Getting to your destination

After you arrive at your destination, the tablet may update the date and time according to your new location. One additional step you may want to take is to set the tablet's time zone. By doing so, you ensure that your schedule adapts properly to your new location.

To change the tablet's time zone, follow these steps:

1. **Open the Settings app.**

2. **Choose Date and Time.**

   On some Samsung tablets, tap the General tab to locate the Date and Time item.

3. **If you find an Automatic Dave & Time setting, ensure that it's active.**

   If so, you're done; the tablet automatically updates its time references. Otherwise, continue with Step 4.

4. **Choose Select Time Zone.**

5. **Pluck the current time zone from the list.**

If you've set appointments for your new location, visit the Calendar app to ensure that their start and end times have been properly adjusted. If you're prompted to update appointment times based on the new zone, do so.

REMEMBER

When you're done traveling or you change your time zone again, make sure that the tablet is updated as well. When the Automatic Time Zone setting isn't available, follow the steps in this section to reset the tablet's time zone.

The Android Tablet Goes Abroad

Yes, your Android tablet works overseas. The two resources you need to consider are how to recharge the battery and how to access Wi-Fi. As long as you have both, you're pretty much set. You also must be careful about mobile data (cellular) roaming surcharges when using an LTE tablet.

Using overseas power

You can easily attach a foreign AC power adapter to your tablet's AC power plug. You don't need a voltage converter — just an adapter. After it's attached, you can plug your tablet into those weirdo overseas power sockets without the risk of blowing up anything. I charged my Android tablet nightly while I spent time in France, and it worked like a charm.

Accessing Wi-Fi in foreign lands

Wi-Fi is pretty universal. The same protocols and standards are used everywhere, so if the tablet can access Wi-Fi at your local Starbucks, it can access Wi-Fi at the Malted Yak Blood Café in Wamboolistan. As long as Wi-Fi is available, your Android tablet can use it.

>> See Chapter 16 for details on using Wi-Fi with your Android tablet.

>> Internet cafés are more popular overseas than in the United States. They are the best locations for connecting your tablet and catching up on life back home.

>> Many overseas hotels offer free Wi-Fi service, although the signal may not reach into every room. Don't be surprised if you can use the Wi-Fi network only while you're in the lobby.

TIP

>> Obtain Skype Credit to use your Android tablet to place phone calls overseas. Skype's international rates are quite reasonable. The calls are made over the Internet, so when the tablet has Wi-Fi access, you're good to go. See Chapter 8 for more information on making Skype calls.

Disabling data roaming

The word *roam* takes on an entirely new meaning when it's applied to an LTE tablet (which features a cellular modem). Whenever you venture outside of your carrier's service area, the tablet may end up latching onto another mobile data network. When that happens, the tablet is roaming.

Roaming sounds handy, but there's a catch: It almost always involves a surcharge for using another mobile data network — an unpleasant surcharge.

Relax: Your cellular tablet alerts you whenever you're roaming. The Roaming icon appears in the status area, similar to the one shown in the margin. You may even see the word *Roaming* on the Lock screen and witness the name of the foreign cellular provider where the local provider's name normally appears.

If you'd like to eschew using the alien mobile network and, potentially, avoid any unpleasant charges, disable the tablet's Data Roaming option. Follow these steps:

1. **Open the Settings app.**

2. **In the Wireless & Networks section, tap the More item.**

   On some Samsung tablets, tap the Connections tab in the Settings app. The More item may be titled More Networks.

3. **Choose Cellular Networks.**

   If you see a Mobile Networks item in the Wireless and Networks area, choose it instead and then choose Global Data Roaming Access.

4. **Ensure that the Data Roaming option is disabled or denied.**

   On some tablets, the option is titled Global Data Roaming Access. Choose it and then choose the option Deny Data Roaming Access.

On some Samsung tablets, follow these steps:

1. **Open the Settings app and choose Mobile Networks.**

2. **Choose Data Roaming Access.**

3. **Select the option Deny Data Roaming Access and tap OK.**

REMEMBER

Your tablet can still access the Internet over the Wi-Fi connection while it's roaming. Connecting to a Wi-Fi network doesn't make you incur extra charges on your cellular bill.

>> Before you travel abroad, contact your cellular provider and ask about overseas data roaming. A subscription service or other options may be available, especially when you plan to stay overseas for an extended length of time.

TIP

>> If roaming concerns you, simply place the tablet into Airplane mode, as covered earlier in this chapter. In Airplane mode, your tablet can access Wi-Fi networks, but its cellular modem is definitely disabled.

Chapter **22**

Maintenance, Troubleshooting, and Help

Maintenance for your Android tablet is a lot easier than it was in the old days. Back in the 1970s, tablet owners were required to completely disassemble their devices and hand-clean every nut and sprocket with solvent and a wire brush. A special cloth was necessary to sop up all the electrical oil. It was a nightmare, which is why most people never did tablet maintenance back then.

Today, things are different. Android tablet maintenance is rather carefree, involving little more than cleaning the thing every so often. No disassembly is required. Beyond covering maintenance, this chapter offers suggestions for using the battery, gives you some helpful tips, and answers some common questions.

The Maintenance Chore

Relax. Maintenance of an Android tablet is simple and quick. Basically, I can summarize it in three words: Keep it clean. Beyond that, another maintenance task worthy of attention is backing up the information stored on your tablet.

Keeping it clean

You probably already keep your Android tablet clean. Perhaps you're one of those people who uses their sleeves to wipe the touchscreen. Of course, better than your sleeve is something called a microfiber cloth. This item can be found at any computer- or office-supply store.

WARNING

>> Never use any liquid to clean the touchscreen — especially ammonia or alcohol. Those harsh chemicals damage the touchscreen, rendering it unable to detect your input. Further, they can smudge the display, making it more difficult to see.

>> Touchscreen-safe screen cleaners are available for those times when your sleeve or even a microfiber cloth won't cut it. Ensure that you get a screen cleaner designed for a touchscreen.

>> If the screen keeps getting dirty, consider adding a *screen protector:* This specially designed cover prevents the screen from getting scratched or dirty but still allows you to use your finger on the touchscreen. Be sure that the screen protector is designed for use with the specific brand and model of your Android tablet.

Backing up your stuff

For a majority of the information on your Android tablet, backup is automatic. Your Google account takes care of Gmail, the calendar, your contacts, and even your apps. If you don't download music, eBooks, or movies, nothing ever needs to be backed up — at least not manually.

To confirm that your account information is being backed up, heed these steps:

1. Open the Settings app and choose Accounts.

On some Samsung tablets, tap the General tab to locate Accounts.

2. Choose Google to access your Google account settings.

3. **Ensure that the master control by each item in the list is enabled.**

   These are the items that synchronize between the tablet and your Google account on the Internet.

   You're not done yet!

4. **Tap the Back navigation icon until you're returned to the main Settings app screen.**

   On some Samsung tablets, you can skip this step because the Settings app displays categories on the left side of the screen.

5. **Choose Backup & Reset.**

6. **Ensure that the item Back Up My Data is On, or enabled.**

Beyond your Google account, which is automatically backed up, the rest of the information can be manually backed up. You can copy files from the tablet's internal storage to the cloud or your computer as a form of backup. See Chapter 17 for information on coordinating files between the Android tablet and a computer.

Yes, I agree: Manual backup isn't an example of technology making your life easier.

Updating the system

Every so often, a new version of the Android tablet's operating system becomes available. It's an Android update because Android is the name of the operating system, not because the Android tablet thinks that it's some type of robot.

When an automatic update occurs, you see an alert or a message, indicating that a system upgrade is available. The message may be as subtle as a notification icon, or it might be a card onscreen informing you that an update is necessary. My advice: Install the update and get it over with. Don't dally.

TIP

To manually check for updates, follow these steps:

1. **Open the Settings app.**

2. **Choose About Tablet.**

   This item may be titled About Device.

3. **Choose System Updates.**

   On some Samsung tablets, the item is titled Download Updates Manually.

If any updates are pending, you see them listed. Tap the RESTART & INSTALL button. Otherwise, you can tap the CHECK FOR UPDATE button — though the button isn't magic, and tapping it doesn't force an update when one isn't available.

>> If possible, connect the tablet to a power source during a software update. You don't want the battery to die in the middle of the operation.

>> Non-Android system updates might also be issued. For example, the tablet's manufacturer may send out an update to the Android tablet's guts. This type of update is often called a *firmware* update. As with Android updates, my advice is to accept all firmware updates.

Battery Care and Feeding

Perhaps the most important item you can monitor and maintain on your Android tablet is its battery. The battery supplies the necessary electrical juice by which the device operates. Without battery power, your tablet is basically an expensive trivet. Keep an eye on the battery.

Monitoring the battery

Android tablets display the current battery status at the top of the screen, in the status area, next to the time. The icons used are similar to those shown in Figure 22-1. They can appear white-on-black or use a charming color scheme, as illustrated in the figure.

FIGURE 22-1: Battery status icons.

Fully charged   Starting to drain   Low— charge soon   Very low— stop using and charge at once!   Charging

You might also see an icon for a dead battery, but for some reason I can't get my Android tablet to turn on and display that icon.

>> Heed those low-battery warnings! The tablet sounds a notification whenever the battery power gets low. Another notification sounds whenever the battery gets very low.

TIP

>> When the battery level is too low, the Android tablet shuts itself off.

>> The best way to deal with low battery power is to connect the tablet to a power source: Either plug it into a wall socket or connect it to a computer by using a USB cable. The tablet begins charging itself immediately; plus, you can use the device while it's charging.

>> The tablet charges more efficiently when it's plugged into a wall socket rather than a computer.

>> You don't have to fully charge the Android tablet to use it. When you have only 20 minutes to charge and you get only a 70 percent battery level, that's great. Well, it's not great, but it's far better than a lower battery level.

TECHNICAL STUFF

>> Battery percentage values are best-guess estimates. Just because you get 8 hours of use from the tablet and the battery meter shows 20 percent remaining doesn't imply that 20 percent equals 2 more hours of use. In practice, the amount of time you have left is much less than that. As a rule, when the battery percentage value gets low, the battery appears to drain faster.

Determining what is drawing power

An Android tablet is smart enough to know which of its features and apps use the most battery power. You can check it out for yourself on the battery usage screen, such as the one shown in Figure 22-2.

To view the battery usage screen on your tablet, follow these steps:

1. **Open the Settings app.**

2. **Choose Battery.**

   On some Samsung tablets, you tap the General tab in the Settings app to locate the Battery item.

Tap an item in the list to view specific details. For some items, the details screen hosts a button that lets you adjust power settings or even disable the feature.

The number and variety of items shown on the battery usage screen depend on what you've been doing with your tablet between charges and how many different apps you've been using. Don't be surprised if an item doesn't show up in the list; not every app consumes a lot of battery power.

Current battery charge and state

Usage and time chart

Items consuming power

Battery

← Battery

⟳ REFRESH ⋮

88% - approx. 2 days left

100%

8/4

8/5

8/6

0%

11:00

18:00

02:00

Use since last full charge

Jazz Radio

6%

Screen

2%

Tablet idle

7%

◁   ○   ▢

FIGURE 22-2:
Things that
drain the
battery.

Tap to view usage specifics or change settings

Extending battery life

A surefire way to make a battery last a good, long time is to never turn on the device in the first place. That's kind of impractical, so rather than let you use your Android tablet as a high-tech sushi tray, I offer a smattering of suggestions you can follow to help prolong tablet battery life:

Dim the screen: Refer to Figure 22-2, and you can see that the display (labeled *Screen*) draws quite a lot of battery power. Although a dim screen can be more difficult to see, especially outdoors, it definitely saves on battery life.

Lower the volume: Consider lowering the volume for the various noises the Android tablet makes, especially notifications.

Disable the vibration options: The tablet's vibration is caused by a teensy motor. Though you don't see much battery savings by disabling the vibration options, it's better than no savings.

Turn off Bluetooth: When you're not using Bluetooth, turn it off. The fastest way to do that is to use the Bluetooth Quick Action.

TIP

Some Android tablets come with battery-saving features. To check for them, open the Settings app and choose Battery or look for a specific Battery Savings or Power Saving Mode item. This feature automatically throttles certain battery-consuming items. It may kick in automatically when the battery gets low, or it might be something you must activate specifically.

>> Refer to Chapter 19 for information on setting screen brightness, sound, and vibration options.

>> If your tablet doesn't come with a Battery Savings item in the Settings app, check Google Play for such an app. See Chapter 15.

Help and Troubleshooting

Wouldn't it be great if you could have an avuncular Mr. Wizard type available at a moment's notice? He could just walk in and, with a happy smile on his face and a reassuring hand on your shoulder, let you know what the problem is and how to fix it. Then he'd give you a cookie. Never mind that such a thing would be creepy — getting helpful advice is worth it.

Fixing random and annoying problems

Here are some typical problems you may encounter on your Android tablet and my suggestions for a solution:

General trouble

For just about any problem or minor quirk, consider restarting the tablet. If the tablet features a Restart action on the Device Options menu, use it. Otherwise, turn off the tablet, and then turn it on again. This procedure will most likely fix a majority of the annoying problems you encounter.

See Chapter 2 for basic tablet on/off instructions.

Connection woes

As you move about, the cellular signal can change. In fact, you may observe the status icon change from 4G LTE to 3G to even the dreaded 1X or — worse — nothing, depending on the strength and availability of the mobile data network.

My advice for random signal weirdness is to wait. Oftentimes, the signal comes back after a few minutes. If it doesn't, the mobile data network might be down, or you may simply be in an area with lousy service. Consider changing your location.

For Wi-Fi connections, ensure that Wi-Fi is set up properly and working. This process usually involves pestering the person who configured the Wi-Fi router or, in a coffee shop, bothering the cheerful person with the tattoos and piercings who serves you coffee.

Perhaps the issue isn't with the tablet at all, but rather with the Wi-Fi network? Some networks have a "lease time" after which your tablet is disconnected. If so, follow the directions in Chapter 16 for turning off the tablet's Wi-Fi and then turn it on again. That often solves the issue.

Another problem I've heard about is that the Wi-Fi router doesn't recognize your Android tablet. In this case, the router might use older technology and it needs to be replaced. Especially if you have a Wi-Fi router over five years old, consider getting a newer router.

Music is playing and you want it to stop

It's awesome that your tablet continues to play music while you do other things. Getting the music to stop quickly, however, requires some skill. You can access the play controls for the Play Music app from a number of locations. They're found on the Lock screen, for example. You can also find them in the notifications drawer.

An app has run amok

Sometimes, apps that misbehave let you know. You see a warning on the screen announcing the app's stubborn disposition. When that happens, tap the Force Quit button to shut down the app. Then say, "Whew!"

To manually shut down an app, refer to Chapter 18.

You've reached your wit's end

When all else fails, you can do the drastic thing and perform a factory data reset on your Android tablet. Before committing to this step, you should contact support as described in the next section.

Refer to Chapter 20 for details on the factory data reset.

Finding help and support

Never discount your Android tablet's manufacturer for assistance when you need it. If you have a cellular tablet, consider contacting the cellular provider. Oh, and you can read the information I've presented in this section while you wait on hold for help and support.

The Help app

Some tablets come supplied with the Help app. It may be called Help or Help Center or something similar, and it may not be the kind of avuncular, well-written assistance you get from this book, but it's better than nothing.

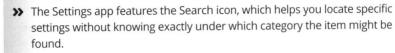

>> A Guided Tour or Tutorial app may also be available, which helps you understand how to work some of the phone's interesting features.

>> Also look for a Help eBook in the Play Books app.

>> The Settings app features the Search icon, which helps you locate specific settings without knowing exactly under which category the item might be found.

Manufacturer support

The tablet's manufacturer owes you support in exchange for your purchase. The support might take the shape of an online Help site, but that's better than nothing. Refer to Table 22-1 for a list of tablet manufacturers and their support websites.

TABLE 22-1   **Android Tablet Manufacturers**

Manufacturer	Website
HTC	www.htc.com/us/support
LG	www.lg.com/us/support
Motorola	www.motorola.com
Samsung	samsung.com/us/mobile/tablets

Cellular support

Assuming that you're a current mobile-data subscriber, consider contacting the cellular provider for tablet issues. Table 22-2 lists contact information for U.S. cellular providers.

TABLE 22-2   **U.S. Cellular Providers**

Provider	Toll-free Number	Website
AT&T	800-331-0500	www.att.com/esupport
Sprint Nextel	800-211-4727	sprint.com
T-Mobile	877-453-1304	www.t-mobile.com/Contact.aspx
Verizon	800-922-0204	verizonwireless.com/support

App support

For app issues, contact the developer. Follow these steps:

1. **Open the Play Store app.**

2. **Tap the Side Menu icon to display the navigation drawer.**

3. **Choose My Apps & Games.**

   If you don't see this item, choose Apps & Games and then repeat Steps 2 and 3.

4. **Tap the entry for the specific app, the one that's bothering you.**

5. **Choose the Send Email item.**

   Swipe the screen from bottom to top to scroll down the app's info screen and find the Send Email item. It's usually one of the last items on the screen.

REMEMBER

Contacting the developer is no guarantee that you'll get a response.

Google Play support

For issues with Google Play itself, contact Google at

```
support.google.com/googleplay
```

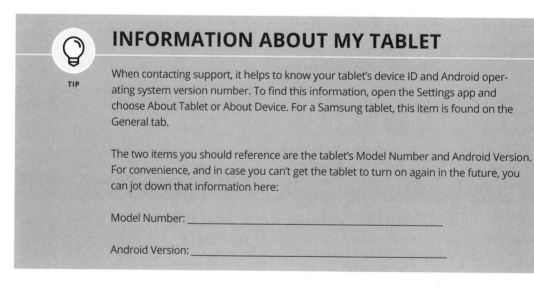

INFORMATION ABOUT MY TABLET

TIP

When contacting support, it helps to know your tablet's device ID and Android operating system version number. To find this information, open the Settings app and choose About Tablet or About Device. For a Samsung tablet, this item is found on the General tab.

The two items you should reference are the tablet's Model Number and Android Version. For convenience, and in case you can't get the tablet to turn on again in the future, you can jot down that information here:

Model Number: _____

Android Version: _____

Valuable Tablet Q&A

I love Q&A! Not only is it an effective way to express certain problems and solutions, but some of the questions might also cover things I've been wanting to ask.

"I can't turn the tablet on (or off)!"

Sometimes an Android tablet locks up. It's frustrating, but I've discovered that if you press and hold the Power/Lock key for about eight seconds, the tablet turns either off or on, depending on which state it's in.

I've had a program lock my tablet tight when the 8-second Power/Lock key trick didn't work. In that case, I waited 12 minutes or so, just letting the tablet sit there and do nothing. Then I pressed and held the Power/Lock key for about 8 seconds, and it turned itself back on.

"The touchscreen doesn't work!"

A touchscreen requires a human finger for proper interaction. The tablet interprets the static potential between the human finger and the device to determine where the touchscreen is being touched. The touchscreen will not work if the screen is damaged. It will not work when you're wearing gloves, unless they're specially designed touchscreen gloves. The touchscreen might fail also when the battery power is low.

"The screen is too dark!"

Android tablets feature a teensy light sensor on the front. If the Adaptive Brightness feature is active, the sensor adjusts the touchscreen's brightness based on the amount of ambient light at your location. If the sensor is covered, the screen can get very, very dark.

Ensure that you don't unintentionally block the light sensor. Avoid buying a case or screen protector that obscures the sensor.

The Automatic Brightness setting might also be vexing you. See Chapter 19 for information on setting screen brightness.

"The battery doesn't charge!"

Start from the source: Is the wall socket providing power? Is the cord plugged in? The cable may be damaged, so try another cable.

When charging from a USB port on a computer, ensure that the computer is turned on. Most computers don't provide USB power when they're turned off. Also, some USB ports may not supply enough power to charge the tablet. If possible, use a port on the computer console (the box) instead of a USB hub.

Some tablets may charge from a special cord, not the USB cable. Check to confirm that your tablet is able to take a charge from the USB cable.

"The tablet gets so hot that it turns itself off!"

Yikes! An overheating gadget can be a nasty problem. Can you hold the tablet in your hand, or is it too hot to hold? When it's too hot to hold, turn off the power. Disconnect it from the power supply. Let it cool.

If the overheating problem continues, have the Android tablet looked at for potential repair. The battery might need to be replaced. As far as I can tell, there's no way to remove and replace the Android tablet battery by yourself.

WARNING

Do not continue to use any gizmo that's too hot! The heat damages the electronics. It can also start a fire.

"My tablet doesn't do Landscape mode!"

Not every app can change its orientation between Portrait and Landscape modes — or even Upside-Down mode. For example, many games present themselves in one orientation only. Some tablets don't rotate their Home screens. So, just because the app doesn't go into Horizontal or Vertical mode doesn't mean that anything is broken.

Confirm that the orientation lock isn't on: Check the Quick Settings. Ensure that the Auto-Rotate or Screen Rotation item is properly set. Also, some eBook reader apps sport their own screen-rotation lock feature. Tap the Action Overflow to determine whether it's enabled.

5

The Part of Tens

Chapter **23**

Ten Tips, Tricks, and Shortcuts

tip is a small suggestion, a word of advice often spoken from bruising experience or knowledge passed along from someone with bruising experience. A *trick*, which is something not many know about, usually causes amazement or surprise. A *shortcut* is a quick way to get home, even though it crosses the old graveyard and you never quite know whether Old Man Witherspoon is the groundskeeper or a zombie.

I'd like to think that just about everything in this book is a tip, trick, or shortcut for using an Android tablet. Even so, I've distilled a list of items in this chapter that are definitely worthy of note.

Quickly Switch Apps

Android apps don't quit. Sure, some of them have a Quit or Sign Out command, but most apps loiter in the tablet's memory while you do other things. The Android operating system may eventually kill off a stale app. Before that happens, you can deftly and quickly switch between all running apps.

The key to making the switch is to use the Recent navigation icon, found at the bottom of the touchscreen. Figure 23-1 illustrates two popular incarnations of the Recent navigation icon.

FIGURE 23-1:
Incarnations
of the Recent
navigation
icon.

Android Nougat   Android Kitkat
Android Marshmallow
Android Lollipop

Tap the Recent navigation icon and choose an app from the list. Swipe the list up or down to peruse what's available. To dismiss the list, tap the Back icon or Home icon.

>> On tablets that lack the Recent icon, long-press the Home navigation icon.

>> To remove an app from the list of recent apps, swipe it left or right. This is effectively the same thing as quitting an app.

>> Some tablets may feature a Task Manager. It's usually a more technical representation of the items you find on the list of recent apps, with the addition of internal apps and services.

>> The list of recent apps is called the *Overview,* though everyone I know calls it the List of Recent Apps.

Install Apps from a Computer

You don't need to use an Android tablet to install apps. Using a computer, you can visit the Google Play website, browse for apps, and have that app installed remotely. It's kind of cool yet kind of scary at the same time. Here's how it works:

1. **Use a computer's web browser to visit the Google Play Store on the Internet:**

   ```
   play.google.com/store
   ```

   Bookmark that site!

2. **Browse for something.**

   You can hunt down apps, books, music — the whole gamut.

3. **Click the INSTALL button or BUY button.**

   If you're prompted to sign in to your Google account, do so. Use the same account as you use on your tablet.

4. **Choose your Android tablet from the Choose a Device menu.**

   If your tablet isn't listed, the app isn't compatible. That happens. Also, the tablet may be listed using its technical name, not the brand name you're used to seeing.

5. **For a free app, click the INSTALL button. For a paid app, click the CONTINUE button, choose your payment source, and then click the BUY button.**

   Installation proceeds.

As if by magic, the app is installed on your Android tablet — even though you used a computer to do it. Heck, the tablet need not even be within sight of you, and the app installs remotely.

Shooting a Panorama

Most variations of the Camera app sport a panoramic shooting mode. The *panorama* is a wide shot — it works by panning the tablet across a scene. The Camera app then stitches together several images to build the panoramic image.

To shoot a panoramic shot, follow these steps in the Camera app:

1. **Choose the Camera app's Panorama mode.**

   For the stock Android Camera app, tap the Side Menu icon (in the upper left corner of the screen), and then tap the Panorama icon, shown in the margin.

   On some Samsung tablets, tap the MODE button and choose Panorama.

2. **Hold the tablet steady, and then tap the Shutter icon.**

3. **Pivot in one direction as shown on the screen, following along with the animation.**

   Watch as the image is rendered and saved.

Panoramas work best for vistas, wide shots, or perhaps for family gatherings where not everyone likes each other.

TIP

Avoid Data Surcharges

An important issue for anyone using an LTE Android tablet is whether they're about to burst through their monthly data quota. Mobile data surcharges can pinch the wallet, but your Android tablet has a handy tool to help you avoid data overages. It's the data usage screen, shown in Figure 23-2.

Data Usage Cycle Action Bar   Usage chart

FIGURE 23-2:
Data usage
(Wi-Fi tablet
version).

Tap to examine the app's data usage or change network settings

To access the data usage screen, follow these steps:

1. **Open the Settings app.**

2. **Choose Data Usage.**

   On some Samsung tablets, the Data Usage item is located on the Connections tab.

If you have an LTE tablet, you see cellular data usage, not the Wi-Fi usage shown in Figure 23-2. To view Wi-Fi usage, tap the Action Overflow and choose Show Wi-Fi. You can then tap the CELLULAR or WI-FI tabs to view separate usage statistics.

To help avoid data surcharges, activate the Set Cellular Data Limit option that appears on the CELLULAR tab (not shown in Figure 23-2); set that option's master control to the On position. You can then adjust the black and red sliders on the chart to create a warning and cutoff values: When the black line is crossed, a warning appears. When the red line is crossed, the tablet ceases using the mobile data network.

>> The line chart (refer to Figure 23-2) informs you of your data usage over a specific period. Tap the Data Usage Cycle Action Bar to set that timespan, for example, matching it up with your cellular provider's monthly billing cycle.

>> My monthly data plan is capped at 10GB. I set the limits (on all my Android devices) to 8GB for the warning (black bar) and 9.5GB for the stop (red bar).

>> Keep in mind that the data usage shown on your tablet may not reflect the same values tracked by the cellular provider.

>> If you notice that the app is using more data than it should, tap the App Settings button. You may be able to adjust some settings to curtail unintended Internet access. For example, you can allow large uploads or downloads only over the Wi-Fi network.

TIP

Share Mobile Data

It's marvelously convenient to have a cellular tablet and be able to use the Internet wherever you roam. If you're feeling benevolent, you can share that mobile data connection in one of two ways: Create a mobile hotspot or tether the connection to a single device, such as a laptop computer.

To create a mobile hotspot, heed these steps:

1. **Turn off the tablet's Wi-Fi radio.**

There's no point in creating a Wi-Fi hotspot where one is already available.

2. **If possible, connect your Android tablet to a power source.**

Running a mobile hotspot draws a lot of power.

3. **Open the Settings app.**

   Some tablets may feature an app named Mobile Hotspot or 4G Hotspot. If so, open it instead.

4. **In the Wireless & Networks area, tap the More item.**

5. **Choose Tethering & Portable Hotspot.**

   The Tethering & Portable Hotspot item might be found on the main Settings app screen. On some Samsung tablets, tap the Connections tab and then choose Tethering and Portable Hotspot.

   You may see text describing the process. If so, dismiss the text.

6. **Activate the Portable Wi-Fi Hotspot item.**

   The item might be titled Mobile Hotspot.

7. **Choose Set Up Wi-Fi Hotspot.**

   On some Samsung tablets, tap the MORE button and choose Configure Mobile Hotspot.

   Give the hotspot a name, or SSID, and review, change, or assign a password. You may need to tap a Configure button to set up these items.

8. **Tap the SAVE or OK button to set your changes.**

To deactivate the mobile hotspot, repeat these steps but deactivate the Portable Wi-Fi Hotspot item in Step 6.

A more direct way to share the mobile data network is to tether the tablet to a computer by using a USB cable. Follow these steps to set up Internet tethering:

1. **Use a USB cable to connect the tablet to a computer or laptop.**

2. **Open the Settings app.**

3. **In the Wireless & Networks are, tap the More item.**

   On some Samsung tablets, tap the Connections tab and choose Tethering.

4. **Activate USB Tethering.**

The other device instantly recognizes the Android tablet as a "modem" with Internet access. Further configuration may be required, which depends on the computer using the tethered connection. For example, you may have to accept the installation of new software when prompted by Windows.

To terminate your Internet tethering session, repeat Steps 2 through 4 to remove the check mark. You can then disconnect the USB cable.

>> You can continue to use the tablet while it's sharing the mobile data connection.

>> Some cellular providers limit your tablet's ability to create a mobile Wi-Fi hotspot unless you pay an extra fee.

>> Sharing the mobile data network connection more rapidly consumes your cellular data quota. Be careful!

Make the Tablet Dream

Does your tablet lock, or does it fall asleep? I prefer to think that the tablet sleeps. That begs the question of whether or not it dreams.

Of course it does! You can even see the dreams, providing that you activate the Daydream feature, that your tablet has this feature, and that you keep it connected to a power source. Heed these steps:

1. **Open the Settings app.**

2. **Choose Display and then Daydream.**

   The Display item is found on the Device tab on some Samsung tablets.

3. **Ensure that the Daydream master control is in the On position.**

4. **Choose which type of daydream you want displayed.**

   Clock is a popular item, though I'm fond of Colors.

   Some daydreams feature the Settings icon. Use it to customize how the daydream appears.

5. **Tap the Action Overflow and choose the When to Daydream button.**

6. **Choose the Either option.**

The daydreaming begins when the screen would normally time-out and lock. So if you've set the tablet to lock after 1 minute of inactivity, it daydreams instead — as long as it's plugged in or docked.

>> To disrupt the dream, swipe the screen.

>> The tablet doesn't lock when it daydreams. To lock the tablet, press the Power/Lock key.

Add Spice to Dictation

I feel that too few people use dictation, despite how handy it can be. Anyway, if you've used dictation, you might notice that it occasionally censors some of the words you utter. Perhaps you're the kind of person who doesn't put up with that kind of s***.

Relax. You can follow these steps to lift the vocal censorship ban:

1. Start the Settings app.

2. Choose Language & Input.

On some Samsung tablets, tap the General tab to locate the Language & Input item. If it's not there, look on the Controls tab.

3. Choose Google Voice Typing.

4. Disable the option Block Offensive Words.

And just what are offensive words? I would think that *censorship* is an offensive word. But no, apparently only a few choice words fall into this category. I won't print them here, because the tablet's censor retains the initial letter and generally makes the foul language easy to guess. D***.

Add a Word to the Dictionary

Betcha didn't know that your tablet sports a dictionary. The dictionary keeps track of words you type — words that may not be recognized as being spelled properly.

Words unknown to the tablet are highlighted on the screen. Sometimes the word is shown in a different color or on a different background, and sometimes it's underlined in red. To add that word to the tablet's dictionary, long-press it. You see the Add Word to Dictionary action, which sticks the word in the tablet's dictionary.

To review or edit the tablet's dictionary, follow these steps:

1. Start the Settings app.

2. Choose Language & Input.

Tap the General tab on some Samsung tablets to locate this item.

3. Choose Personal Dictionary.

This action may not be obvious on some tablets: Try choosing the keyboard first, and then choose either the Dictionary or User Dictionary command.

With the dictionary visible, you can review words, edit them, remove them, or manually add new ones. To edit or delete a word, long-press it. To add a word, tap the Add icon.

Add Useful Widgets

Your tablet features a wide assortment of widgets with which to festoon the Home screen. They can be exceedingly handy, although you may not realize it because the sample widgets often included with the tablet are weak and unimpressive.

Good widgets to add include navigation, contact, eBook, and web page favorites. Adding any of these widgets starts out the same. Here are the brief directions:

1. **Long-press a Home screen page that has room for a widget.**

   The widget's sizes are shown on the widget's screen, as described in Chapter 18.

2. **Choose Widgets.**

3. **Drag a widget to the Home screen.**

4. **Complete the process.**

   The process is specific for each type of widget suggestion in this section.

Directions widget

The Maps/Directions widget allows you to quickly summon directions to a specific location from wherever you happen to be. After you add the widget to the Home screen, select a traveling method and destination. You can type a contact name, an address, a business name, and so on. Add a shortcut name, which is a brief description to fit under the widget on the Home screen. Tap the SAVE button.

Tap the Directions widget to use it. Instantly, the Maps app starts and enters Navigation mode, steering you from wherever you are to the location referenced by the widget.

Contact widget

For your most popular contacts, consider adding a contact widget: Add the Contact widget to the Home screen, and then select the specific contact from the tablet's address book. A widget representing the contact (with the contact's picture, if available) appears on the Home screen. Tap the widget to display information about the contact, along with an email link, a phone number, a map location, and other details supplied for that contact.

eBook widget

When you're mired in the middle of that latest potboiler, put a Google Play Books/Book shortcut on the Home screen: Choose the Book widget, and then select which eBooks in your digital library you want to access. Tap the widget to open the Play Books app and jump right into the book at the spot where you were last reading.

Web bookmark widget

For your favorite websites, consider adding a Home page widget. You can use a bookmarks widget, such as Chrome/Chrome Bookmarks, found on the Widgets screen. Even so, an easier shortcut is to open the web browser app, navigate to the page you desire, and then tap the Action Overflow and choose Add to Home Screen.

Take a Screen Shot

A screen shot, also called a *screen cap* (for *cap*ture), is a picture of your tablet's touchscreen. So if you see something interesting on the screen or you just want to take a quick pic of your tablet life, you take a screen shot.

The stock Android method of shooting the screen is to press and hold both the Volume Down and Power/Lock keys at the same time. Upon success, the touchscreen image reduces in size, you may hear a shutter sound, and the screen shot is saved.

>> Screen shots are accessed through the Photos app. If your tablet uses the old Gallery app, you'll find screen shots in their own album.

>> Some Samsung tablets use the Motion command to capture the screen: Hold your hand perpendicular to the tablet, like you're giving it a karate chop. Swipe the edge of your palm over the screen, right-to-left or left-to-right. Upon success, you hear a shutter sound.

TECHNICAL STUFF

>> Internally, screen shots are stored in the Pictures/Screenshots folder. They're created in the PNG graphics file format.

Chapter **24**

Ten Things to Remember

Have you ever tried to tie a string around your finger to remember something? I've not attempted that technique just yet. The main reason is that I keep forgetting to buy string and I have no way to remind myself.

For your Android tablet, some things are definitely worth remembering. From that long, long list, I've come up with ten good ones.

Dictate Text

Dictation is such a handy feature — don't forget to use it! You can dictate most text instead of typing it. Just tap the Microphone key on the keyboard — or anywhere you see the Microphone icon — and begin speaking. Your utterances are translated to text. In most cases, the translation is instantaneous.

» See Chapter 4 for more information on Android tablet dictation.

» Google Now doesn't require you to tap the Microphone icon. Instead, utter the phrase "OK Google," and it starts listening.

Change the Tablet's Orientation

Larger-format Android tablets have a natural horizontal orientation. Smaller tablets beg to be held vertically. You won't break any law by changing the tablet's orientation.

Apps such as Chrome and Gmail can look much better in the horizontal orientation, whereas apps such as Play Books and Play Music can look much better in the vertical orientation. The key to changing orientation is to rotate the tablet to view the app the way you like best.

TIP

» If you prefer a specific orientation, use the Quick Settings item that sets the tablet's orientation. See Chapter 3.

» Not every app changes its orientation. Some apps — specifically, games — present themselves in one orientation only: landscape or portrait.

REMEMBER

» eBook reader apps have screen rotation settings that let you lock the orientation to the way you want, regardless of what the tablet is doing.

Work the Quick Settings

Many tablet controls are available at a single, handy location: the Quick Settings drawer. Pull it down to turn tablet features on or off, such as Wi-Fi, Bluetooth, screen orientation, and other On–Off settings. Using the Quick Settings drawer is far more expedient than visiting the Settings app.

» Some tablets feature a vast array of Quick Settings, only a handful of which appear at a time. Try swiping the Quick Settings left or right to see more.

» As a bonus, you may find the Settings app shortcut in the Quick Settings drawer.

Employ Keyboard Suggestions

Don't forget to take advantage of the predictive-text suggestions that appear above the onscreen keyboard while you're typing text. In fact, you don't even need to tap a suggestion; to replace your text with the highlighted suggestion, simply touch the onscreen keyboard's Space key. Zap! The word appears.

Refer to Chapter 4 for information on using the keyboard suggestions.

Avoid the Battery Hogs

Three items on an Android tablet suck down battery power faster than a massive alien fleet is defeated by a plucky antihero who only wants the girl:

>> The display

>> Navigation

>> Wireless radios

The display is obviously a most necessary part of your Android tablet — but it's also a tremendous power hog. The Adaptive Brightness (also called Auto Brightness) setting is your best friend for saving power with the display. See Chapter 19.

Navigation is certainly handy, but the battery drains rapidly because the tablet's touchscreen is on the entire time and the speaker is dictating your directions. If possible, plug the tablet into the car's power socket when you're navigating.

Wireless radios include Wi-Fi networking, Bluetooth, and GPS. Though they require extra power, they aren't real power hogs, like navigation and the display. Still, when power is getting low, consider disabling those items.

See Chapter 22 for more information on managing the tablet's battery.

Unlock and Launch

Quite a few Android tablets feature special Lock screen icons. For example, you may see an icon representing the Camera app. Samsung tablets can sport several app icons on the Lock screen. To unlock and launch an app, swipe the icon across the screen. That app instantly runs.

>> Depending on the screen lock that's installed, the app may run but the tablet won't unlock. To do anything other than run the app, you must work the screen lock.

>> Samsung tablet lock-screen icons are enabled only when the swipe lock is set.

Make Phone Calls

Yeah, I know: It's not a phone. Even Android tablets that use the mobile data network can't make phone calls. Why let that stop you?

Both the Hangouts and Skype apps let you place phone calls and video-chat with your friends. Boost your Skype account with some coinage and you can even dial into real phones. See Chapter 8 for details.

Check Your Schedule

The Calendar app reminds you of upcoming dates and generally keeps you on schedule. A great way to augment the calendar is to employ the Calendar widget on the Home screen.

The Calendar widget lists the current date and then a long list of upcoming appointments. It's a great way to check your schedule, especially when you use your tablet all the time. I recommend sticking the Calendar widget right on the main or center Home screen panel.

TIP

>> See Chapter 18 for information on adding widgets to the Home screen; Chapter 14 covers the Calendar app.

>> As long as I'm handing out tips, remember to specify location information when you set up an appointment in the Calendar app. Type the information just as though you were using the Maps app to search. You can then quickly navigate to your next appointment by touching the location item when you review the event.

Snap a Pic of That Contact

Here's something I always forget: Whenever you're near one of your contacts, take the person's picture. Sure, some people are bashful, but most folks are flat-tered. The idea is to build up the tablet's address book so that all your contacts have photos.

REMEMBER

When taking a picture, be sure to show it to the person before you assign it to the contact. Let them decide whether it's good enough.

Use Google Now

Google is known worldwide for its searching capabilities and its popular website. By gum, the word *Google* is synonymous with searching. So please don't forget that your Android tablet, which uses Google's Android operating system, has a powerful search — nay, *knowledge* — command. It's called Google Now.

» On many Android tablets, you access Google Now from the far left Home screen page.

» The Google Search widget on the Home screen provides a shortcut into Google Now.

» The Google Now app is titled Google.

» Review Chapter 14 for details on various Google Now commands.

» Beyond Google Now, you can take advantage of the various Search icons found in just about every app on an Android tablet. Use this icon to search for information, locations, people — you name it. It's handy.

Chapter **25**

Ten Nifty Apps

Nothing stirs up controversy like choosing only ten free apps out of the million-plus apps available at Google Play. Even so, when I started out with my first smartphone 30 years ago, I wanted to see a list of worthy apps, or even apps recommended by friends. Lamentably, that was long before anyone else had a smartphone of any type, so I was forced to wait. Thanks to the suggestions here, you don't have to wait to get started with apps on your Android tablet.

Airline Apps

All the major airlines have apps, and those apps have improved greatly over the years. Today, you use an airline app not only to make a reservation and check on flight status, but the app — and your tablet — serve as the boarding pass. The only downside to a digital boarding pass is that the airport security people have nothing to scribble on after they check your ID.

Perhaps the most convenient thing about an airline app are the updates. I had a flight change its departure gate (from one terminal to another) and then get canceled. The app informed me of the gate change and then automatically told me on which alternative flight I'd been re-booked. I found that amazing.

Games

It's not a question of whether or not the tablet can play games. The question is which games to choose. The selection is overwhelming, almost to the point where you're unwilling to give a game a chance because more exist. So rather than speed-date some games, here are my suggestions:

>> *Angry Birds*. Perhaps the most viral of the mobile gaming apps, it spawned an entire series of games and even a silly movie. Still, the original game is lots of fun.

>> *Crossy Road*. This game is similar to the old arcade game Frogger, but it's just insane. Crossy Road is easy to learn and play, addictive, and it's a great short-time waster.

>> *Plants Versus Zombies*. Shown in Figure 25-1, this game is a lot of fun and somewhat strategic.

>> *X-Plane*. This flight simulator is easy to learn, though you must download the maps before you can play. I keep forgetting that when I want to play X-Plane on a real airplane without an Internet connection.

>> *Sudoku Daily*. If you're a puzzle addict, specifically the Sudoku puzzle, then you'll enjoy this version of the popular game. It makes new puzzles available each day, with a wide range of skill sets, hints, cheats, and anything a Sudoku addict would enjoy.

>> *Jet Car Stunts*. This paid game is enjoyable from a road-racing standpoint as well as a flight simulator. It's quite challenging and it saved me from hours of boredom during a flight overseas.

>> *Threes!*. A strategy game, Threes! is delightful. It's quick to learn, but increases in frustration quickly. It's best to play when you have a friend who also plays so that you can compare scores.

This list is by no means complete; I have dozens more games installed on my tablet. I'm not into sports games, and some of the more complex games become too involved for me to get interested.

FIGURE 25-1:
The popular game Plants Versus Zombies.

REMEMBER

Free or Lite versions of paid games are available in Google Play. Even so, a paid game is generally 99 cents. Treat yourself to a new paid game a month, or buy one before you leave on a trip to help keep yourself entertained.

Google Docs

In previous editions of this book, I would recommend a specific note-taking app for jotting down information, lists, or other text on your tablet. Using such an app is no longer necessary because your Android tablet comes with Google Docs.

Google Docs is really an entire Office suite of apps, including word processing, a spreadsheet, and a presentation program. I know quite a few businesses that use Google Docs exclusively, specifically because it allows for better document sharing than Microsoft Office.

On my tablet, I use Google Docs to write quick notes and keep lists. For example, my shopping list is on a Google Doc. To access it, I open the Docs app, then choose a document thumbnail. I can read or edit the document. Also, because the documents are linked to my Google account, I can edit or view the document on any computer, laptop, or another Internet gizmo.

Kindle

Yes, your Android tablet comes with the Google Play Books app. Sometimes that's not enough. Consider getting the Kindle app as well. You don't need to use it exclusively, it's just good to have options available.

Obtain the Kindle app from Google Play. Use your Amazon account to sign in. If you already have Kindle books, they'll appear in the library. If not, go out and buy some books. The Kindle store often contains books not available from Google Play.

Movies by Flixster

The Movies by Flixster app is your tablet's gateway to Hollywood. It lists currently running films, premieres and openings, and it has links to your local theaters with show times and other information. The app is also tied into the popular Rotten Tomatoes website for reviews and feedback. If you enjoy going to the movies, you'll find the Movies app a valuable addition to your tablet's app library.

Sky Map

Ever look up into the night sky and say, "What the heck is that?" Unless it's a bird, an airplane, a satellite, or a UFO, the Sky Map can help you discover mysterious objects aloft. It may turn out that a particularly bright star in the sky is, in fact, the planet Jupiter.

The Sky Map app works like a window you can look through to identify things in the night sky. Just start the app and hold up your tablet. Pan and tilt the device to identify planets, stars, and constellations.

Television Alternatives

When you're ready to cut the cable, your Android tablet is more than eager to step up to the plate and offer you a host of alternative TV and movie-watching resources. These apps offer media choices beyond what's available at Google Play and viewable in the Play Movies & TV app. Here are my suggestions:

» *Netflix.* The app is free, but you must have a Netflix subscription to access the content. When you do, you'll be able to view the entire Netflix library of movies, TV shows, and documentaries on your Android tablet.

» *Hulu.* Similar to Netflix, Hulu offers current TV show episodes, movies, foreign films, and other unique content to its subscription holders.

» *HBO Now.* If you cut the cable but miss *Game of Thrones*, you can obtain the HBO Now app and subscribe directly to the service. HBO Now offers every series ever broadcast on the network, as well as its current slate of movie offerings.

» *CBSN.* When you miss live news, consider getting the CBSN app, which shows a live feed of CBS news. The app is free.

Other apps are available, but often to view shows or events you must concurrently have a cable TV subscription. This burden isn't required for the above-listed apps. For example, the ESPN and CBS apps let you watch sports and live TV, but only when you have an active cable subscription. This restriction may change in the future.

Translate

Not only does Google's Translate app assist with other apps in translating foreign tongues into English, you can use the app directly to help you pass 3rd period French. I'm serious: I took an Italian course at a community college and just about everyone used this app to help them get a C in that course. Why a C? Because although the translation is okay, it's not perfect — and the professor knows when you've used it. Even so, it's fun to play with and brush up on anything from Chinese to Russian.

Voice Recorder

All Android tablets have a microphone and speakers, so where is the voice recorder app? Don't bother looking. If you need to record your blurts, conversations, or that new song you composed on the ukulele, get the Voice Recorder app. It has an elegant and simple interface: Touch the big Record button to start recording. Make a note for yourself or record a friend doing his Daffy Duck impression.

Previous recordings are stored in a list on the Voice Recorder's main screen. Each recording is shown with its title, the date and time of the recording, and the recording duration.

Several voice recording apps can be found at Google Play. I recommend the one by Mamoru Tokashiki.

Zedge

The Zedge program is a helpful resource for finding wallpapers and ringtones — millions of them. It's a sharing app, so you can access wallpapers and ringtones created by other Android users as well as share your own. If you're looking for a specific sound or something special for Home screen wallpaper, Zedge is the best place to start your search.

In Figure 25-2, you see a list of popular ringtones available from Zedge. Choose one to preview. If you like it, you can download the ringtone to your tablet and configure it as the main notification ringtone or set it as a ringtone for a specific app.

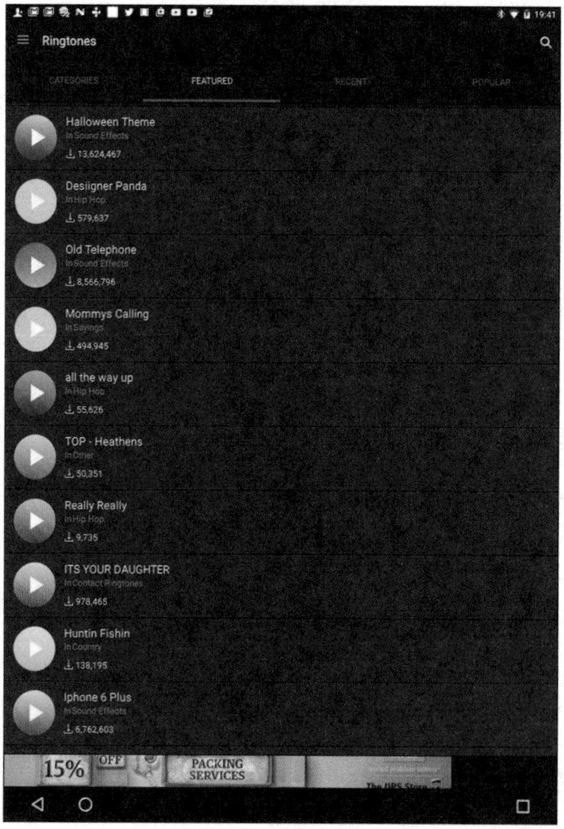

FIGURE 25-2:
The Zedge app lists popular ringtones.

REMEMBER

When you install a media app like Zedge, you will see the default app card displayed when you choose a ringtone or select wallpaper. The choices you're presented with include Tablet Media and Zedge, plus any other media apps. You can choose a default app, such as Zedge, or be prompted every time. For more information on this decision, see Chapter 18.

Index

Symbols and Numerics

~[< key, 50
1X, 202
3G, 202
4G LTE, 202
4G SIM card holder, 11
1234 key, 50

A

A icon, 182
ABC key, 50
AC adapter, 264, 266–267
accelerometer, 33–34
ACCEPT button, 190
accessing
  data usage screen, 286–287
  foreign Wi-Fi, 267
  Google Play, 188
  Home screen pages, 37
  Quick Settings, 39
  special characters, 50–51
  Twitter app navigation drawer, 115
accessories
  included, 10–11
  optional, 16–17
accounts
  adding, 25–26
  corporate email, 77
  email, 75–76, 77, 85
  kid's user, 261–262
Action Bar icon, 44
Action Overflow icon, 44, 80
activating
  Bluetooth, 208–209
  keyboard gestures, 249

  location technology, 123
  predictive text, 248–249
  self-timer, 140
  Wi-Fi, 203
adapter, 11, 15, 264, 266–267
Adaptive Brightness setting, 246
Add icon, 44
Add Photo icon (Facebook), 112
Add Video icon (Facebook), 112
adding
  accounts, 25–26
  app launchers to folders, 233
  apps to Home screen, 228–229
  contact's pictures, 68–69
  corporate email accounts, 77
  email accounts, 75–76
  Lock screen shortcuts, 247
  owner info text, 255–256
  people to Hangouts app, 101
  print services, 220–221
  users, 259–261
  widgets, 291–292
  words to dictionary, 290–291
address book
  about, 61–62
  adding contact's pictures, 68–69
  creating contacts from email messages, 66–67
  creating favorites, 69–70
  editing contacts, 68
  importing contacts from computer, 67
  joining identical contacts, 70–71
  managing, 68–72
  removing contacts, 71–72
  separating contacts, 71
  sorting contacts, 64
  using, 62–64

Downloading Complete notification, 95
Download(s) folder, 83
drag, 30, 89
Dummies (website), 5

E

earphones, 17
eBook reader, 180–182
eBook widget, 292
Edit Bookmark card, 91
Edit icon, 45, 151
editing
 contacts, 68
 images, 151–155
 text, 55–58
email. *See also* Email app; Gmail app
 about, 73–74
 adding accounts, 76
 configuring, 84–86
 creating contacts from, 66–67
 creating signatures, 85–86
 getting messages, 77–78
 reading, 79–80
 sending, 63, 82
 setting primary accounts, 86
 setting up first account, 74
Email app
 about, 73–74
 attachments, 82–84
 on Home screen, 229
 reading email, 79–80
 setting up, 74–75
 writing messages, 80–82
enabling
 Bluetooth, 208–209
 keyboard gestures, 249
 location technology, 123
 predictive text, 248–249
 self-timer, 140
encryption, 252, 258

End Call icon, 104
ending
 Internet tethering, 288–289
 video chats, 103
events, creating, 178–179
Exchange Server, 76, 77
Exit command, 41
exiting
 Airplane mode, 265
 from Navigation mode, 133
extending battery life, 274–275
external storage slot, 14

F

Face Unlock, 252
Facebook app
 about, 109–110
 changing ringtone, 114
 on Home screen, 229
 running, 110–111
 setting status, 111–112
 uploading pictures/videos, 112–113
factory data resets, performing, 258–259, 276
Favorite (Star) icon, 45, 70
favorites
 creating in address book, 69–70
 removing, 70
 searching for in Maps app, 130
Favorites Tray, 36, 229
File Transfers mode, 214
files. *See also* folders
 about, 217–218
 adding print services, 220–221
 downloading, 95
 managing, 225
 printing, 221
 sharing on the cloud, 218–219
 streaming media, 221–223
 transferring using USB cable, 219–220

R

Notes

Notes

Notes

Notes

About the Author

Dan Gookin has been writing about technology for over 25 years. He combines his love of writing with his gizmo fascination to create books that are informative, entertaining, and not boring. Having written over 130 titles, with 12 million copies in print and translated into over 30 languages, Dan can attest that his method of crafting computer tomes seems to work.

Perhaps his most famous title is the original *DOS For Dummies,* published in 1991. It became the world's fastest-selling computer book, at one time moving more copies per week than the *New York Times* number-one bestseller (though, as a reference, it could not be listed on the *Times'* Best Sellers list). That book spawned the entire line of *For Dummies* books, which remains a publishing phenomenon to this day.

Dan's most popular titles include *PCs For Dummies, Word For Dummies, Laptops For Dummies,* and *Android Phones For Dummies.* He also maintains the vast and helpful website www.wambooli.com.

Dan holds a degree in Communications/Visual Arts from the University of California, San Diego. He lives in the Pacific Northwest, where he enjoys spending time with his sons playing video games indoors while they enjoy the gentle woods of Idaho.

Publisher's Acknowledgments

Acquisitions Editor: Katie Mohr
Senior Project Editor: Paul Levesque
Copy Editor: Becky Whitney
Editorial Assistant: Serena Novosel
Sr. Editorial Assistant: Cherie Case

Production Editor: Tamilmani Varadharaj
Cover Image: kirill_makarov/Shutterstock

Apple & Mac

iPad For Dummies,
5th Edition
978-1-118-72306-7

iPhone For Dummies,
7th Edition
978-1-118-69083-3

Macs All-in-One
For Dummies, 4th Edition
978-1-118-82210-4

OS X Mavericks
For Dummies
978-1-118-69188-5

Blogging & Social Media

Facebook For Dummies,
5th Edition
978-1-118-63312-0

Social Media Engagement
For Dummies
978-1-118-53019-1

WordPress For Dummies,
6th Edition
978-1-118-79161-5

Business

Stock Investing
For Dummies, 4th Edition
978-1-118-37678-2

Investing For Dummies,
6th Edition
978-0-470-90545-6

Personal Finance
For Dummies, 7th Edition
978-1-118-11785-9

QuickBooks 2014
For Dummies
978-1-118-72005-9

Small Business Marketing
Kit For Dummies,
3rd Edition
978-1-118-31183-7

Careers

Job Interviews
For Dummies, 4th Edition
978-1-118-11290-8

Job Searching with Social
Media For Dummies,
2nd Edition
978-1-118-67856-5

Personal Branding
For Dummies
978-1-118-11792-7

Resumes For Dummies,
6th Edition
978-0-470-87361-8

Starting an Etsy Business
For Dummies, 2nd Edition
978-1-118-59024-9

Diet & Nutrition

Belly Fat Diet For Dummies
978-1-118-34585-6

Mediterranean Diet
For Dummies
978-1-118-71525-3

Nutrition For Dummies,
5th Edition
978-0-470-93231-5

Digital Photography

Digital SLR Photography
All-in-One For Dummies,
2nd Edition
978-1-118-59082-9

Digital SLR Video &
Filmmaking For Dummies
978-1-118-36598-4

Photoshop Elements 12
For Dummies
978-1-118-72714-0

Gardening

Herb Gardening
For Dummies, 2nd Edition
978-0-470-61778-6

Gardening with Free-Range
Chickens For Dummies
978-1-118-54754-0

Health

Boosting Your Immunity
For Dummies
978-1-118-40200-9

Diabetes For Dummies,
4th Edition
978-1-118-29447-5

Living Paleo For Dummies
978-1-118-29405-5

Big Data

Big Data For Dummies
978-1-118-50422-2

Data Visualization
For Dummies
978-1-118-50289-1

Hadoop For Dummies
978-1-118-60755-8

Language &
Foreign Language

500 Spanish Verbs
For Dummies
978-1-118-02382-2

English Grammar
For Dummies, 2nd Edition
978-0-470-54664-2

French All-in-One
For Dummies
978-1-118-22815-9

German Essentials
For Dummies
978-1-118-18422-6

Italian For Dummies,
2nd Edition
978-1-118-00465-4

Available in print and e-book formats.

Available wherever books are sold. **For more information or to order direct visit www.dummies.com**

Math & Science

Algebra I For Dummies,
2nd Edition
978-0-470-55964-2

Anatomy and Physiology
For Dummies, 2nd Edition
978-0-470-92326-9

Astronomy For Dummies,
3rd Edition
978-1-118-37697-3

Biology For Dummies,
2nd Edition
978-0-470-59875-7

Chemistry For Dummies,
2nd Edition
978-1-118-00730-3

1001 Algebra II Practice
Problems For Dummies
978-1-118-44662-1

Microsoft Office

Excel 2013 For Dummies
978-1-118-51012-4

Office 2013 All-in-One
For Dummies
978-1-118-51636-2

PowerPoint 2013
For Dummies
978-1-118-50253-2

Word 2013 For Dummies
978-1-118-49123-2

Music

Blues Harmonica
For Dummies
978-1-118-25269-7

Guitar For Dummies,
3rd Edition
978-1-118-11554-1

iPod & iTunes
For Dummies, 10th Edition
978-1-118-50864-0

Programming

Beginning Programming
with C For Dummies
978-1-118-73763-7

Excel VBA Programming
For Dummies, 3rd Edition
978-1-118-49037-2

Java For Dummies,
6th Edition
978-1-118-40780-6

Religion & Inspiration

The Bible For Dummies
978-0-7645-5296-0

Buddhism For Dummies,
2nd Edition
978-1-118-02379-2

Catholicism For Dummies,
2nd Edition
978-1-118-07778-8

Self-Help & Relationships

Beating Sugar Addiction
For Dummies
978-1-118-54645-1

Meditation For Dummies,
3rd Edition
978-1-118-29144-3

Seniors

Laptops For Seniors
For Dummies, 3rd Edition
978-1-118-71105-7

Computers For Seniors
For Dummies, 3rd Edition
978-1-118-11553-4

iPad For Seniors
For Dummies, 6th Edition
978-1-118-72826-0

Social Security
For Dummies
978-1-118-20573-0

Smartphones & Tablets

Android Phones
For Dummies, 2nd Edition
978-1-118-72030-1

Nexus Tablets
For Dummies
978-1-118-77243-0

Samsung Galaxy S 4
For Dummies
978-1-118-64222-1

Samsung Galaxy Tabs
For Dummies
978-1-118-77294-2

Test Prep

ACT For Dummies,
5th Edition
978-1-118-01259-8

ASVAB For Dummies,
3rd Edition
978-0-470-63760-9

GRE For Dummies,
7th Edition
978-0-470-88921-3

Officer Candidate Tests
For Dummies
978-0-470-59876-4

Physician's Assistant Exam
For Dummies
978-1-118-11556-5

Series 7 Exam For Dummies
978-0-470-09932-2

Windows 8

Windows 8.1 All-in-One
For Dummies
978-1-118-82087-2

Windows 8.1 For Dummies
978-1-118-82121-3

Windows 8.1 For Dummies,
Book + DVD Bundle
978-1-118-82107-7

e Available in print and e-book formats.

Available wherever books are sold. **For more information or to order direct visit www.dummies.com**

Take Dummies with you everywhere you go!

Whether you are excited about e-books, want more from the web, must have your mobile apps, or are swept up in social media, Dummies makes everything easier.

Leverage the Power

For Dummies is the global leader in the reference category and one of the most trusted and highly regarded brands in the world. No longer just focused on books, customers now have access to the For Dummies content they need in the format they want. Let us help you develop a solution that will fit your brand and help you connect with your customers.

Advertising & Sponsorships

Connect with an engaged audience on a powerful multimedia site, and position your message alongside expert how-to content.

Targeted ads • Video • Email marketing • Microsites • Sweepstakes sponsorship

Custom Publishing

Reach a global audience in any language by creating a solution that will
differentiate you from competitors, amplify your message,
and encourage customers to make a buying decision.

Apps • Books • eBooks • Video • Audio • Webinars

Brand Licensing & Content

Leverage the strength of the world's most popular reference brand to reach
new audiences and channels of distribution.

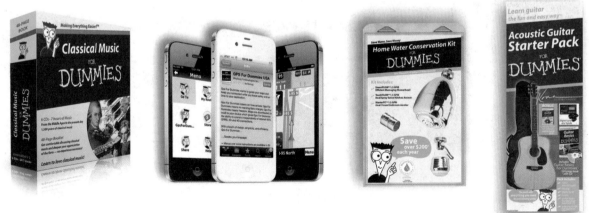

For more information, visit www.Dummies.com/biz

A Wiley Brand

Dummies products make life easier!

- DIY
- Consumer Electronics
- Crafts
- Software
- Cookware
- Hobbies
- Videos
- Music
- Games
- and More!

For more information, go to **Dummies.com** and search the store by category.

A Wiley Brand